Sunset

Australia
TRAVEL GUIDE

By the Editors of Sunset Books
and Sunset Magazine

Lane Publishing Co. • **Menlo Park, California**

Edited by **Joan Erickson**

Design: **Cynthia Hanson**

Illustrations & Maps: **Joe Seney**

Cover: Sydney's sculptural Opera House, overlooking the harbor, has become an internationally known landmark of Australia. Photographed by Darrow M. Watt.

Sunset Books
   Editor: David E. Clark
   Managing Editor: Elizabeth L. Hogan

First printing January 1987

Acknowledgments

For assistance in the gathering of information and manuscript checking, we would like to thank the following: Australian Tourist Commission, New South Wales Tourist Commission, Canberra Tourist Bureau, Victorian Tourism Commission, Tasmanian Department of Tourism, South Australian Department of Tourism, Western Australian Tourism Commission, Northern Territory Tourist Commission, and Queensland Tourist & Travel Corporation.

Photographers

Australian Information Service: 71 top left. **Australian Tourist Commission:** 6, 11 top left, 14 bottom, 19 top right and bottom, 38 bottom, 51 all, 54, 59 bottom, 62, 66 top, 79 all, 87 top, 90 top, 95, 98 bottom, 106 top right, 111, 119, 122. **Dave Bartruff:** 35 right. **Margaret Betchart:** 43 bottom right. **Brian Brake, Photo Researchers, Inc.:** 11 bottom, 90 bottom. **Canberra Tourist Bureau:** 46. **Ken Castle:** 82, 87 bottom, 106 top left. **Joan Erickson:** 30 top, 38 top, 43 left, 59 top, 66 bottom, 71 top right, 74, 103. **James Gebbie:** 98 top. **George Holton, Photo Researchers, Inc.:** 19 top left. **Esther Litton:** 106 bottom. **Bruce Moss:** 43 top right, 114 bottom. **New South Wales Department of Tourism:** 71 bottom. **Qantas Airways Ltd.:** 3, 11 top right, 127. **Richard Rowan:** 27 bottom, 35 left. **Joan Storey:** 14 top left, 27 top. **Marie Ueda, S.F. Photo Network:** 30 bottom. **Darrow M. Watt:** 22, 114 top. **Nikolay Zurek:** 14 top right.

Maps have been provided in each chapter for the purpose of highlighting significant regions, routes, and attractions in the area. For detailed road maps of Australia, check with automobile clubs, insurance or travel agencies, or government tourist offices.

Square is one of Brisbane's showplaces. For a good overall view of the city and surrounding countryside, take the lift to the observation platform at the top of the clock tower. City Hall contains an impressive collection of paintings and historic treasures, and a grand organ said to be one of the finest in the Southern Hemisphere.

Parliament House, Alice and George streets, opened in 1868. This building is an imposing example of French Renaissance architecture. A newer annex now towers above the original structure.

The Observatory, Wickham Terrace, dates from 1829. Built by convict labor, it was designed to operate as a windmill, but the sails never worked so it was converted to a convict-manned treadmill.

John Oxley Memorial, an obelisk between Victoria and William Jolly bridges, marks the spot where Lt. John Oxley landed in 1823, establishing the site of Brisbane.

Newstead Park is the site of Brisbane's oldest residence, Newstead House, open Monday through Thursday from 11 A.M. to 3 P.M. and Sunday from 2 to 5. A memorial at Lyndon B. Johnson Place in the park was erected by the people of Queensland as a tribute to the United States. (During the Pacific crisis in World War II, General Douglas MacArthur made his base in Brisbane.)

Miegunyah, on Jordan Terrace in Bowen Hills, is a fine example of colonial architecture, memorializing Australia's pioneer women. Furnished in the manner of the late 1800s, it holds many relics of those early days. You can view the exhibit Tuesdays, Wednesdays, Saturdays, and Sundays from 10:30 A.M. to 4 P.M.

Early Street, 75 McIlwraith Avenue, Norman Park, re-creates a pioneer town. From 10 A.M. to 5 P.M. daily, visitors may inspect an old-time pub, a coach house, a settler's cottage, and an Aboriginal *gunyah* (a type of primitive shelter).

Museums and galleries. Queensland Art Gallery, M.I.M. Building, 160 Ann Street, houses a small but good collection of works by Australian contemporary painters. The gallery is open Monday through Saturday from 10 A.M. to 5 P.M. and Sundays from 2 to 5.

Visitors with a special interest in art may wish to visit the Ray Hughes Gallery, McInnes Galleries, the Town Gallery, and Philip Bacon Galleries as well.

Design Art Centre features pottery and applied arts as well as paintings and drawings. Jewelry, sculpture, and paintings by Australian and international artists are on view at New Central Galleries. The Potters' Gallery is also worth a visit. A colony of arts and crafts showplaces has grown among the old narrow streets of Spring Hill close to the city. The Queensland Government Travel Centre can provide a list of interesting places to visit on a stroll through the district.

The Queensland Cultural Centre, located on the south bank of the Brisbane River, is the hub of the state's cultural activities. The Performing Arts Centre and Art Gallery are currently open, with the State Museum and Library to be completed soon. The complex is open daily from 10 A.M. to 5 P.M., and until 8 P.M. on Wednesdays.

Gardens and parks. Botanic Gardens—20 hectares/50 acres of flowers, shrubs, and trees—borders the Brisbane River next to Parliament House. The gardens are open daily from sunrise to sunset.

New Farm Park, alongside the Brisbane River east of the city, is a favorite with flower lovers. Some 12,000 rose bushes bloom here from September through November.

(Continued on page 122)

Will your boomerang come back?

For decades, the Australian Aborigines used the boomerang for hunting and warfare. The Aborigines are believed to have developed the returning boomerang, but nonreturning boomerangs were used by hunters in other parts of the world as well. Even North American Indians used a form of nonreturning boomerang.

Today, Australia's returning boomerang has evolved into a plaything, and throwing it has become a sport. There's even a national boomerang throwing championship held annually in New South Wales.

During your travels in Australia you might have an opportunity to learn how to throw a boomerang, and the first thing you'll learn is that it's not as easy as it looks. Here are a few tips that might help make your returning boomerang come back as it's supposed to.

First, do your boomerang throwing in a clear, open area. Hold the boomerang vertically by one of its tips, with the flat side of it facing away from you. Bring your arm back behind your head and then throw the boomerang forward toward the horizon. The trick of a good throw is the snap you give the boomerang as you let it go after your arm is fully extended in front of you. This snap creates a spin that's necessary for the boomerang to gain lift. If there's too much lift, though, the boomerang will climb too quickly and eventually plummet to the ground—a good way to break a boomerang.

If you've thrown correctly, the boomerang will make a wide circle and then return to you in a horizontal position. As it nears you it may make several more small spins, or hover before it lands near your feet. A skilled boomerang thrower can send a boomerang into a 45-meter/50-yard-wide circle before it returns.

If you don't succeed the first time, keep practicing, remembering that it's the snap that counts.

You can purchase souvenir boomerangs throughout Australia, some of them decorated with Aboriginal designs. For a close-up look at how boomerangs are made, take a tour of the Hawes Boomerang Farm near Brisbane (see page 125).

Queensland

CORAL SEA

Cape

York

Peninsula

Gulf of

Carpentaria

GREAT

Cooktown

Mossman

Port Douglas

Atherton
Tableland

Kuranda

Cairns

Innisfail

Normanton

Ingham

BARRIER

SOUTH

Townsville

Charters Towers

Proserpine

PACIFIC

Camooweal

Mt. Isa

Cloncurry

Flinders

Hwy

(18)

(78)

Mackay

REEF

Winton

(66)

(71)

Boulia

Landsborough

Hwy

Clermont

Longreach

Emerald

(64)

Capricorn

(1)

Hwy

Rockhampton

OCEAN

Gladstone

SIMPSON
DESERT
NATL.
PARK

Jundah

(66)

Bundaberg

Windorah

Fraser Island

Maryborough

Quilpie

Charleville

Warrego

Roma

Kingaroy

Gympie

(71)

Hwy

(54)

Sunshine Coast

Thargomindah

Cunnamulla

BUNYA MTNS
NATL. PARK

Ipswich

Brisbane

St. George

Toowoomba

Gold Coast

Goondiwindi

Warwick

(15)

Kilometers

| 0 | 50 | 125 |

| 0 | 50 | 125 |

Miles

Principal Roads (sealed)
Secondary Roads (sealed)
Unsealed Roads

Sun worshippers *flock to the golden sands of Surfers Paradise, a large resort area on the Gold Coast.*

...Continued from page 120

In October and November, jacaranda and bougainvillea are in bloom. Red poinciana trees blossom in November and December.

Oasis Tourist Garden at Sunnybank is a much-enjoyed spot with landscaped gardens, trimmed lawns, aviaries, swimming pools, and a garden cafe.

Exhibition Grounds, Bowen Hills, annually hosts the Royal National Show (Queensland's equivalent of a state fair), usually beginning the second week of August. A highlight of the winter season, the fair attracts great crowds from surrounding districts.

Shopping suggestions

Brisbane's main shopping area is bounded by Elizabeth, Edward, Adelaide and George streets. Here you'll find arcades, specialty shops, boutiques, and major department stores. The main department stores, David Jones, Myer's, and Barry and Roberts, can be found on Queen Street. A traffic-free pedestrian mall stretches along Queen Street between Albert and Edward streets.

In the heart of Brisbane, next to City Hall, is City Plaza, an impressive complex of specialty shops and open-air cafes opening onto plazas and courtyards. Access to pedestrians is from George, Ann, and Adelaide streets.

Many gift shops specialize in souvenir items—rugs, garments, and bags made from hides and skins; curios from Queensland woods; and jewelry from local gemstones (rubies, sapphires, and opals). You'll find the best selection of native handicrafts and artifacts at Queensland Aboriginal Creations on George Street, open from 9 A.M. to 4:30 P.M. Monday through Friday.

Antique hunters will have a field day in Brisbane and its suburbs. Ian Still features a variety of Papua New Guinea and Oceania primitive art in addition to a mixed stock of antiques. More than 20 other dealers round out the antique scene in Brisbane. At the Brisbane Antique and Art Centre in Clayfield, 35 antique dealers have shops under one roof.

Entertainment

Though Brisbane is not a lively nighttime city, several theaters stage professional or amateur productions; rock, jazz, and folk groups are featured; and there are theater-restaurants and a few discos.

The S.G.I.O. Theatre on Turbot Street is the home of the Queensland State Theatre Company. Her Majesty's Theatre on Queen Street features professional artists, many from overseas. Amateur groups stage productions at the Brisbane Art Theatre, 250 Petrie Terrace; La Boite, 57 Hale Street; Rialto Theatre, West End; and Twelfth Night Theatre, 4 Cintra Road, Bowen Hills. The Festival Hall on Charlotte Street offers operas, concerts, and ballets featuring overseas and local stars. The Living Room, a theater-restaurant, presents a dinner show nightly Tuesdays through Saturdays.

In late September/early October, Brisbane takes on a carnival air during "Warana"—a week-long spring festival with parades, concerts, art shows, beauty contests, and other events.

Things to do outdoors

For a relaxing break from travel tensions, stroll through one of Brisbane's city parks. Several are described on pages 120 and 122. Near the city's center, Victoria Park extends over 78 hectares/193 acres, providing playing grounds for many sports. Included in the park are the Municipal Golf Links and the Centenary Swimming Pool, an Olympic-size pool open September through April.

Also in pleasant park settings are the swimming pools of the Acacia Tourist Garden and Oasis Tourist Garden in Sunnybank.

Brisbane's leading golf clubs usually permit visitors to play when introduced by a member. Some have reciprocal arrangements with overseas clubs. These championship courses are open to visitors: Brisbane Golf Club, Indooroopilly Golf Cluf, Cailes Golf Club, and Royal Queensland Golf Club. Public golf clubs, in addition to the one at Victoria Park, are Pacific and Redcliffe.

Major tennis matches are held at Milton, home of the Queensland Lawn Tennis Association. For information about where to play, contact the association.

Horse racing ranks as the number one spectator sport in Brisbane. The Stradbroke Handicap and Brisbane Cup in June and the Doomben Ten Thousand and Doomben Cup in July are the chief races. Meets are held at the Queensland Turf Club at Eagle Farm, and at Doomben (Albion Park), and Bundamba. Trotting races are held at Albion Park. Greyhounds race at Woolloongabba.

Major cricket matches are those between the Australian states for the Sheffield Shield. These matches, at Woolloongabba, are 4 days long, usually starting on a Friday or Saturday. The season runs from October to February.

Rugby matches are played at Lang Park.

Brisbane River sailors test their skills in frequent yacht races down the river and across Moreton Bay. For sun, surf, and sand, it's hard to top the beaches of the Sunshine Coast to the north and the Gold Coast to the south.

Excursions in Brisbane's environs

Many day, half-day, and extended tours and cruises operate from Brisbane. A sampling is given here. For folders and additional possibilities, visit the Queensland Government Travel Centre in Brisbane.

Mount Coot-tha Forest Park

From this oasis of tall eucalypts and native shrubs only 8 km/5 miles from the city center, you can look out over Brisbane and the surrounding countryside to Moreton Bay and sometimes as far as the Glasshouse Mountains, 80 km/50 miles away. Within the park are the Mount Coot-tha Botanic Gardens. More than 2,000 native and exotic plants are on view in its Tropical Display Dome. Also featured are a cactus garden, fragrance garden, and the Sir Thomas Brisbane Planetarium.

Lone Pine Koala Sanctuary

One of Brisbane's top attractions, this privately owned acreage on the banks of the Brisbane River was the first koala sanctuary established in Australia. Its koala colony of about 100 is the largest on public display anywhere.

Koalas breed freely here; the owners release their surplus stock each year to state forests and national parks in an effort to re-establish the koala in its natural environment. One group of Lone Pine koalas now resides in California's San Diego Zoo.

You can reach the sanctuary by car in 15 minutes. Bus tours include it, often with a stop at Mount Coot-tha for a view of the city. Launches travel upriver from Brisbane's Hayles Wharf to the sanctuary and back.

In the sanctuary, you can have your picture taken holding one of the cuddly koalas. You'll also meet kangaroos, wallabies, wombats, Tasmanian devils, dingoes, a platypus, and a fascinating assortment of native birds.

Moreton Bay district

After it passes through the city, the Brisbane River swings northeast and empties into Moreton Bay, a huge body of water sheltered by Moreton and Stradbroke islands. The protected waters of the bay are well known to Brisbane residents, who have camped, fished, gone crabbing, and enjoyed the bay's water sports for years.

Moreton Island, about 32 km/20 miles east of the mouth of the river, is 39 km/24 miles long and boasts the world's highest permanent sand dunes—Mount Tempest (279 meters/914 feet) and Storm Mountain (267 meters/875 feet). From Brisbane you can reach Moreton Island by launch or light aircraft (Tangalooma Air Taxis). You can visit the island's main resort, Tangalooma, on a day cruise. For those who wish to stay longer, the resort offers comfortable accommodations. Island activities include swimming, surfing, riding, sand-hill tobogganing, tennis, fishing, and skin diving.

Stradbroke Island, just south of Moreton Island, is really two islands. North and South Stradbroke stretch south for 61 km/38 miles—almost to Surfers Paradise. Launches, vehicular ferries, and light aircraft provide access to North Stradbroke Island and its sparkling white beaches, fresh-water lakes, wildlife sanctuary, and small resorts.

Other activity centers include Wellington Point, Cleveland, and Victoria Point resorts along the southern mainland shores of Moreton Bay, and Bribie and Bishop islands, both popular picnicking and camping spots. You can swim, sun-bathe, or fish at any of the many beaches and resorts along the Redcliffe Peninsula.

The essentials

A capsule version of what you need to know about getting to and around Brisbane, and enjoying your stay there.

Getting there. Brisbane is served by air, rail, and bus. For services to northern Queensland, see page 112.

Air. International service to Brisbane by Qantas and foreign-flag carriers. Domestic flights to Brisbane and Coolangatta (Gold Coast) by Ansett, Australian, East-West, and Air New South Wales from Sydney and other Australian cities. Connecting flights from Brisbane to other Queensland cities also available. Brisbane International Airport is 8 km/5 miles from town by bus or taxi.

Rail. Brisbane Limited Express to Brisbane from Sydney, one train in each direction daily, leaving late afternoon, arriving the next morning; trip takes about 15½ hours.

Bus. Daily service from Sydney to Brisbane with stops at intermediate coastal towns.

Accommodations. Among the many major hotels in the Brisbane area are Brisbane Parkroyal, Crest International, Gateway, Gazebo Ramada, Lennons Brisbane, Sheraton Brisbane, Hilton Brisbane, and Brisbane City Travelodge. South of Brisbane, there are accommodations along the Gold and Sunshine coasts.

Food and drink. Wide range of ethnic restaurants in Brisbane and on Gold Coast. Local specialties: Queensland mudcrab, Moreton Bay bugs (a kind of crayfish, cooked and served in the shell), fresh seafood from Great Barrier Reef, beef from central Queensland, tropical fruits in season. Local beers include Castlemaine.

Most restaurants are licensed to serve wine, ales, and spirits. You can take your own beverages to unlicensed restaurants (called BYO restaurants). You'll be charged a small corkage fee.

Getting around. City-operated buses operate throughout Brisbane. For a small fee, Day Rover Tickets allow unlimited bus travel on the day ticket is purchased. Private bus lines supplement the city system; there's train service to the suburbs. Ferry service is provided across the Brisbane River between the Creek Street Landing and Park Avenue in East Brisbane, and between the Botanic Gardens and Kangaroo Point.

Tours: Half-day and full-day tours of city and to Gold Coast (this page), Sunshine Coast (page 125), Mount Coot-tha and Lone Pine (page 123), Mount Tamborine (page 126), Toowoomba and Darling Downs (page 126), Noosa Heads (page 125), and Lamington National Park (page 126). River cruises on Brisbane River and to Moreton Bay and Lone Pine.

For more information. Queensland Government Travel Centre, 196 Adelaide Street, Brisbane 4000.

Surf & sand, a coastal journey

Brisbane is the gateway to Australia's vacation country—the golden beaches that edge the continent north and south of the city. In less than 2 hours, you can reach the sand, surf, and swinging resort life of the Gold Coast or the somewhat more subdued Sunshine Coast, Queensland's most popular family resort area.

The Gold Coast

More than 5 million pleasure-seekers flock to the beaches of the Gold Coast every year. This highly developed stretch of coastline is Australia's answer to Florida's Miami, Hawaii's Waikiki, and Europe's Riviera.

The Gold Coast begins at Southport, about 80 km/50 miles south of Brisbane, and curves south in a series of beaches and bays to Coolangatta. It comprises a long string of beach communities that are officially one city with one mayor.

The golden sands are backed by a ribbon of resort development culminating in the skyscrapers of Surfers Paradise. Inland from the Gold Coast Highway are canals and waterways where picnicking, fishing, and boating are popular. Farther afield, in the lofty MacPherson Range, is a mountainous hinterland of lush rain forests. (See Lamington National Park, page 126, and Mount Tamborine, page 126.)

You can reach the Gold Coast easily by road or plane. There's bus service from Brisbane (1½ hours), and there's daily air service to Coolangatta. Local buses travel the coast between resort areas.

The Gold Coast can be explored in a day excursion from Brisbane, but if you wish to spend more time, you'll find a full range of accommodations. The Queensland Government Tourist Bureau publishes a guide to them.

For those who tire of the surf and sand, there are golf courses, tennis and squash courts, greyhound and horse races, trail rides into the bush, and deep-sea fishing trips. Other manmade tourist attractions include marine life shows, a wildlife sanctuary, a bird sanctuary, an auto museum, and a zoo. Launch and paddle boat tours operate from Surfers Paradise along the Nerang River. There are coffee houses, night clubs, and discos. You can dine *al fresco* on meals prepared by Continental chefs or pick up fish and chips or a hamburger at a beachside stand.

Sea World occupies 20 hectares/50 acres on a finger of land called The Spit that juts north from Surfers Paradise. Half the area is a manmade lake system. Here you can enjoy the antics of dolphins and sea lions; see sharks being fed; pet turtles and dolphins; ride a paddle wheeler, miniature train, or helicopter; watch a water-ski show; and swim in a large salt-water pool. It's open daily, 9 A.M. to 5 P.M.

Nearby attractions, a short distance from Sea World, include Fishermans Wharf and Bird Life Park.

Fishermans Wharf, on Sea World Drive, is a waterfront complex of seafood restaurants, taverns, and shops specializing in sports and casual fashions. Water tours also depart from here.

Bird Life Park, next to Sea World, presents a special

selection of wildlife in a natural setting. The park has a free-flight aviary, plus kangaroos, and koalas. There are also shows, informative talks, and presentations about these animals of Australia, plus a special area where you can pet and hand-feed some of them. The park is open daily, 9 A.M. to 5 P.M.

Springbrook side trip. This lush plateau offers some of the hinterland's most beautiful scenery—pasturelands, gorges, rain forests, mountain streams, and waterfalls. To explore this lofty region, on a spur of the MacPherson Range above the coast, take the road to Mudgeeraba from Burleigh Heads or Broadbeach.

At Mudgeeraba, you can learn the art of boomerang throwing at Hawes Boomerang Farm. Boomerangs are made, displayed, and sold here. Visitors can watch exhibition throwing, receive instruction, and try their skills on a practice field. There are a boomerang museum, a boomerang-shaped lake (spanned by a 9-meter/30-foot model of the Sydney Harbour Bridge), and a manmade opal mine where visitors can try their luck at finding opal chips. The farm is open daily except Saturday.

Two national parks, Gwongorella and Warrie, have pleasant picnic areas and networks of graded trails leading to view points. In Gwongorella National Park, you can hike to the edge of Purlingbrook Falls and look down into the fern-filled gorge below. Canyon Lookout above Warrie National Park offers views out to the coast.

At Wunburra on the Springbrook Road, a link road branches into scenic Numinbah Valley, a long, rich valley that lies between the sheer face of the Springbrook spur and the densely wooded slopes of Lamington National Park.

Currumbin Bird Sanctuary is just south of Currumbin Creek. Large flocks of wild birds—mostly brilliantly colored lorikeets—fly into the sanctuary from the bush each day to be fed bread and honey on plates held by visitors. There are morning and afternoon feedings.

Chewing Gum Field Aircraft Museum, on Guineas Creek Road, 6 km/4 miles from Currumbin Bird Sanctuary, is dedicated to military memorabilia. Within a World War II hangar are an extensive collection of ex-service aircraft, plus guns, uniforms, models, and engines. The museum is open daily from 9 A.M. to 5 P.M.

Gilltrap's Yesteryear World at Kirra is a unique auto museum where visitors can not only see vintage and veteran cars displayed but also can observe some of them in action and even ride in them. Four hour-long shows are given daily. The museum is open daily from 9 A.M. to 5:30 P.M.

Natureland, on the New South Wales side of the border, is Australia's third largest zoo, with a fine collection of the usual zoo birds and animals. It is open daily from 9 A.M. to 5 P.M.

Captain Cook Memorial and Lighthouse, an imposing landmark on Point Danger, Coolangatta, commemorates Cook's discovery of the east coast of Australia. It contains the world's first laser lighthouse beam.

The Sunshine Coast

Moving north along the coast from Brisbane, sun lovers will discover a long chain of splendid surfing beaches, appropriately named the Sunshine Coast, stretching from Caloundra to Noosa Heads and beyond. Relatively undeveloped, this area offers quiet relaxation on uncrowded beaches—a restful complement to the commercialized atmosphere of the Gold Coast.

The Sunshine Coast (about 80 km/50 miles from Brisbane) is easily reached by car, bus, or train. Light planes fly into the airport at Maroochydore.

The largest resort is Caloundra (109 km/68 miles north of Brisbane). Other major resorts include Mooloolaba, Maroochydore, Coolum Beach, Peregian Beach, and Noosa Heads.

Though the choice of accommodations is considerably more limited than on the Gold Coast, the northern resort facilities are certainly comfortable—and, in some cases, luxurious.

The Glasshouse Mountains rise abruptly from near-level countryside a few miles west of Caloundra. Captain Cook named the striking trachyte pillars in 1770; he chose the name because he thought they resembled the glass furnaces of his native Yorkshire. Beerwah (an Aboriginal word meaning "up in the sky") looms the highest at 555 meters/1,823 feet.

Kondalilla National Park boasts an oddity—the curious "lung fish" (*Neoceratodus fosteri*), a living fossil that subsists in deep pools in the park. Kondalilla also offers a sparkling waterfall and 75 hectares/185 acres of lush tropical rain forests.

The Noosa Heads area has a reputation for exceptionally beautiful coastal scenery: Witches' Cauldron, Hell's Gates, Devil's Kitchen, and Paradise Caves are a few of the spots you won't want to miss. Sunshine Beach at Noosa Heads draws surfboard champions from all over the world. Noosa National Park is a rugged, scenic coastal area with trails and picnic sites.

North of Tewantin, tidal salt-water lakes and fresh-water Lake Cooloola provide good fishing and an opportunity to view black swans, cranes, and other waterfowl.

A ginger factory and a sugar cane train are interesting stops on the drive along the coast. The only ginger factory in the Southern Hemisphere operates at Buderim; visitors are welcome to tour the plant, where ginger products may be purchased. South of Nambour, at Sunshine Plantation, you can ride on a sugar cane train through plantings of pineapples, bananas, passion fruit, and avocados, and visit an adjacent macadamia nut processing plant.

Fraser Island

The waters of Hervey Bay are sheltered by 145-km/90-mile-long Fraser Island, the largest island off the Queensland coast. It is known for its sweeping beaches, good fishing, surfing, swimming, fresh-water lakes, flora and fauna reserves, and Aboriginal relics.

The main resort is the Polynesian-style Orchid Beach Village, facing the Pacific on the island's extreme northeastern tip. All of the village buildings follow a basic Samoan *fale* (thatched hut) architectural design, featuring natural timbers and Polynesian decor. Self-contained fales and hillside units with private bath, some air-conditioned, accommodate 73 guests. From some units, you enjoy a view of bushland gardens; from others, you look across the waters of Marloo Bay.

(Continued on page 126)

...Continued from page 125

There's direct air service to Fraser Island from Brisbane, and charter flights take off from Maryborough and Hervey Bay. Launches serve the island from Hervey Bay, and there's vehicular barge service from Inskip Point.

Other interesting side trips

If you have time for more excursions from Brisbane, or perhaps a side trip from the Gold Coast, these destinations are worth considering. Each has its own distinctive features. All can be sampled in a full day, but to explore the areas leisurely, you may want more time.

The Darling Downs

A checkerboard of farmlands due west of Brisbane, the Darling Downs comprises 69,948 square km/27,000 square miles of black soil plains. Here climate and topography combine with fertile soil to make one of the country's richest agricultural districts.

Three main routes open this scenic country to motorists. From Brisbane, the Warrego Highway leads northwest through Toowoomba to Oakey, Dalby, and the far western centers. Cunningham Highway goes over Cunningham's Gap to Warwick and continues west via Inglewood and Goondiwindi. The New England Highway starts at Yarraman and heads southwest through Toowoomba and Warwick to the state border.

Toowoomba, Queensland's largest inland settlement and the commercial center for the area, is perched at 610 meters/2,000 feet on the crest of the Great Dividing Range 129 km/80 miles west of Brisbane. It is the state's "Garden City." During its annual Carnival of Flowers in September, floral decorations enhance public buildings, and flower-decked floats are featured in a carnival parade.

Toowoomba's Lionel Lindsay Art Gallery, 27 Jellicoe Street, commemorates this Australian artist with many of his paintings, woodcuts, and etchings, and displays the works of other Australian artists.

At the corner of James and Water streets, the Cobb & Co. Museum contains another interesting Australiana collection, including relics of horse and buggy days. A well-landscaped historical garden next to the museum includes trees and shrubs from foreign lands.

Creative 92, at 92 Margaret Street, presents a comprehensive display of crafts, ceramics, and showings by Queensland artists.

For a good look at Toowoomba and views of the Darling Downs, follow the signed Blue Arrow Route, a scenic 52-km/32-mile drive through the city and along the escarpment of the MacPherson Range. It will take you to Mt. Kynoch and Mt. Lofty for panoramic views of the city, and past Redwood Park, a bird and animal sanctuary.

Don't miss the view from Picnic Point, a gigantic headland on the crest of the range. You look out over Table Top Mountain—an extinct volcano capped with a flat, grassy plateau and clad with trees—across the coastal lowlands to the majestic heights of the border ranges.

Warwick, second largest city on the Darling Downs, occupies a quiet setting 84 km/52 miles south of Toowoomba on the banks of the Condamine River. The first of Queensland's sheep flocks were bred here on the southern Downs, and three of the earliest sheep stations—South Toolburra, Canning Downs, and Rosenthal—are still in existence. Today some of Australia's finest race horses are bred in this region.

Pringle Cottage on Dragon Street, built in 1863, displays relics of pioneering days; it is open daily, afternoons only.

Mount Tamborine

A full-day tour south from Brisbane takes you to this popular mountain resort, through subtropical vine jungles, past waterfalls veiled in mist, and into the rich vegetation of the rain forest.

Here the trees grow tall, and their heavy top foliage provides filtered shade for creepers, palms, ferns, orchids, and lilies. Strange carrabeeb trees thrive in the rain forests. On the western slopes of the mountains, you can see prolific stands of macrozamia palm trees, a species of cycad dating back millions of years. Some individual trees at Tamborine are thought to be 1,000 years old.

Butterflies are bred at the Butterfly Farm on Long Road (open daily summer months only). A walk-through path into the netted enclosure gives visitors a close-up look.

For a nominal fee, you can fossick for gemstones at Jasper Farm, Wonga Wallen, upper Coomera; or at Thunderbird Park, Cedar Creek. Both are open daily.

Lamington National Park

Another favorite mountain resort area, Lamington National Park lies some 113 km/70 miles south of Brisbane amid the cloudy peaks of the rugged MacPherson Range. This is a land of awesome chasms, unexplored tablelands, forests of ancient Antarctic beech trees, and views stretching to the coast and south into New South Wales.

Many coastal streams have their origins in the park's mountains. At Moran's Falls, tons of sparkling water plunge into a deep gorge.

Masses of wildflowers bloom in the spring, and the park is alive with bird and animal life. On a hike you may glimpse the Rufus scrub bird (a ventriloquist) or the magnificently plumed male Albert lyrebird. Pademelons (small wallabies) and possums feed near the lodges in the mornings and evenings.

Two simple but comfortable guest houses offer accommodations within the park boundaries. O'Reilly's "Green Mountains" resort is situated on the western summit of the park. Binna Burra Lodge is near the northeastern boundary.

Hiking trails radiate from both lodges. Binna Burra Lodge offers guided hikes, rock climbing lessons, and horseback rides. A special feature at Binna Burra is the Senses Trail developed for the blind; a rope along the circular trail makes the route easy to follow, and signs in Braille help the hiker to experience the forest surroundings by means of touch, smell, and hearing.

Climate in this mountain region is mild, but visitors should be prepared for chilly evenings even in summer. The lodges are popular; book well ahead for holiday periods or long weekends.

Silhouetted against the light, koala and kangaroo pause briefly for a fast-shooting photographer.

INDEX

INTRODUCING AUSTRALIA

An ancient continent filled with inviting contrasts

Australia is a faraway country of sun-burnt red earth. It's a city called Sydney and an ultramodern Opera House. It's kangaroos and koalas, bleating sheep and well-tanned cattle drovers. Australia is all of this and much, much more—nearly 8 million square km/3 million square miles, in fact—and filled with a remarkable range of travel experiences.

Comparable in size to the United States (excluding Alaska), Australia is an island continent in the South Pacific. It's the only continent with just one nation on it, and, geologically, it's believed to be the oldest continent on the earth. In the northwest corner of Western Australia, researchers recently found a fossil-laden rock 3.5 billion years old: the oldest known evidence of life on the globe.

Separated from other land masses early in its youth, Australia developed separately. Unique plant and animal life, native only to Australia, resulted from this separate development. One of the most unusual feats of Mother Nature is the country's marsupials: kangaroos, koalas, wombats, and Tasmanian devils. Raucous kookaburras, beautiful lyrebirds, and graceful black swans also claim Australia as their native home. Along with unusual fauna are fascinating flora like the eucalypt (gum tree). Varieties of these trees are found all over the world today, but they had their beginnings in Australia. For more information on Australia flora, see page 70.

A land of contrasts

The country offers a myriad of topography and color—rich red plains, blue green mountains, deep green pasturelands, and turquoise lagoons. Much of Australia's center, though, is a flat plateau of red earth occupying about three-fourths of the continent. Little rain falls in this outback area to nourish the vegetation. Though maps

Masters of the situation, these hard-working sheep dogs help rider herd flock of Merinos around twisted gum tree. Pastoral scene is repeated throughout world's top wool-producing country.

show many rivers flowing into central Australia, most streams go dry before they reach the huge salt flats that are called lakes, but which fill with water only in the wettest years.

Yet even in this apparently monotonous landscape there is striking beauty in the rocky peaks and red-walled chasms of the MacDonnell Ranges or the hulklike mass of Ayers Rock. To the south of these attractions the treeless Nullarbor Plain breaks off into dramatic, sheer cliffs of the Great Australian Bight.

Variety in landscape

The continent's principal mountain chain, the Great Dividing Range, is also varied in character. Paralleling the country's eastern coast for almost 4,023 km/2,500 miles, the Great Dividing Range includes the alpine peaks of the Snowy Mountains near Canberra, the gum-tree-covered Blue Mountains of New South Wales, and the jungle-clad mountains of Queensland. The country's most important river, the Murray, begins in the Great Dividing Range, then flows about 2,575 km/1,600 miles along the New South Wales-Victoria border and through South Australia to the Indian Ocean.

The well-watered foothills of the Great Dividing Range contain fertile farmlands and rich, tree-dotted pastures of grazing sheep and cattle. Here you'll find fast-running streams, leafy glades, and tumbling waterfalls.

In contrast, Australia's coastline (nearly 37,047 km/ 23,021 miles) contains miles of golden sand beaches, secluded coves, expansive bays, and dramatic headlands. It rates high on the country's list of scenic attractions. The eastern and southeastern coast is home for many Australians. In fact, all but one of the country's capital cities—Canberra— have the ocean at their doorsteps.

Then there are the tropical rain forests of the northern section of Australia which lie in the tropics above the Tropic of Capricorn. Here you'll find forests reminiscent of those in Asia and Africa where orchids grow wild and leafy tree ferns thrive. Brilliantly colored birds flit through these vine-tangled forests and even a crocodile or two might lurk in a swampy clearing.

One of Australia's great natural wonders—The Great

Barrier Reef—lies in this tropical region. Stretching in lazy arcs along the Queensland coast, the reef is really a series of reefs and underwater shoals. It includes one of the largest coral collections in the world—more than 350 varieties. In these clear, warm ocean waters, the reef supports a fascinating array of flora and fauna; it's a living laboratory for those who study marine life.

Varying climates

Seasons in Australia are the reverse of those in the Northern Hemisphere. Summer lasts from December through February, autumn from March through May, winter from June through August, and spring from September through November.

As the landscape of Australia varies, so does the climate. Summers in semi-tropical Sydney can be more humid than in Melbourne, and Melbourne's winters can be cooler than Sydney's. In both cities, sunshine intermingled with moderate rainfall can be expected the year around.

As you travel farther inland, the climate becomes warmer and much drier. In the arid interior, winter temperatures average 23°C/73°F, while summer temperatures can soar to 43°C/118°F or even higher. Rainfalls are few and far between.

The tropical northern coastal areas of Australia are hot and humid the year around, with temperatures averaging between 27°C/80°F and 33°C/91°F. Darwin, on the north coast, really has only two seasons—"the wet" and "the dry." The wet or monsoon season runs from November to April, and the dry season from April to October.

Australia's people

Of Australia's 15½ million people, 7 out of every 10 live in the country's major cities. As city people, they enjoy things that urban life can provide—modern shopping complexes, good restaurants, and an array of cultural events. Although they may work in the heart of the city, they live in sprawling nearby suburbs, in homes complete with gardens and outdoor barbecues much like those of the American West.

Beyond the cities and their suburban sprawl is the vast, little-populated outback of Australia. This is a land of rambling sheep and cattle stations—some of them bigger than some European countries. The men and women who live on these stations are tough and self-sufficient. The nearest neighbor might be a several-hour drive away from the veranda-trimmed homestead, light aircraft the best way to get into town. Station children learn their lessons by radio—the School of the Air (see page 107).

The good life. Australia is a country rich in natural resources. It's the world's leading producer of lead and zinc; it also exports copper in large quantities. Discoveries of vast iron ore deposits in Western Australia add to this mineral wealth. In addition the country is the world's biggest wool producer.

All this wealth contributes to the good life that many Australians enjoy. To most Australians, work is only part of their lives. With long hours of sunshine and pleasant weather much of the year, Australians want time to enjoy the outdoors and to enjoy their country.

Although many Australians don't live in the bush or the outback, the beautiful country beyond the city's doorstep is never far from mind. On weekends and during vacations, Australians love to escape to the country to fish, bushwalk, camp, or picnic. The "bush" is considered the wild country just beyond the city. The "outback" is farther away and far more desolate and rugged. Both hold an attraction for city-dwelling Australians.

Australians love outdoor sport whether it be bushwalking, swimming, sailing, golf, or tennis. When they are not playing, they are enthusiastically watching such outdoor sports as soccer, rugby, or Australian Rules football.

Along with this love of sports goes a love of gambling. Betting the horses is extremely popular. Nearly every Australian has purchased a lottery ticket at some time.

Roots in England. Many Australians come from British stock. Australia is part of the British Commonwealth, and the influence of England is evident in the fact that Australians drive on the left side of the road, and enjoy morning and afternoon tea.

The distinctive British pattern of speech is also evident, though altered somewhat by vigorous Australian idioms and pronunciation changes. As in England, apartments are "flats," candies are "lollies," and crackers are "biscuits." Then there are Aussie terms like "back of beyond" which means far away in the outback and "dinkum" which means honest or genuine.

Cosmopolitan influences. Many newcomers—immigrants from Europe since World War II—have added zest and an international flavor to Australia. Nearly one-third of Australia's people are first or second-generation immigrants. A large portion of these new arrivals are from the British Isles; other immigrants include Europeans (Dutch, Italians, Greeks, Yugoslavs, Spaniards, Scandinavians, Hungarians, Czechoslovaks, Turks, Poles, and Icelanders), North and South Americans, Asians, and Arabs.

Something for everyone

With Australia's diversity in landscape and lifestyle, the country can accommodate its many visitors with varied interests—from the person who enjoys the cosmopolitan life of the big city to the person who wants to ride a camel through the outback and sleep under the stars.

Big city offerings

Australia's larger cities—Sydney, Melbourne, Adelaide, Perth, Canberra, and Brisbane—offer high-rise hotels, gourmet restaurants, and cultural opportunities. Visitors can attend a performance of the opera at Sydney's famous Opera House or a concert at Melbourne's Victorian Arts Centre. The Adelaide Festival, held in March on even-numbered years, offers visitors a bonus of 22 days of cultural performances and art exhibits. Sydney's Australian Museum provides a glimpse of Aboriginal artifacts, and Fremantle's Maritime Museum near Perth takes you back to the 16th century, with relics of Dutch explorers. Canberra's National Gallery houses Australian, European, Oriental, and American art.

(Continued on page 10)

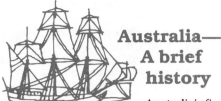

Australia— A brief history

Australia's first inhabitants came from Asia about 40,000 years ago. Some traveled across a land bridge (now submerged); others came by raft or canoe. Descendants of these first Aborigines still live in Australia today.

Thousands of years later, 2nd century European geographers were suggesting that a large land mass existed at the southern end of the world. Otherwise, they said, the earth couldn't possibly remain upright. They called this southern land mass "Terra Australis Incognita," which appropriately means "Unknown South Land."

The discovery. As early as the 1500s, Portuguese exploring the East Indies may have sighted Australia. A Portuguese navigator, Pedro de Quiros, thought he had found the "southern continent" when he discovered the New Hebrides in 1606. That same year Willem Jansz of the Dutch East India Company discovered and charted 322 km/200 miles of the north Australian coast. This is the first recorded discovery of Australia.

During the 17th century, Portuguese, Dutch, and British navigators carried out preliminary explorations and charting of the country's northern and western coastline. Abel Tasman discovered the island of Tasmania in 1642 and named it Van Dieman's Land. These early explorers gave dour accounts of the country, characterizing it as "the barrenest spot upon the globe." It was dismissed as being an improbable area for development, with nothing of commercial value, so interest in the continent lapsed for three-quarters of a century.

Credit for the "rediscovery" of Australia goes to the intrepid English explorer, Captain James Cook. On April 29, 1770, Cook cast anchor in Botany Bay near the site of Sydney's present-day airport. He charted the whole eastern coast and took possession of it for the British calling it New Wales. Having seen Australia's lush east coast, he was able to send glowing reports back about possibilities for colonization.

Settling Australia. With the American Revolution, England lost a place to transport the overflow of convicts from its innumerable prisons. England's jails and prison ships were overcrowded, and the country was in search of new territory to settle. Australia seemed a good alternative, so Britain sent a shipment of convicts under the command of Captain Arthur Phillip to establish a settlement in Australia. In a simple ceremony on January 26, 1788, Phillip unfurled the Union Jack at what is now Sydney, drank to the King's health, and set to work building the colony of New South Wales.

During the next 80 years, another 100,000 convicts were transported to Australia. With them were free settlers willing to endure the hardships of a strange land to make a new life. At first the going was rough. Crops failed, stock escaped, supply ships were delayed. But slowly, painfully, the colonists succeeded in the most difficult pioneering effort in history.

One of the most important developments during the country's early history came from the experiments of Captain John MacArthur. In 1801, he began breeding sheep for a fine wool. The results of his experiments— the Australian Merino—produce some of the finest wool in the world.

Exploring a strange land. Australia's first settlements were along the coast and transportation between them was primarily by boat—the inland regions seemed too inhospitable for overland travel. Gradually, however, Australians began to see what was beyond their "back door." In 1813 William C. Wentworth's expedition crossed the Blue Mountains west of Sydney. Between 1827 and 1829 Charles Sturt charted much of the Darling River and its tributaries, and in 1841 Edward Eyre walked the entire southern coast of Australia across the Nullarbor Plain to the west coast.

Along with the success of these first explorations, there were some tragic failures. Ludwig Leichardt and his party disappeared in 1848 while attempting to travel overland from Queensland to Perth. The Burke and Wills expedition ended in death for both men during their 1860 attempt to cross Australia from south to north.

Beginnings of a nation. The discovery of gold by Edward Hargreaves in 1851 brought a tide of immigration that doubled the population in 10 years. New South Wales peacefully achieved responsible self-government in 1855, and by 1890 the rest of the colonies had followed suit. Federation came quickly—January 1, 1901, saw the birth of the Commonwealth of Australia.

With the exception of a brief uprising during the gold rush period, the nation's history has been one of unbroken domestic tranquility. The city of Darwin was bombed by the Japanese in 1942, but no enemy troops have ever set foot on Australian soil. Australian troops fought with distinction in two world wars and in conflicts in Korea and Vietnam.

The government. Since 1901 Australia has been governed as a federal commonwealth, with both federal and state parliaments modeled on a thoughtful mixture of British, American, Canadian, and Swiss democracies. A prime minister heads the national government, and a premier leads each of its six states: New South Wales, Victoria, Queensland, South Australia, Western Australia, and Tasmania. Governors in each of the states, along with a governor general, represent the British Crown in Australia.

In addition to states, Australia has several territories. On mainland Australia are the Northern Territory and the Australian Capital Territory (A.C.T.), site of Canberra, the nation's capital city. Six more territories— ranging in size from tiny Christmas Island to Australia's holdings in the Antarctic—lie outside the continent.

One feature of Australian politics is that enfranchised adults are required to vote, under penalty of fine.

...*Continued from page 8*

Outdoor enthusiasts will love the many parks and waterways of Australia's cities. You can row a canoe on the Yarra River in Melbourne or the Swan River in Perth, or sail a boat on Sydney's beautiful harbor. Golf, tennis, cycling, and jogging are among activities available.

A glimpse of history

Sights throughout Australia speak of Australia's early days. The Rocks, one of Sydney's restored areas, is where a nation began after Captain Phillip's convict ships anchored in Sydney Cove in 1788. To the south in Tasmania, other convicts toiled under harsh conditions at Port Arthur's penal colony.

Australia also has a number of folk museums that show life the way it was in Australia's early years. Swan Hill's Pioneer Settlement in northern Victoria is a re-creation of a 19th century Australian inland river town. Sovereign Hill Goldmining Township, also in Victoria, evokes memories of Australia's gold rush era. This historical park re-creates the town of Ballarat during its first 10 years of development following the discovery of gold in the area in 1851. For a real gold rush ghost town, journey out to Coolgardie in Western Australia. During its heyday, this town was considered queen of the gold fields.

A taste of the grape

Wine-country touring in Australia can be every bit as interesting, educational, and fun as it is in France or California. Australia's wines are diverse. So are the wineries; they range from small to large and family-owned to cooperative, some in historic chateaux, others in modern, functional structures.

You'll find most of the wine-producing vineyards concentrated in three states—South Australia, New South Wales, and Victoria. Other smaller wine-producing areas are located in Western Australia, Queensland, and Tasmania. No matter which of these regions you visit, you'll find that wine people are friendly and enjoy sharing with you the story of how they make their wines; and frequently they'll allow you to sample their product.

Heading the list of wine-producing regions is the Barossa Valley just north of Adelaide in South Australia. Other South Australia wine regions you can tour include the Clare Valley, Southern Vales, Coonawarra, and Murray River. In New South Wales you can go touring and tasting in the Hunter River Valley or the Riverina District. In Victoria take a trip to Rutherglen or the Great Western District.

The lure of the wild

Lovers of the great out-of-doors will not lack opportunity to commune with nature in Australia. The country has 500 national parks, from the rugged, rocky beauty of the Flinders Ranges to the white sands of the Great Barrier Reef islands, set aside to preserve and protect a variety of terrain, vegetation, and wildlife.

In Australia's many fauna parks you can feed a kangaroo or lorikeet, or hold a koala. Especially noteworthy are the Cleland Conservation Park near Adelaide, the Currumbin Bird Sanctuary on the Queensland Gold Coast, and the Lone Pine Koala Sanctuary near Brisbane.

Still other outdoor experiences include adventure tours in the outback or a tropical rain forest. These Australian adventure tours are numerous and varied (see page 15 for more information on them).

Rockhounds with an inclination to strike it rich can take their picks to remote opal mining areas like Coober Pedy, Andamooka, or Lightning Ridge. Lovers of farming and ranching can spend time at one of Australia's many cattle or sheep stations.

Traveling Down Under

You can reach Australia from North America, Europe, Southeast Asia, the Orient, many South Pacific Islands, New Zealand, and South Africa. More frequent air service has made access quick and easy; more than two dozen international air carriers serve the country.

Air travel has made a voyage by ship a rare experience, though many cruise lines still call at several Australian ports.

Tours to Australia are numerous. You can choose from escorted tours, independent tours, special interest tours, and adventure tours. The choice depends on what you want to spend and what you want to see and do. Because of the number of options available for your trip to Australia, it's wise to seek the advice of a knowledgeable travel agent to help plan your trip.

Getting there by air

Both direct and connecting flights link Sydney with major North American cities. Airlines providing service from the United States include Qantas, Continental, Air New Zealand, United, and UTA French Airlines. Qantas, Canadian Pacific, Continental, and Air New Zealand provide service from Canada.

Sydney, Melbourne, Cairns, and Brisbane are important arrival cities for international flights from North America, but Darwin, Perth, Townsville, Adelaide, and Hobart all have international airports too.

A variety of discount air fares are now available to travelers heading for Australia. Traveling independently, visitors can take advantage of several Advance Purchase Excursion (APEX) fares. The seasons you travel will dictate the round-trip cost. There are different low, shoulder, and peak season rates for each direction of travel. Air fares fluctuate a great deal; the amount of time spent in Australia and the miles traveled will affect the cost of your ticket. Consult a travel agent for specific rates.

Getting there by boat

In this jet age, not many passenger ships sailing from the United States stop at Australian ports. A number of cruise lines—Royal Viking, P & O, Salen Linblad Cruising, Society Expeditions, Cunard, Sitmar, Royal Cruise Line, and Princess Cruises—include Australia in their world or circle-Pacific cruise itineraries. These cruises often stop at some South Pacific islands and at least one New Zealand port. Sydney, Melbourne, Adelaide, Perth, Darwin, and Hobart are the usual Australian ports-of-call.

Aboriginal drovers *herd cattle (above) on a station in Northern Territory outback. Some Australian stations are larger than some countries.*

Grim determination *shows on faces of lifeguards marching with military precision (right) at summer surf carnival. After parade, guards take to boats in a show of speed and skill.*

Sleek horses and groomed sheep *parade toward reviewing stand at a Royal Show (below). Annual event is renowned for livestock and agricultural exhibits.*

Sports— A way of life

To Australians, sports are more than a mere pastime or form of recreation— they're a way of life. A zest for living only partially explains their sports-mindedness. Their fanatical loyalty and competitive spirit develop from rigorous physical training at school, a continuing drive to beat the other fellow, and the double advantage of a favorable climate and a high standard of living.

Sports to watch

You can learn a great deal about the Australian's love for sports if your travels include a sports event. Popular spectator sports in Australia include horse racing, football (Australian Rules, rugby League, rugby Union, and soccer), and cricket.

Horse racing. Most pervasive of the spectator sports is horse racing. Many Australians have a natural love for gambling and this sport of kings allows them to place their bets. Throughout the year, you'll find races being run somewhere—from small country meetings to colorful major events attracting thousands of spectators. Races are usually run on Saturday, but you'll also find them held mid-week. (In Canberra, races are run on Sunday as well.)

The biggest horse race—in number of spectators and impact on Australians—is the Melbourne Cup (see page 63). Other major racing events during the year include the AJC (Australia Jockey Club) Derby held at Randwick Racecourse in Sydney in October, and Melbourne's Caulfield Cup also in October. These big meets are always sellouts requiring advance arrangements; your travel agent can usually make them for you.

You place your bets for the races at windows operated by the Totalizator Agency Board (TAB), the state-controlled betting organization which uses the pari-mutuel machine, an Australian invention. (The Aussies also were the first to introduce the photo-finish camera.) You'll also find TAB "shops"—betting agencies—in most cities throughout the country, enabling you to bet on the big races whether or not you can attend.

On a smaller scale are the bush or picnic meetings, and they provide an even better way to get to known Australians. Bush horse racing has no season; races are held throughout the year. Some of these bush meets are on race tracks with stands, while others are simply a course marked out with stakes. Often the picnic is almost as important as the race, with sumptuous spreads for frontier appetites.

Still another form of horse racing is harness racing— called "trotting." With the advent of night race meetings and legalized betting, this sport has increased in popular-

ity. The harness-racing season runs from October through July.

Football mania. Each year many Australians are gripped with a seasonal passion second to none when it comes to numbers of avid, highly partisan followers. Australian Rules football is said to have greater support per person than any other field sport in the world today, though it's played only in Australia where it was invented.

The game's most avid followers are perhaps in Victoria where Melbourne is the center for club matches that can draw 100,000 spectators. The area's twelve professional league teams do battle in 6 league games each Saturday from April to September. The finals, held in September, attract even greater crowds. "Aussie Rules" is also played and enthusiastically supported in each of Australia's other states.

Still another football game—League (professional) rugby—has its own group of strong supporters in New South Wales and Queensland. Union (amateur) rugby finds fans in rural areas. Soccer (association football) is played throughout Australia.

Cricket. This English game has an avid following in Australia during the summer season (October to March). It was first played in Sydney in 1803, but not until 1877 did the Australians feel qualified to hold their first test match with England. Their first victory on English soil came in 1882, and since then they've bested the English at their own game a number of times.

International Test Matches—Australia versus England or another cricket-playing country—are held in capital cities every second year from December to February. All states except Tasmania play each other twice a season (at home and away) for the Sheffield Shield, symbol of cricket supremacy in Australia.

Lawn bowls. Every Saturday, and often on workdays as well, you can watch white-clad members of lawn bowling teams rolling their black balls down immaculately kept greens toward a white "kitty" or "jack"—the target. The point of the game is to get as close to the target as you can with your black ball.

Bowling greens seem to be everywhere—in capital cities and in small country towns. As a visitor, you're welcome to watch; and if you're interested, it's relatively easy to get an invitation to participate. However, you must wear traditional whites for tournament play. The sport's major event, the Australian Gold Coast Winter Bowls Carnival, is held in July along the Gold Coast and attracts more than 1,000 entries.

Sports to play

With more than 80 sports enthusiastically played down under, there's something for everyone, so you shouldn't miss the opportunity to enjoy your favorite sport while in Australia.

Tennis. Australians are avid tennis players. This fact is evident in the number of top players the country has produced. In all major city areas, you'll find a wealth of public and private courts with equipment for hire. There are both hard courts and beautifully maintained lawn courts. If you belong to a club at home, you can almost always get honorary privileges at clubs in Australia.

Golf. Australia's golf courses challenge every type of golfer, from the tournament-hardened professional to the casual amateur. As Australia's big cities enlarged, the greenbelt of golf courses remained where they were placed 40 to 60 years ago. As a result, many of the top golf courses are less than a 30-minute drive from a city center.

You can choose your style, playing a round on a public course or on a private course with a club member. Capital cities have a number of excellent public courses where green fees are modest and clubs can be hired. Leading country clubs welcome visitors introduced by a member and some have reciprocal arrangements with overseas clubs. If you are a member of a club at home, ask your club's secretary-manager for a letter of introduction to the Australian club and have him include your handicap.

Deep-sea fishing. The incredible variety of fish in the seas surrounding Australia attracts fishermen from around the world. The best season is between November and May, though sharks are caught the year around. Fishermen claim the prime area is along Australia's eastern and southeastern coast—particularly off Queensland, New South Wales, South Australia, and Tasmania.

The best ocean fishing is in the waters off northern and southern Queensland; the waters of southern New South Wales—around Sydney and the Bermagui-Eden area; and off Tasmania's rugged southeastern coast. In South Australia, most favored waters are Streaky Bay; the mouth of Spencer Gulf near Port Lincoln; and the prolific waters of Backstairs Passage, between Kangaroo Island and the mainland. Tuna fishing is so good around the island of Tasmania and off the South Australia coast that annual tuna tournaments are held at both places—off Eaglehawk Neck in Tasmania in March or April and at Port Lincoln, South Australia, in January.

Numerous game fishing charter boats and water safaris are available. Charter and tariff information is available from the Australian Tourist Commission.

Stream and lake fishing. The Australian Alps, lying between New South Wales and Victoria, offer many mountain streams and lakes teeming with good-size brown and rainbow trout. Among the best of these spots is massive Lake Eucumbene, formed by the big Snowy Mountain hydroelectric scheme southwest of Canberra. Thousands of fingerling trout are released each year into this huge reservoir by the New South Wales Fisheries Department.

Still another good fishing spot is Tasmania. Some of Tasmania's good fishing streams and lakes are rarely visited by fishermen, and the quality and size of trout are very high. Best Tasmanian haunts are the northwest coastal rivers, the highlands, the Huon Valley area in the south, and the upper reaches of the Derwent River.

An inland fishing license is compulsory. Regulations governing closed season and bag limits vary from state to state. In most states the fishing season is from September through April. In Tasmania, the season is from November to April on lakes, and from September through April for inland streams and estuaries. At Lake Eucumbene there's fishing year around.

Skiing. Australia's snowfields are skiable from June through September. Well-known ski resorts include Thredbo Village, Perisher Valley, and Smiggin Holes—all in the Snowy Mountains of New South Wales. In Victoria, areas such as Falls Creek and Mounts Buller, Hotham, and Buffalo offer good skiing.

Skiers will find lodging, shops, restaurants, and ski schools at the resorts. Slopes are reached by chairlifts, T-bars, Poma lifts, and rope tows.

The surf world

Australia has beaches to suit everyone—from wading children to daring surfers to people who just want to relax and bake in the sunshine. During Australia's warm summer months—November to March—people flock to the beaches to do just that. This is also the time of the surf carnival (see page 28).

Surfing. Australians love to surf. Body surfing became popular in the early 1900s, but it wasn't until 1915 that Hawaii's Duke Kahanamoku introduced board riding at Freshwater Beach, Sydney.

Surfers may be reluctant to tell you their favorite beaches (preferring to keep the traffic to a minimum), but the eastern coast, from Melbourne to north of Brisbane, has good surfing beaches as does the western coast near Perth.

Skin and scuba diving. Stretching 2,012 km/1,250 miles north and south along the Queensland coast, Australia's Great Barrier Reef provides a paradise for skin divers and underwater photographers. Bright sunlight shafts down into the coral-studded depths, providing an almost ethereal atmosphere for divers. Fascinating coral grottoes and colorful tropical fish provide an enthralling setting.

Heron Island and Green Island, the major coral island resorts along the reef, are the two main areas for skin divers and photographers. Divers prefer them for the marine life, ease of accessibility, and availability of equipment and service. A number of diveboats journey out to the Great Barrier Reef, providing day trips from the mainland and island resorts, as well as extended trips where you live on board overnight or longer.

Yachting. You'll find this sport nearly as popular as surfing. On weekends, the country's harbors, bays, and rivers come alive with sailboats. Club and interclub races are exciting to watch.

Good sailing areas include Sydney Harbour, the Derwent River at Hobart, Adelaide's Gulf St. Vincent, Perth's Swan River, Melbourne's Port Phillip Bay, and Brisbane's Moreton Bay and Brisbane River. One of the best places to sail is the Whitsunday Passage off the Queensland coast.

If you are a member of a yacht club at home, you may be given facilities privileges at an Australian sailing club. Those with sailing know-how can charter a boat with or without a crew.

Waves crash on headland facing Bermagui, a quiet village known for its excellent fishing. Popular for holidays, town is near the lively resort of Narooma.

Sydney Tower's golden capsule offers observation floors and restaurants, lofty perches for viewing city's mix of historic and modern architecture.

Day's changing light adds muted brilliance to the Olgas (below), massive weathered rocks rising above flat central plains.

A word about tours

There's a multitude of packaged tours on the market today, so before planning your trip to Australia, investigate the types of tours available. With some tour packages, you travel in a group escorted by a tour guide and have a set itinerary. Still other tours offer you the independence of designing your own trip and setting your own pace at package discount prices. For those of you with special interests, there are trips designed with you in mind.

Escorted tours. Varying in length from about 18 to 36 days, these tours can feature Australia only, or Australia and New Zealand, or even Australia, New Zealand, Tahiti, and Fiji. Some even include Papua New Guinea in the country combination. Tours featuring a number of destinations usually include only a few of Australia's highlights—Sydney, the Snowy Mountains, Melbourne, and Canberra. Tours focusing just on Australia include a number of capital cities as well as the Alice Springs area and the Great Barrier Reef.

These escorted tours usually include transportation, accommodations, some meals, and sightseeing.

Traveling independently. There are fly/drive tours, fly/coach tours, fly/camper-van tours, fly/rail tours, and fly/tour packages available. With these packages you get a round-trip ticket to Australia, a pass for the type of transportation you want to use, and a pass for selected hotels (except on the camper-van tour). You set the pace you want to travel and select your destinations.

Special interest tours. Whether you're an avid golfer, an enthusiastic rockhound, or a cattle rancher who wants to learn more about cattle raising Down Under, Australia's expansive country has something to offer. Special golf tours feature play on Australia's top courses. Ranchers can learn more about Australia's agricultural development on tours to sheep and cattle properties; skin divers can explore the beauty of the Great Barrier Reef on diving tours designed especially for them. Tours for rockhounds include fossicking in the opal fields of Coober Pedy and Lightning Ridge. Tasting tours for wine connoisseurs go to two of Australia's wine regions—the Hunter and Barossa valleys. There are tours for horse breeders, bird watchers, anglers, and horticulturists.

These tours often include round-trip air fare, accommodations, and transportation within the country, as well as a tour guide.

Adventure tours. For the person who likes to rough it a little, there are adventure tours in Australia to the outback and country areas. You travel away from tourist roads and accommodations consist of a sleeping bag and tent. There are four-wheel-drive safari trips into North Queensland's rain forests, white-water raft trips on the upper Murray River in Victoria, camel treks into South Australia's North Flinders Ranges, alpine hikes into the Snowy Mountains, and bicycle trips around Tasmania.

A place to stay

Accommodations in Australia are as varied as the landscape itself and range from modern high-rise hotels with first-class facilities to comfortable motels, serviced apartments, resort cabins, youth hostels, trailer parks (the Australians call them caravan parks), and campgrounds.

In general, travelers can expect a more limited choice of lodgings outside the major urban and resort centers. Outback facilities cannot always offer air-conditioning and private bathrooms; but they often compensate with good home cooking and a family atmosphere. Your hosts can offer valuable information about local attractions and road conditions.

It's advisable to make advance bookings for accommodations since Australians enjoy traveling themselves and accommodations are sometimes tight, especially during holiday periods. Though varying from state to state, these holiday periods are generally the summer holidays—a week or two before Christmas through the end of January; May holidays—one or two weeks in mid-May; August holidays—two or three weeks beginning mid-August to late August, mid-September (Queensland and Western Australia), or early October (Northern Territory); Easter—a few days before and after Easter. If you are planning your trip during any of these periods, confirmed reservations are essential, particularly in vacation areas. This applies not only to accommodations but also to transportation from place to place.

Accommodation bookings can be made with your travel agent before you leave for Australia or, upon your arrival, with the state tourist board office or a local travel agent.

Note that standard check-out time in Australia is generally 10 A.M. (some hotels 11 A.M.).

Hotels, motels & serviced apartments

The wide choice of accommodations in and near Australia's major cities and resort areas is tailored to every taste and budget. There are high-rise hotels featuring restaurants, shops, and cocktail lounges. The Wrest Point Hotel-Casino in Hobart, Tasmania, includes a gambling casino; you'll find similar hotel-casinos in Launceston, Tasmania; in Townsville and on Queensland's Gold Coast; and in Alice Springs and Darwin in the Northern Territory. (Adelaide has a casino without adjoining hotel.)

In addition to plush hotels, there are simple but comfortable private hotels, guest houses, and cottages.

Built mainly in recent years, Australian motels, motor lodges, and motor inns enjoy a high reputation. You'll find them in and near major cities, in smaller towns, and in resort areas. They range from four or five-unit "family" motels to luxurious high-rise establishments. Most motel rooms—like many hotels—provide refrigerators and facilities for preparing coffee and tea; restaurants are often attached to the motel. A unique room service feature in many motels is a special delivery hatch for your tray. Your food is delivered through the outer door of this hatch which is then closed, you can then open the inside door to retrieve your meal in complete privacy.

The serviced apartment is another accommodation option in capital cities and major resort areas. Consisting of one to three rooms, as well as a bathroom and a kitchen, these apartments are generally fully equipped with cooking and eating utensils and linens. Prepared meals are not usually available on the premises.

Youth hostels

Affiliated with the International Youth Hostel Federation, the nearly 130 hostels in Australia vary in size and in the facilities they offer. You'll find youth hostels in every state; for more information, write to the Youth Hostels Association, 118 Alfred Street, Milsons Point, New South Wales 2061. You'll also find additional accommodations at YMCA and YWCA facilities.

For more information contact...

The Australian Tourist Commission (ATC) can be a helpful source of trip-planning information.

In the United States, ATC offices are located at 3550 Wilshire Boulevard, Suite 1740, Los Angeles, CA 90010 and at 489 Fifth Avenue, 31st Floor, New York, NY 10017.

The Australian Tourist Commission's head office is located at 324 St. Kilda Road, Melbourne, Victoria 3004, Australia.

For information on visa applications, contact the nearest Australian consular office (see page 20).

Each of Australia's states and territories operates a tourist bureau or travel center in the United States (see below). For addresses of state tourist offices in Australia, check "The essentials" feature in each chapter.

New South Wales Tourist Commission
2049 Century Park East, Suite 2250
Los Angeles, CA 90067

Victorian Tourism Commission
3550 Wilshire Boulevard, Suite 1736
Los Angeles, CA 90010

Northern Territory Tourist Commission
3550 Wilshire Boulevard, Suite 1610
Los Angeles, CA 90010

Queensland Tourist & Travel Corporation
3550 Wilshire Boulevard, Suite 1738
Los Angeles, CA 90010

South Australian Department of Tourism
3550 Wilshire Boulevard, Suite 1740
Los Angeles, CA 90010

Western Australian Tourism Commission
3550 Wilshire Boulevard, Suite 1610
Los Angeles, CA 90010

Tasmanian Department of Tourism
3550 Wilshire Boulevard, Suite 1740
Los Angeles, CA 90010

Australian Home Accommodation
209 Toorak Road, Suite 4
South Yarra, Victoria 3141, Australia

Farm Holidays
9 Fletcher Street
Woollahra, N.S.W. 2025, Australia

Host Farms Association
'Fairview'
Gnarwarre, Victoria 3221, Australia

Camping out in Australia

A number of trailer parks—caravan parks—are located near big cities and towns as well as out in the country. You can enjoy the economy of these parks without having to haul along your own trailer: many of the parks have on-site vans (house trailers) for hire at very reasonable rates. These are usually equipped with stove, refrigerator, eating and cooking utensils, linens, etc.

If you want to travel in a camper-van, a number of rental car agencies have camper-vans for hire that are fully equipped (sometimes at a small extra charge).

Some caravan parks have specially designated areas for tent camping. You'll also find regular campgrounds throughout Australia and in some of the country's many national parks.

Farm holidays

If you want to enjoy the country life, you can choose from a number of farms (stations) that offer accommodations. It's an excellent way to meet Australians and enjoy some warm hospitality.

Accommodations on these stations can vary from very plush to very spartan. In some places, you might stay in your own separate cottage; in others you might be in the station owner's home, eating with the family and sharing their bathroom facilities.

While on the farm, you're on your own to do whatever you wish, including the farm chores. You can also fish in a nearby creek, swim in the family swimming pool (or waterhole), or go for a horseback ride.

A list of stations offering farm holidays is available from each state's tourist board and from the addresses at left.

Meet an Australian

There are several "bed and breakfast" plans that feature a stay with a local family. Your accommodations might be a waterfront home near Sydney, a beach-side house on the Gold Coast, or a sheep property in Victoria.

For more information, contact Bed and Breakfast International (Australia), 396 Kent Street, Sydney, N.S.W. 2000, Australia.

Traveling around a vast country

Australia is a vast land of nearly 8 million square km/3 million square miles, much of it sparsely populated because people tend to live in or near capital cities. The distances between these centers are great, but seem even greater because of their empty openness.

The quickest way from city to city is by air. Roads between cities generally have only two lanes.

The following tells you the length of time it takes to travel between certain cities. From Sydney to Alice Springs, it takes about 3 hours by air and 56 hours by bus. The trip from Sydney to Brisbane takes a little over an hour by air and almost 18 hours by bus. The distance between Sydney and Melbourne can be covered in little over an hour by air, but takes 14½ hours by bus.

Flying around Australia

Early in Australia's history, the country realized the importance of air service in linking isolated towns. The first route flown was between Geraldton and Derby in Western Australia in 1921. In 1922, Queensland and Northern Territories Aerial Services Limited (now known as Qantas, the country's international carrier) began flights between Cloncurry and Charleville, Queensland.

Today, frequent air service links all of Australia's cities and many smaller towns. Both Ansett Airlines and Australian Airlines (formerly Trans-Australia) have routes throughout Australia. East-West Airlines has an extensive network in New South Wales with additional service to other states. Kendell Airlines connects cities and towns in New South Wales, South Australia, and Victoria.

Air New South Wales flies to points within New South Wales, and to Ayers Rock. Ansett N.T. covers the Northern Territory and flies to Cairns. Ansett W.A. connects the vast reaches of Western Australia to Darwin and Alice Springs. Air Queensland provides service within this state. In addition to these larger airline companies, numerous small airlines provide regional services.

Discounts. Although Australia's airline services can be convenient, they also can be expensive. Several discount packages are available to help reduce the costs of Australian air transportation. We mention a few of the available discounts below. Since fares vary from season to season—and even from week to week—always consult a travel agent for the latest information on ticket fares and restrictions.

Airlines offering discount packages include Ansett Airlines, Australian Airlines, East-West Airlines, Air New South Wales, and Kendell Airlines. Many of the discounted fares are offered only to persons holding international airline tickets. In some cases, these tickets must be either an excursion or promotional airfare to qualify for the domestic air carrier discount. These discount tickets may have to be purchased prior to arrival.

Both airpasses and discount airfares are available. Some airpasses allow unlimited mileage on the carrier's routes with a maximum number of days to complete the journey. Still other airpasses set limitations on the number of miles traveled within a specified time frame. Stopover restrictions may also apply. Airfare discounts usually range from 20 to 35 percent and a minimum number of sectors may be required.

Reservations. As with hotel accommodations, it is advisable to make advance reservations for flights, especially during holiday periods. You can make your reservations through your travel agent or, in Australia, with the airline office concerned.

Riding the rails

Australia's network of rail lines provides numerous rail travel opportunities. The principal lines follow the east and south coasts, linking the principal cities of Cairns, Brisbane, Sydney, Melbourne, and Adelaide. Lines from Adelaide connect with the line between Sydney and Perth—the famous *Indian-Pacific* run (see page 96)—and with a line to Alice Springs.

In addition to this major network of interstate rail service, there is intrastate service as well as suburban rail service in metropolitan areas.

Discounts. If you plan to travel a good deal on Australia's trains, you might want to purchase an Austrailpass entitling you to unlimited, first or budget-class rail travel on interstate, intrastate, and metropolitan trains. Sleeping berths and meals are extra. You can purchase a pass for 14 days (with a 7-day extension available), or 1, 2, and 3 months, depending on your needs. The pass must be purchased before you go to Australia. The agent is Tour Pacific/Australian Travel Service, 1101 E. Broadway, Glendale, CA 91205.

In addition to the Austrailpass, there are all-lines tickets which offer unlimited rail travel within a particular

Speaking Australian

The rollicking dialect and salty slang of the Australians reflect a nimble-witted humor unique to Australia. Although English is the country's official language, an Australian's interpretation of this language might prove mind-boggling to a visitor.

First, the pronunciation of words can be different. The letter *A* takes a long sound, either as long *i* (eye) or somewhere between *a* and *i*. Thus, "Good day, mate" is pronounced "Goo'dye, mite." More obvious in pronunciation is the disappearance of the letter *r* in the middle or last syllable of a word. Thus Melbourne is pronounced Mel'bun.

A number of Australia's colorful words and expressions might put you *up a gum tree* (in a quandary). *Bo-peep* (take a look at) some of the words and expressions listed in the next paragraph and *give it a burl* (try it) yourself.

One of the most commonly heard expressions is *fair dinkum* which means absolutely true or genuine. Other vigorous Aussie terms you might hear include *beaut* (an exclamation of approval), *galah* (a fool), *wowser* (a straight-laced person, a spoil sport), *crook* (sick), *cobber* (a friend, also *mate, sport*), *squatter* (large landowner), *jumbuck* (sheep), *billabong* (water hole), *tucker* (food), or *drink with the flies* (drink alone). Of all Aussie slang terms, *bloody* is the most commonplace. You hear it everywhere except in polite English households—where youngsters, particularly, bloody well better not use it.

Aussie expressions can be an enjoyable challenge. Just remember that the key to communications is friendliness. Smile, and somewhere along the way you're bound to hear the friendly greeting: "Goo'dye mite; 'owyer goin'? Can I shout yer a beer (buy you a beer)?"

state for a designated period of time. Check with the state Public Transport Commission office or the state tourist office for more information. These can be purchased after your arrival in Australia. Some states also feature package tours using public transportation.

Making reservations. Australia's rail services are also popular with Australian travelers, so it is important to book in advance, if possible. This is especially true of the *Indian-Pacific* run between Sydney and Perth.

For reservations, contact your travel agent or the Railway Booking office in the capital city where your first rail trip begins.

Taking to the road by bus

Whether you want to sightsee your way through Australia, or just travel between a few major cities and see a little scenery along the way, Australia has three bus companies to fill your needs. Traveling the highways and byways of Australia are Ansett Pioneer, Greyhound, and Deluxe coachlines. Coaches usually have air conditioning, toilet facilities, fully adjustable seats, picture windows, and a driver versed in sights along the way.

Part of the fun of traveling by bus is planning your own itinerary and stopping where you want. It's also a great way to meet Australians.

Discounts. If you plan extensive bus travel in Australia, investigate the various special plans. Periods of validity vary by company and plan, but most range between 10 and 90 days. Most must be purchased before arriving in Australia.

Ansett Pioneer Express offers the "Aussiepass" and "Super Aussiepass", covering fast inter-city service on its coaches throughout Australia (including Tasmania, on Redline coaches); some sightseeing is also included. The "Super Aussiepass" includes limited accommodations at Flag Inns.

Deluxe Coachlines' "Koalapass" offers unlimited travel on its express network for periods from 10 to 90 days.

Greyhound's "Aussie Explorer" offers a series of wideranging circular tours on express coaches, valid for up to 12 months; you begin the journey anywhere along the route but must travel in one direction without backtracking. The Greyhound Bus Pass offers unlimited travel over its express coach network. Both plans include discounts on selected accommodations, sightseeing tours, and rental cars.

Tours. A variety of package tours which include daylight transportation, informed commentaries, and accommodations depart from capital cities regularly. Run by a number of different bus companies, these tours can range from 2 or 3 days to 8 weeks.

Still another bus tour features camping out. Rather than hotels, you stay in a tent you pitch yourself and help with the cookout. These tours can range from a long weekend to a 44-day tour around the country.

Reservations. Talk to your travel agent about discount passes and reservations. As with train and air travel, buses are a popular form of local transportation, particularly during holiday periods. In Australia, you can make bus reservations through the office of the bus line on which you want to travel.

Taking to the road by car

Cars are especially convenient for day trips out of major cities and resort areas. They give you the freedom to explore what you want at the pace you want. However, be prepared to drive on the left side of the road and on two-lane thoroughfares in many areas. Major highways linking capital cities are paved, but you'll find that roads between smaller towns can be gravel, and in remote outback areas the road might be nothing more than a two-wheel track.

If you are thinking of exploring all of Australia by car, bear in mind that beyond cities, distances are great and towns sometimes few and far between. For longer journeys, it might be best to take an air-conditioned train or bus or a domestic plane flight.

Renting a car. You'll find rental car agencies throughout Australia. Companies include Avis, Budget, Hertz, Letz, Natcar, and Thrifty.

To rent a car you'll need a valid driver's license from home. Minimum rental-age varies from 21 years old to 25 depending on the rental agency. Foreign car insurance is not valid in Australia. Compulsory third party insurance will be automatically added to your car rental charges.

All sizes of automobiles are available for hire. In the warmer climates of Alice Springs, Cairns, or the Gold Coast, you might want to rent a mini-moke. This openair, jeeplike vehicle is an economical, breezy way to travel short trips. Some rental car agencies also rent self-contained camper-vans accommodating up to 5 people.

Driving tips. First—fasten your seat belt. It's against the law not to wear your seat belt; and failure to do so can result in a fine.

Next, remember that you drive on the left side of the road. If you're a pedestrian, you look to your right instead of left before you step off the curb to cross the street. Speed limits are generally 60 km/36 miles per hour in cities and towns and 100 km/60 miles per hour in Australia's open country.

Traveling in the remote outback on dirt tracks is not really advisable for the inexperienced. Tracks can sometimes become confusing or disappear. Flash floods are not uncommon. If you must head into rough country on a dirt track, check out road conditions with local residents before you go, and leave your destination and time of arrival with someone before you leave. Take along an extra supply of water and gas, and if your car does break down, stay near it, don't wander off.

A word of warning about Australia's wildlife. In the country areas—on both paved and unpaved roads—kangaroos as well as domestic livestock have been known to stray onto the road at dusk and become blinded by headlights. Hitting a 2-meter/6-foot kangaroo can be very damaging to you and your car. Australians who travel country roads often have steel guards on the front of their cars as protection against wandering wildlife.

Going for a cruise

Don't overlook the possibility of seeing some of Australia by boat. The *M.V. Abel Tasman*, an 850-passenger/car ferry, sails between Melbourne and Devonport, Tasmania. The

Angler nets catch in New South Wales stream. Trout fishing, good in many spots throughout Australia, is particularly rewarding in the state of Tasmania.

Immaculately clad members of local lawn bowling team roll balls down well-kept turf during tournament.

Brightly colored sails catch the wind. Weekends find eager yachters hoisting spinnakers in Sydney Harbour.

overnight sailing, which takes about 14½ hours, can be rough at times.

Still another water option is a calm, leisurely 5 or 5½-day cruise aboard a paddle wheel boat on the Murray River. Amenities include comfortable cabins, pleasant sun decks, and good food. There are also shorter day trips on the Murray.

If you want to skipper your own boat, you can rent a houseboat in several places, including the Hawkesbury River near Sydney and the Murray River. These houseboats come fully equipped with stove, refrigerator, toilet, water supplies, cooking and eating utensils, linens, etc.

Dozens of fully equipped, big-game fishing boats, available for charter, dock at Cairns, Port Lincoln, and Kangaroo Island (South Australia), and at Tasmanian harbors. In most of the major coastal cities, you can charter yachts or boats for light fishing or cruising.

Know before you go

The following pertinent information will help you plan your trip—from documents you'll need to enter the country to items you should pack in your suitcase.

Entry formalities

In order to enter Australia, you'll need a valid passport and a visa. Visitor visa application forms are available from Australian consular offices in Los Angeles, San Francisco, New York, Chicago, Washington, D.C., Honolulu, Houston, Ottawa, Toronto, and Vancouver.

Inoculations. Only visitors arriving from an area infected with smallpox, yellow fever, or cholera are required to have a valid International Certificate of Vaccination showing inoculation against these diseases.

Customs. The only duty-free items you're allowed to bring into Australia are your personal effects including 200 cigarettes or 250 grams (approximately a half-pound) of tobacco or cigars as well as a liter (approximately a quart) of liquor.

Sporting equipment and camping gear are admitted without duty, but the importation of firearms and ammunition is restricted, subject to approval by state police authorities. Reasonable limits are placed on the importation of radios, tape recorders, tape players, dictating machines, and record players.

Strict controls are maintained on the importation of animals and plants and on the transport of plants between the various Australian states.

Currency. Australia has a decimal currency system. As in the United States, $1 equals 100 cents. Australian notes come in denominations of $2, $5, $10, $20, $50, and $100; coins are minted in denominations of 1 cent, 2 cents, 5 cents, 20 cents, 50 cents, and $1. You may bring in any amount of personal funds into the country, but you can't take out more than the amount you brought in.

International credit cards that are accepted include American Express, Diners Club, Carte Blanche, Visa, Mastercard, and their affiliates. Usage may be restricted in small shops and in smaller towns and country areas.

Departure tax. A A$20 departure tax is assessed departing travelers, payable in Australian currency. Transit passengers are exempt from payment of the tax.

What to pack

Except for business and certain evening functions, casual, informal clothing is the rule. Australians reserve their formal attire for opening nights and diplomatic functions. Men might want to bring along a coat and tie for dinner at more elegant restaurants in the larger cities.

Remember that the seasons are reversed in the Southern Hemisphere. If you visit Australia between November and March (summer), be sure to include lightweight clothes for warm weather, a sweater for air-conditioned rooms, and your swimsuit, sunglasses, and suntan lotion. It's warm all year in the northern tropical areas of Australia, but winters in the southeastern states can be cool and rainy, so bring along warm clothing, a lined raincoat, and an umbrella.

Some useful items. If you are traveling into Australia's Centre (Alice Springs area), bring along durable, casual clothes, good walking shoes, and a sunhat. Winter evenings in this area can be chilly. People going to the Great Barrier Reef will want to bring along a pair of tennis shoes for reef walking. Still another useful item is insect repellent to ward off flies and mosquitoes.

Electrical appliances. Electric current in Australia is 220-240 volts A.C., and 50 cycles. Leading hotels usually have 110 volt outlets for razors and small appliances, but for larger appliances such as hairdryers, you'll need to bring along a converter and a special flat three-pin adapter plug to fit into outlets.

A few other details

Here are still more helpful items of information to familiarize you with Australia.

What time is it? When it's noon in Perth, it's 1:30 P.M. in Darwin and Adelaide and 2 P.M. from Cairns down to Hobart. Australia has three time zones: Eastern Standard Time is 10 hours ahead of Greenwich mean time; Central Australian Standard Time is 9½ hours ahead; and Western Standard Time is 8 hours ahead.

During the summer months, most of Australia (except Queensland, Western Australia, and Northern Territory) set their clocks ahead for daylight savings time.

There's an 18-hour time difference between Sydney and San Francisco, which means that when it is 10 A.M. Monday in Sydney, it is 4 P.M. Sunday in San Francisco. This time difference will vary with daylight savings time.

To tip or not to tip. In Australia, tipping is a reward for good service. It is the customer's prerogative; restaurants do not add a service charge to the bill. A tip of 10 to 15 percent is customary at first-class restaurants if you feel you've had good service. You can tip baggage porters about A20 to A30 cents per suitcase.

Measuring up. Some years ago Australia converted to the metric system of weights and measures, so a small, wallet-size conversion table might be helpful in your travels.

Australia's many special events

Whether you prefer concerts or rodeos, flower shows or football, you'll find plenty of activities to suit your taste on Australia's calendar of events. The major regularly scheduled events are covered below.

January—March

New Year's Day (January 1). This public holiday is celebrated with surf carnivals and horse race meetings (including Perth Cup in Western Australia).

Festival of Sydney. A month-long series of art and cultural events held in January.

Australia Day. A national holiday observed the last Monday in January, it commemorates the founding of the first settlement at Sydney in 1788. Events include the Royal Sydney Anniversary Regatta in Sydney Harbour plus ceremonies and parades throughout the country.

Royal Hobart Regatta. In early February, this several-day aquatic carnival in Tasmania features sailing, swimming, and rowing events plus fireworks and parades.

Festival of Perth. Held mid-February to mid-March, this cultural festival in Western Australia includes a foreign film festival, concerts, opera, and ballet.

Moomba Festival. An annual event held in Melbourne in late February or early March, the festival features art exhibitions, concerts, street theater, and a parade.

Adelaide Festival. This festival is held in March on even-numbered years. It is a 3-week concentration of art exhibits plus performances in music, drama, and dance by visiting international artists and Australian artists.

Canberra Festival. This 10-day March festival celebrating Canberra's birthday includes cultural and sports events.

April—June

Royal Easter Show. The most popular of the country's agricultural shows, it is held in Sydney in early to mid-April.

Anzac Day. On April 25 this solemn holiday commemorates the 1915 landing of the Australian and New Zealand Army Corps (ANZAC) at Gallipoli in Turkey during World War I. War heroes of this and later conflicts are remembered with massive parades, memorial services, speeches, and sporting events.

Barossa Valley Vintage Festival. Held during late April in odd-numbered years, this festival heralds the harvest of this area's wine grapes.

Bangtail Muster. Horse racing, a rodeo, and cattle roundup are features of this event held in early May in Alice Springs.

Camel Cup. In May this well-known camel race is held in Alice Springs.

Beer Can Regatta. Beer cans are the building materials for speedboats, sailboats, and rafts that race on Darwin Harbour on this public holiday in June.

July—September

Doomben Ten Thousand. In the first half of July, this winter carnival horse race is held in Brisbane.

Royal Shows. Held in August, the Brisbane Royal Show is noted for its unusual display of Queensland's tropical plants and flowers. Other Royal Shows featuring agricultural displays are held in September in Melbourne, Adelaide, and Perth.

Henley-on-Todd Regatta. This yacht race is held on a dry riverbed in Alice Springs at the end of August.

Rugby football finals. Rugby League and rugby Union grand final competitions are held at Sydney Cricket Ground in September.

Australian Rules football finals. Some 100,000 spectators turn out at Melbourne Cricket Ground to watch the four September games of these fast-moving finals.

October—December

Royal Hobart Show. An agricultural show, it is held in mid-October in Tasmania.

Jacaranda Festival. Events at this October festival in Grafton, New South Wales, include parades, floral displays, and sporting events.

Spring Racing Carnival. A week-long series of horse races in Melbourne culminates in the Melbourne Cup in early November.

Melbourne Cup. Australia's richest handicap race, it is held on the first Tuesday of November at Flemington Race Course in Melbourne.

Cricket matches. They are held November through March in cities and towns across the country; international matches are held in state capitals from late December to early February.

Surf carnivals. Teams of volunteer lifeguards give spectacular displays of lifesaving techniques (see page 28). On weekends and holidays, December through March, on beaches in New South Wales, Queensland, Victoria, and South and Western Australia.

Carols by candlelight. Outdoor caroling in Melbourne's Myer Music Bowl, Sydney's Hyde Park, and in other cities and towns throughout Australia in mid-December.

Boxing Day. A national holiday, it falls on December 26 and marks the start of the Sydney-Hobart Yacht Race, Australia's yachting classic for ocean cruisers.

SYDNEY

In New South Wales, urban bustle or rural quiet

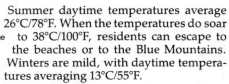

The heart of New South Wales is Sydney, the state's capital and the largest city in Australia. With a population of three million, Sydney is a bustling center for industry, business, and manufacturing as well as a major world port. Spreading over about 1,736 square km/ 670 square miles, the city seems to stretch from an undulating coastline in the east to the horizon in the west, north, and south.

Where the city's thriving metropolitan area ends, the bush of New South Wales begins. Since most of the state's residents live in the Sydney metropolitan area, the rest of the state's 803,109 square km/310,000 square miles are wide-open spaces—a playground for those who want to enjoy the outdoors.

New South Wales's superb coastline—including golden beaches, dramatic headlands, and quiet bays and river estuaries—are a haven for swimmers, surfers, and fishers. Bushwalkers can enjoy the Blue Mountains just west of Sydney or travel north to the New England area where trees turn vibrant red and gold in the fall. Throughout the state are numerous national parks where visitors can enjoy Australia's outdoor offerings.

Sydney—A zestful city

The key to Sydney's splendor is its harbor. It gives the city a pronounced maritime character and an immense vitality. From a number of vantage points throughout the city you can enjoy the harbor's beauty—its quiet coves, its dramatic headlands, and its wooded peninsulas. Beyond the water of the harbor are the coastal beaches—alluring expanses of golden sand that stretch north and south along the Pacific Ocean.

All this water plus a warm, subtropical climate makes Sydney an outdoor city. The residents are outdoor people who enjoy such pastimes as surfing, swimming, boating, fishing, water-skiing, and sun-bathing.

The sail-shaped roofline of Sydney's Opera House provides a dramatic backdrop for outdoor dining. The complex includes concert and opera halls and a playhouse.

Summer daytime temperatures average 26°C/78°F. When the temperatures do soar to 38°C/100°F, residents can escape to the beaches or to the Blue Mountains. Winters are mild, with daytime temperatures averaging 13°C/55°F.

The feeling of Sydney is vital, breezy, brash, and busy. It's a place with a zest for life.

Getting your bearings

Geographically Sydney is divided into Sydney proper on one side of the harbor and North Sydney on the other. The city's famous Harbour Bridge spans the bay to link these two metropolitan areas.

Many of the sights are clustered in the central city area—Sydney proper; those in North Sydney can be easily reached by ferry from Circular Quay, or by train. In fact the heart of Sydney seems to be Circular Quay (pronounced *key*).

Within minutes you can walk from the quay to the Opera House and Harbour Bridge and to one of Sydney's best viewing spots—the 48-story Australia Square Tower on George Street—where you can survey the entire city in a painless orientation course.

Australia Square Tower—a round building in Australia Square—has its observation terrace on the 48th floor. From here, you have an impressive, 360-degree view of the city, including the bustling harbor, the historic Rocks area, and the constantly changing downtown skyline. The terrace is open daily from 10 A.M. to 10 P.M.

Sydney Tower, atop the Centrepoint commercial complex on Pitt Street, provides another vantage point. The 298-meter/984-foot tower's central shaft is topped with a golden capsule. Inside this capsule is an observation deck, open daily, and a pair of revolving restaurants.

Seeing the city

Like many of the world's major cities, Sydney is a contrast of old and new. There are soaring glass and steel skyscrapers and the dramatic white sails of the Opera House, offset by interesting old historical buildings.

Captain Arthur Phillip and 1,000 convicts set foot on the shores of Sydney Cove in 1788. Today, you can see some of this settlement's buildings in The Rocks—a his-

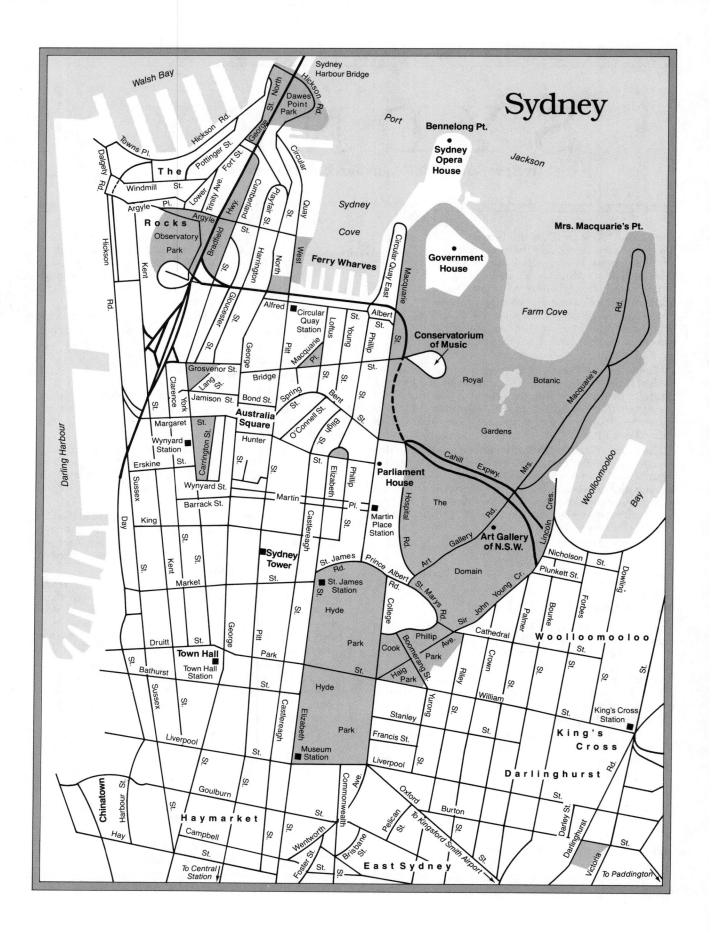

Sydney

toric area of Sydney that is being restored. In other sections of Sydney you'll see some of convict-architect Francis Greenway's buildings, as well as some of Sydney's early gracious mansions.

Besides historic offerings, Sydney has a number of modern shopping centers for visitors to browse through, and museums and galleries to enjoy. Sydney's entertainment scene runs the gamut from the bright neon lights of King's Cross to drama and opera productions at the Opera House.

Sydney Opera House

An improbable collection of curving walls that soar 70 meters/230 feet above Bennelong Point, this may be the most talked-about building in the world. Certainly it has become an international symbol of Australia, surpassing with ease the kangaroo and the koala. From its inception in 1956 to its completion in 1973, the building was the source of endless local arguments and discussions.

It all started when the New South Wales government

The essentials

Australia's largest and most internationally minded city is well endowed with ample comforts for the traveler.

Getting there. Australia's internal and external transportation networks have their hubs at Sydney.

Air. International service to and from Sydney is by Qantas and foreign flag carriers from New Zealand, the United Kingdom, continental Europe, the Orient, Southeast Asia, and North America.

Domestic flights by Ansett, Australian and East-West airlines link Sydney and other state capitals. Other New South Wales towns are served by Air New South Wales and East-West Airlines.

Kingsford Smith International Airport is about 30 minutes south of downtown by taxi or bus.

Sea. Pacific cruise ships call at Sydney, most of them docking downtown at Sydney Cove.

Rail. Direct routes link Sydney with Brisbane, Perth, Canberra, and Melbourne. Weekly luxury train service on the "Alice" connects Sydney with Alice Springs to the west. Train connections west can also be made from Melbourne to Adelaide, Alice Springs, and Perth.

Accommodations. Like most Australian cities, Sydney has a welcome concentration of hotels and restaurants in the main shopping and business districts.

Major hotels include Boulevard, Central Plaza Quality Inn, Chateau, Hilton Sydney, Holiday Inn Menzies, Hyatt Kingsgate, Inter-Continental, Old Sydney Parkroyal, Regent of Sydney, Sebel Town House, Sheraton Wentworth, Southern Cross, and Wynyard Travelodge.

Food and drink. An unofficial census gives Sydney 3,000 restaurants, a number that includes at least one for every major ethnic cuisine in the world. Sydney's own chief claims for gastronomy center around local seafoods, especially Sydney rock oysters, a white-fleshed fish called John Dory, snapper, and salt-water crayfish. Sydney's reigning dish for everyman is the meat pie, as common here as the hamburger is in Chicago.

The most prestigious wines of New South Wales come from nearby Hunter River Valley, the reds mostly Shiraz, the whites mostly Semillon. Producers include old standbys Lindemans and McWilliams, and such smaller cellars as Tyrrells and Lake's Folly.

Tooheys and KB Reschs are popular Sydney beers.

Getting around. Central Sydney is so compact that feet can do most of the traveling, but an excellent public transport system is there to be used.

A loop subway stops at Town Hall, Wynyard, Circular Quay, Martin Place, St. James, and Museum stations; another line links Martin Place (downtown) with King's Cross and Bondi Junction.

The Sydney Explorer Bus travels an 18 km/11 mile loop around the city daily from 9:30 A.M. to 5 P.M., stopping at 20 tourist attractions en route. Full-day tickets can be purchased on the bus or from the Travel Centre of New South Wales.

Ferries provide quick cross-harbor service and routes to ocean beaches (see page 29).

Public transportation maps are available from the Urban Transit Authority, 11 York Street, or the Travel Centre of New South Wales, 16 Spring Street.

Taxis and rental cars are abundant.

Tours. Half and full-day bus tours cover city sights, southern beaches, northern suburbs, Blue Mountains (see page 39), Hawkesbury River (page 40), and Hunter Valley (page 41). Most tours leave from Circular Quay West. Hotel pickup can also be arranged.

Half and full-day train tours take in the Blue Mountains, Old Sydney Town, Hawkesbury River, and Hunter Valley.

For a bird's-eye-view of the city, try a helicopter or bi-plane flight over the harbor and northern beaches. Scenic seaplane flights are also available.

For more information. The Travel Centre of New South Wales, 16 Spring Street, Sydney 2000, is open weekdays from 8:30 A.M. to 5 P.M.

decided to build an opera house on Bennelong Point—a beautiful headland bounded by Sydney Harbour on three sides and the Royal Botanic Gardens on the fourth. The government asked architects from around the world to submit designs for a building on the site. From the 223 entries submitted, that of Danish architect Joern Utzon was selected.

Utzon's sketches showed a building unlike any other in the world, its soaring roof structure resembling a cluster of billowing sails, a fitting design for a building nearly surrounded by a harbor alive with boats. But Utzon's submission was only a schematic presentation of sketches. He had not been required to submit any final plans with such particulars as engineering details and cost estimates.

Though Utzon's design was free as the wind on paper, the concrete problems of constructing it were another matter. From inception to completion, the building took 17 years. Part way through the project Utzon resigned. Costs, originally estimated at $12 million, rose through the years to more than $100 million. (Sydney proved it is a sporting town; a lottery paid the bills in just 2 years.)

The final results of all the years of problems and frustrations is one of the most exciting buildings in the world. It's a vast complex housing some 90 rooms under its soaring roofs: a concert hall seating 2,700, an opera hall accommodating more than 1,500, a playhouse seating 600, and smaller halls for recitals and receptions. There are also two restaurants on the premises.

To get a feeling for the building, take the long stroll around it to study its form and shape. You'll note upon closer inspection that the roof tiles that create the white soaring sails of the Opera House aren't really white at all. Instead they are an intermingling of off-white glossy tiles with buff-colored matte tiles, a combination that reflects the mood of the daytime hours—from early morning until dusk.

After your leisurely stroll around the outside, take one of the guided tours offered, Monday through Friday from 9 A.M. to 4 P.M. to see how some of the unconventional qualities of Utzon's exterior have been matched by uncommon touches in the great concert halls by Australian architect Peter Hall. In the symphony hall, finished with thousands of narrow, vertical strips of wood, a narrow tier of seats runs behind the orchestra, allowing conductor watchers an unparalleled opportunity to see (if not hear) the shadings of orchestral playing. The opera theater, contrarily, has its front and side walls and the backs of all its seats painted mat black, so as to focus every bit of attention on the stage.

Good as the tours are, the Sydney Opera House is at its best when crowded for a performance. The outer halls were deliberately underplayed to put audiences into the forefront just as the inner halls were shaped and finished to benefit the performers.

You can book a package tour, dinner, and performance as much as 12 months in advance through travel agents or Qantas, or you may book directly by writing to Tourism Marketing Section, Sydney Opera House, GPO Box 4274, Sydney 2001. For schedules of performances in the current year, write the Australian Tourist Commission. (For additional information on types of performances given in the Opera House, see "The lively arts," page 33.)

On Sundays—weather permitting—there is free outdoor entertainment around the Opera House between noon and 8 P.M. You'll see everything from street theater to jazz bands.

There is no parking at the Opera House. If you're driving into town to attend a performance, park your car at the Domain Parking Station. A special bus will take you to the front steps.

Sydney on The Rocks

If you want to discover what Sydney's architecture was like in the early days, before the advent of soaring glass-and-steel skyscrapers, take a trip to The Rocks. To Sydneysiders, this area includes the entire western promontory of Sydney Cove. It was here that working parties of convicts from Captain Phillip's First Fleet began to chisel out the beginnings of a town.

The history of this area of Sydney has not always shown man at his best, but it has been colorful. The area's rocky terrain stifled development. Good roads and decent drainage were impossible. Instead a series of alleyways and dead end streets appeared. Soon these were lined with taverns, hovels, flophouses, gaming houses, and brothels. In 1855 The Rocks had 37 taverns with intriguing names like "Hit and Miss" and "Live and Let Live." The area became the haunt of sailors, harpies, whores, and bands of thugs. The 1900s brought bubonic plague to the area, and in the rat hunts that followed, whole areas of The Rocks were razed. Still further destruction took place in the 1920s, when more buildings were destroyed to make way for the Sydney Harbour Bridge approaches. In the 1970s the Sydney Cove Redevelopment Authority was formed to salvage what was left of The Rocks and revitalize and renovate it.

As you stroll the streets of The Rocks, you'll see this redevelopment. Many buildings have already been partly or fully restored. Courtyards have been paved, and gas lamps added. Many buildings now house antique stores, arts and crafts shops, galleries, and restaurants.

The best way to explore The Rocks is on foot. Start your explorations at The Rocks Visitors' Centre at 104 George Street. It's open from 8:30 A.M. to 4:30 P.M. weekdays, and 10 to 5 on weekends and public holidays. Here you can see a film on The Rocks and get a useful map and other information on the area. There are guided tours of The Rocks daily from the Argyle Centre on Argyle Street. Phone ahead (27-6678) for tour reservations.

The following are some points of interest you'll want to see during your Rocks exploration. (You'll also want to take a look at nearby Pier One, Sydney's oldest shipping terminal. It's now an entertainment complex with a variety of shops and restaurants.)

Along George Street. Sprinkled along George Street are a number of bars, sandwich shops, and specialty shops including a shop for left-handed people and a shop selling seashells. The Orient Hotel, at the corner of Argyle and George streets, was built in 1850 and has been faithfully restored.

The Geological and Mining Museum, 36 George Street, contains one of the best displays of geological specimens in the Southern Hemisphere. Here you'll see mineral ores, fossils, and gemstones. The building was built in 1902 as an electric light station. Hours are 9:30 A.M.

Lingering over lunch, *shoppers enjoy an oasis created by leafy trees and curtains of water. King's Cross area, center of nighttime activity, abounds with noise and neon.*

Future lifeguards *enjoy surf and sand at one of 34 grand beaches within easy reach of downtown Sydney.*

Surf carnival time

It's a warm summer day at the beach and the scene about to unfold is uniquely Australian. Several groups of bronzed lifeguards in distinctive swim suits and headgear march along the beach with military precision. At the head of each column, a member carries the club pennant. The groups come to a stop and stand at parade rest. Then the action begins. The lifeguards launch surf boats into the pounding surf, stage demonstration rescues of swimmers in distress, and race boats.

The event is a surf carnival whose participants are volunteer members of surf lifesaving clubs. You'll find one or more such carnivals on the beaches of Sydney almost any weekend from December through March, and less frequently during the summer on other beaches in New South Wales, Queensland, Victoria, South Australia, and Western Australia.

The first lifesaving club was originated at Bondi Beach in Sydney in 1907 (with the motto "Vigilance and Service") to help save swimmers who tired in the rough surf or were caught in the riptide. Today there are 160 affiliated clubs with more than 25,000 members and an amazing record of rescues—more than 7,000 yearly.

Surf rescues are carried out by several methods including by belt and reel and by boat.

Belt and reel rescue squads are seven-man teams. One member, wearing a belt and trailing a light line attached to a large reel on shore, swims out to a swimmer in trouble. While he holds the swimmer, the reel men bring them both back to the beach. In a surf carnival, competing teams are judged on precision and speed.

Surf boat squads are five-man teams (four rowers and a helmsman). Boats are used when the surf is too rough for a lifeguard or when the swimmer is too far offshore. The five life-jacketed members launch their boats into the crashing surf and row through the breakers to reach the swimmer in distress. The most thrilling event for spectators at a surf carnival occurs when these surf boat teams row out through the breakers, round a buoy, and race back to the beach.

---

to 4 P.M. weekdays, 1 to 4 P.M. on Saturdays, and 11 A.M. to 4 P.M. on Sundays.

Lower Fort Street. Next, head out to Dawes Point Park at the tip of the promontory. From here you get a good view of The Rocks, including the peaked roofs of the remodeled Campbell's Storehouses, home of the Australian Wine Centre. You can also see the Opera House.

High above Dawes Point Park's grassy expanse tower the approaches to the Sydney Harbour Bridge. Walk under the bridge and over to Lower Fort Street. Several gracious old Georgian buildings line this street—an area where prosperous merchants lived. Numbers 59 and 61 are particularly elegant, and so is Bligh House (number 43). Built in 1833, this was the home of Robert Campbell Jr., son of the colony's first merchant. Today, this historic building is occupied by the Australian College of General Practitioners.

Of an entirely different order is the Hero of Waterloo Hotel, a pub with an interesting history. During the 1800s, ships' crews were hard to find. It is said that a trapdoor in the floor of this bar helped to fill a few captains' orders. Unwary imbibers were dropped into a tunnel below and hauled off to sea. Note that some of the windows of the hotel are only painted on—when the hotel was built, there was a tax on window glass.

Argyle Place. Continuing another block up Lower Fort Street, you'll come to Argyle Place, a delightful corner of old Sydney just below Observatory Park. Terrace houses and cottages trimmed in a variety of iron lace border a true village green that is shaded by giant trees and lighted by gas lamps. The restored houses on this street were built between 1830 and 1880.

Sydney's second oldest church stands facing one corner of the green. The cornerstone of the Church of the Holy Trinity—better known as Garrison Church—was laid in 1840. After its completion, it became the official garrison church for the English Queen's Regiments stationed at Dawes Point. Note the beautiful stained-glass east window that depicts the Holy Trinity.

Observatory Park. This rolling stretch of parkland shaded by large Moreton Bay fig trees overlooks Argyle Place and the harbor. From this sandstone bluff, you get a good view of Sydney Harbour Bridge. The Observatory, built in 1858, is open 10 A.M. to noon weekdays (except Wednesday when it closes at 5 P.M.), and weekends from 1 to 5 P.M. You can get to the park by climbing the flight of stairs located opposite the Argyle Place green.

Argyle Cut. Descending the stairs, head down Argyle Street through the damp Argyle Cut. Construction began on this tunnel in 1843. Pick-wielding convicts struggled to hew the tunnel out of solid rock. It was later widened to accommodate cars.

Argyle Arts Centre. Just beyond the tunnel is the brick Argyle Arts Centre. It's located in the old bond stores built between 1828 and 1881. At one time goods were delivered into the cobblestone central courtyard by horse and carriage. Today, the Argyle Arts Centre, open daily from 10 A.M. to 5:30 P.M., features a number of shops where browsers can watch craftspeople at work on silverware, copperware, leather goods, pottery, stained glass, and art enamels.

Cadman's Cottage. On George Street, not far from where Argyle Street intersects it, is Cadman's Cottage—a simple, cream colored building dating from about 1816 and believed to be the oldest building still standing in the city of Sydney. Originally called the Coxswains' Barracks, it was home for the government boatswains, including John Cadman, the Overseer of Government Craft, who gave it his name.

Heart of the harbor

Sydney Harbour is huge, one of the world's largest. But the heart of it nestles in the few hundred meters of shore-line between the Opera House and The Rocks. Sydney had its origins in this cove in 1788, when Captain Phillips landed on the spot. The first pier was called Semicircular Quay. Today, the main one is Circular Quay. It's only a name—the quay is not even semicircular.

Circular Quay may be the heart of the city as well as the harbor. At least this is where many of its arteries of transportation come together. Ferries and hydrofoils depart from six jetties for destinations as close as straight across the harbor or as distant as its mouth, 11 km/7 miles east. Passenger ships dock just alongside. In front of the ferry building, elevated commuter train tracks lead into Sydney. Higher still, Harbour Bridge looms against the skyline, the quick connection to North Sydney.

The Circular Quay is currently undergoing redevelop-

Cruising Sydney Harbour

Sydney has one of the most beautiful harbors in the world. In size alone it outdoes the harbors of some other major world cities, its watery expanse lapping against more than 290 km/180 miles of shoreline. There are secluded beaches, quiet coves, inviting bays, soaring headlands. In some places, homes march to the shore's edge and marinas extend their arms into the water. In other places, wild native bushland reaches to the bay's edge, and man is but a visitor.

To enjoy this exceptional harbor, as well as get a different perspective of Sydney's skyline, take a ride on a tour boat or one of the ferry boats leaving from Circular Quay.

The city's ferries sail at frequent intervals daily until 11 P.M. Some of their routes are as scenic for sightseeing as they are efficient for commuting, and they let you rub elbows with a variety of Sydneysiders. During commute hours, business people travel to and from their jobs on ferries. In the afternoons, legions of schoolboys wearing short flannel pants and caps with sewn-on insignias use the ferries to head for playing fields or home. On weekends, families and outing groups board the ferries for relaxing excursions.

Short ferry trips. Two ferry lines leave from Number 6 Jetty. The shortest ride goes to Kirribilli and gives you a panorama of the city skyline, the Opera House, and the Harbour Bridge—all on a round trip taking only 20 minutes.

Another ferry stops at Lavender Bay, across the harbor from Circular Quay, and then goes to McMahon's Point.

From Number 5 Jetty, ferries leave for Taronga Zoo and Hunter's Hill. At the zoo you can see such Australian natives as the koala, kangaroo, and emu, along with performing seals and dolphins and a host of other creatures (see page 34).

The ferry to Hunter's Hill takes you under the Sydney Harbour Bridge (an impressive view) and makes stops at Darling Street Wharf, Balmain, Long Nose Point Wharf, Parramatta Wharf, and Valentia Street at Hunter's Hill.

From Number 4 Jetty, one ferry goes to Kirribilli and on to Neutral Bay. Another crosses the harbor to Mossman, with stops at Musgrave Street, Cremorne Point, and Old Cremorne. On this trip you have spectacular views of the Opera House, the bridge, and the eastern suburbs of Double Bay and Watson's Bay.

The longest regular ferryboat run is the trip from Number 3 Jetty to Manly, covering 11 km/7 miles in 35 minutes. You can also get to Manly by hydrofoil from Number 2 Jetty in about 17 minutes. To better see the harbor, it's good to travel one way by ferry. At Manly, there are a number of beaches to explore.

Harbor cruises. The Urban Transit Authority has a 1½-hour Sydney Harbour scenic cruise that leaves from Circular Quay at 1:30 P.M. on Wednesday, 2:30 P.M. on Saturday and Sunday. You sail along the southern shores of Port Jackson and cruise up Middle Harbour before returning to Circular Quay by way of the north shores of the main harbor. Another scenic cruise operating at 2 P.M. on Sunday covers the Upper Harbour and the Lane Cove and Parramatta rivers.

Captain Cook and Southern Cross cruises offer an assortment of harbor cruises that include the Parramatta and Lane Cove rivers. Interesting commentary accompanies each cruise. Most of the cruises last 2 hours, though several are longer. Captain Cook has morning and afternoon coffee cruises, plus luncheon and dinner cruises, and on the M.V. *Southern Cross* there are morning coffee, luncheon, and dinner cruises.

The *Sydney Harbour Explorer* catamaran cruise schedules stops along the way so passengers can disembark for a swim or lunch.

All cruises leave from Circular Quay.

For more information on cruise details, contact the Travel Centre of New South Wales (see page 25).

Fine view of Sydney and its harbor diverts attention from performing seal at Taronga Zoo. Ferries from Circular Quay bring visitors daily to spend some time among the park's inhabitants.

Humpback Sydney Harbour Bridge, dubbed "the coat hanger" by locals, links the glittering lights of the downtown area with suburban North Sydney.

ment to improve harbor views. The promenade leading to the Opera House is being redone, and the bus loading area west of the quay is being moved underground.

Harbour Bridge. Just west of Sydney Cove and Circular Quay, this bridge looms on the skyline. Called "the coat hanger" by Australians, this mass of metal is the world's second largest single-span bridge after the Kill van Kull Bridge between New Jersey and Staten Island, New York. The views from the bridge are worth a walk across it. You can take a train back from Milson's Point station.

Fort Denison. Within view of the Opera House stands a stone fortress on a tiny rock island in the middle of Sydney Harbour.

The island, nothing more than a bleak lump of rock, was first used as a place of confinement for incorrigible convicts. A fort was built on the island in 1857, during the Crimean War, to protect Sydney from invasion.

Today, the island fort serves as a maritime tide observation station. Tours of the island, conducted by the Maritime Services Board Tuesday through Saturday, must be booked in advance by calling 240-2111 ext. 2036. Sights to see at the fort include old cannons and stairways too narrow for an invader to swing a cutlass.

Greenway was here

The Opera House was not Sydney's first controversial building, Utzon not its only flamboyant imported architect. Early in the 19th century, Francis Greenway set an example that remains impressive. Some of the best of his work is along Macquarie Street, within easy walking distance of the Opera House.

Greenway arrived in Australia as a convict, his original death sentence for fraud having been commuted by the English courts to 14 years' transportation to New South Wales. The exiled architect befriended New South Wales's Governor Macquarie, who soon discovered his talents. Greenway became Acting Government Architect, and quickly demonstrated the temperament that put him in Australia.

The governor's desire for grandeur and Greenway's desire to produce it left a rich legacy of buildings.

Conservatorium of Music. When it was built in 1817, this elaborate white building was to be the stable for the governor's horses. An even more elaborate building was planned as the governor's house. The colonists were horrified at the useless ornateness of the stable that Francis Greenway designed.

In 1914 the stable was converted and became a center for musical instruction for New South Wales. Regular concerts are held at the conservatorium.

Hyde Park Barracks. This building, at the end of Macquarie Street on Queen's Square, was designed in 1819 by Greenway as a convict barracks. Governor Macquarie was so pleased with the building that he granted Greenway a full pardon. Today, the barracks is a museum of the state's history. A model of the original barracks is included among the displays.

St. James' Church. Built on Queen's Square in 1819, it is one of the few churches designed by Greenway. It is a fine example of Georgian architecture and is noted for its cop-

per-sheathed spire and its pleasing proportions. This symbol of another architectural era contrasts sharply with surrounding glass and steel skyscrapers that tower high above it.

Grandeur other than Greenway's

Besides the work of Francis Greenway, Sydney has preserved a number of other buildings of architectural merit and historical interest.

The Old Mint. On Macquarie Street not far from Hyde Park Barracks, this is one of the surviving wings of the Old Rum Hospital—so named because the three colonists who built it (between 1811 and 1816) did so in exchange for a virtual monopoly on the colony's rum trade. The structure's simple design and side verandas are typical of buildings constructed in the British colonies during this era.

From 1855 to 1926, the building was part of the Royal Mint. Today, it houses a museum.

Parliament House. The central portion of this building, on Macquarie Street a short distance from the Old Mint, is also part of the Old Rum Hospital. (The section of the Old Rum Hospital between Parliament House and the Old Mint was torn down and replaced by Sydney Hospital.)

First occupied by the State Legislature in 1829, Parliament House has an interesting interior. You can arrange to visit Parliament House by phoning the Deputy Sergeant-at-Arms.

General Post Office. A monumental example of Renaissance-inspired architecture by James Barnet, this massive building extends along Martin Place between Pitt and George streets.

In 1942 the building's clock was dismantled and stored away. It was feared that Japanese raiders during World War II could use the tower as a landmark. Finally, in 1964—with some difficulty in fitting all the pieces—the tower was reconstructed.

Town Hall. You'll find the seat of Sydney's city government three blocks west of Hyde Park. Located on the corner of George and Park streets, the building was begun in 1866. It includes a large concert and assembly hall and one of the world's finest pipe organs. Until the advent of the Opera House, this building was the city's main concert hall. Town Hall is open weekdays from 9 A.M. until 5 P.M.

Stately homes

During the 1800s many elegant mansions were built in Sydney. Surrounded by gardens, they were showcases, centers of Sydney's social life. A few of these graceful ghosts from the past have been preserved to be enjoyed today.

Elizabeth Bay House. Built in 1838 for the colonial secretary of New South Wales, Elizabeth Bay House is one of the city's most graceful mansions. John Verge designed the Regency house, open Tuesday through Friday, 10 A.M. to 4:30 P.M.; Saturday 10 A.M. to 5 P.M.; and Sunday noon to 5 P.M. The house is located at 7 Onslow Avenue, Elizabeth Bay.

Vaucluse House. This colonial-style house was once the home of William Charles Wentworth, chief architect of the New South Wales Constitution. You approach the house through beautifully landscaped grounds featuring palm trees, ferns, gum trees, and Moreton Bay figs. The interior of the house is decorated with 1800s period pieces. There's even a wine cellar complete with wine press, as well as a coach house with a display of antique carriages.

Servants' quarters near the stable have been converted into a history museum. In four rooms are displayed portraits of governors; memorabilia of the Blue Mountains Expedition that Wentworth participated in; Wentworth family possessions; and items of Sir Henry Browne Hayes, the first owner of the Vaucluse property. (The small house he built on the property was incorporated into Wentworth's larger house.) Vaucluse House is open daily, except Mondays, from 10 A.M. to 4:30 P.M.

Museums & galleries

In just three stops, visitors to Sydney can look into the continent's natural history, its art—both Aboriginal and Western—and some of the odder moments of the history of flight.

Australian Museum. Located near the corner of College and William streets across from Hyde Park, this museum features Australian natural history and includes an extensive Aborigine section. Don't miss the Hall of Fossils' impressive stegosaurus skeleton or the Marine Hall with its large aquarium, wave tank, and mangrove and coral reef dioramas.

The museum is open Tuesday through Sunday from 10 A.M. to 5 P.M., and Monday from noon to 5 P.M.

The Power House Museum. The Ultimo Power Station, on Mary Ann Street in Ultimo, provided Sydney's electricity from 1900 to 1964. Today, it is a museum with exhibits on science and the applied arts. The enormous exhibition halls and galleries provide a unique setting for such diverse displays as a vintage car from the 1920s, a monoplane, an assortment of box kites, a complete railway station and New South Wales' first locomotive, one of Australia's first manufactured cars, a collection of Japanese swords, and numerous gadgets from Australian inventors. There are also several participatory science exhibits—good activities for travelers with children.

Guided tours through the Power House Museum are available, but feel free to explore on your own. After viewing the exhibits, you'll want to investigate the museum's other facilities: a library, a cafeteria, and a gift shop crammed with unusual souvenirs. The building itself has an interesting history; you can take in a film that describes its progression from power station to museum.

The museum is open daily from 10 A.M. to 5 P.M.

Art Gallery of New South Wales. Appropriately, this building is located on Art Gallery Road in the center of The Domain. Its permanent collection includes many paintings by Australians as well as Europeans. You can visit the gallery Monday through Saturday from 10 A.M. to 5 P.M., and on Sunday from noon to 5.

Shopping around

Sydney is a mecca of shopping centers. Nearly every new high-rise building in the downtown area seems to have an underground shopping arcade filled with colorful shops offering a fascinating variety of merchandise. Things to shop for in the Sydney area include opals, Aboriginal woodcarvings, and sheepskin products.

Downtown shopping. Sydney's main shopping district is bounded by Martin Place, George, Park, and Elizabeth streets. Within this area you'll find large department stores like David Jones, Grace Brothers, and Waltons, as well as sprawling shopping arcades such as Piccadilly, Imperial, Strand, Royal, and MLC Centre. One of the area's largest is the four-level Centrepoint Shopping Arcade that runs between Pitt and Castlereagh streets and connects Grace Brothers and David Jones department stores.

Martin Place, extending from George Street to Macquarie Street, provides a resting place for foot-weary shoppers. The paved pedestrian plaza has seats intermingled with trees, flowers, and a fountain. At lunch time on weekdays, workers and shoppers alike gather to hear free entertainment in the plaza's amphitheater.

The Cenotaph on Martin Place memorializes Australians who died in war. Every Thursday at 12:30 P.M. there is a changing of the guard ceremony here.

Market days. Paddy's Market, located at the Darling Harbour end of Liverpool Street, offers a variety of goods, including fresh produce, confections, flowers, pets, art, jewelry, clothing, and leather goods. The market is open Saturday and Sunday from 9 A.M. to 4:30 P.M.

In Flemington, the Flemington Markets' 1,172 stands offer fruit, vegetables, and goods of every description. It's open Fridays, Saturday mornings, and Sundays.

Neighborhoods of note

Beyond the city's central district, you'll find other destinations worth a visit. Though they're not far from downtown, unless you're a dedicated walker it's best to seek out these spots by bus or taxi. City sights bus tours also include them in their itineraries.

Paddington. Once you've arrived in this charming suburb 5 km/3 miles southeast of downtown, a good way to explore it is on foot. Called "Paddo" by locals, this charming community offers visitors narrow streets lined with beautifully restored Victorian terrace houses as well as restaurants, antique shops, and art galleries.

The area—a former working-class suburb—has in recent years become a fashionable place to live that is close to the city. The area's narrow terrace homes sharing common walls have been elegantly restored to their former 1800s grandeur, complete with iron lace balconies.

Chinatown. You can enjoy the sights, sounds, and smells of China in this bustling neighborhood around Harbour and Hay streets. The area is packed with locals Friday through Sunday—so schedule your visit on a Monday, Tuesday, Wednesday, or Thursday.

You'll see some nice terrace houses on Jersey Road (off Oxford Street), Queen Road, Five Ways, Union, Stafford, Healey, Goodhope, Gurner, and Cambridge streets.

On Oxford Street you'll see the immense Victoria Barracks—a good example of colonial military architecture. Built in the 1840s by convict labor (as were many of the buildings of this period), the barracks is still used by the military. There's a changing of the guard ceremony at 10:30 A.M. Tuesdays (February to November). Following the ceremony is a tour of the barracks and military museum. The museum is also open the first Sunday of the month.

Darlinghurst. The major points of interest in this suburb are the Old Gaol and Darlinghurst Court House.

In the 19th century the Old Gaol was notorious for harshness. Public hangings here attracted large crowds. The building on Forbes Street is now part of East Sydney Technical College. Begun in 1835, the Old Gaol consists of a massive wall surrounding a collection of austere buildings that radiate from a round house that once was a chapel. Patterned after the Eastern Penitentiary in Philadelphia, the sandstone gaol was constructed over a long period by the inmates.

Next door to the Old Gaol you'll find the Darlinghurst Court on Taylor Square. The central portion of this impressive colonnaded building—reminiscent of Greek Revival architecture—was designed by Mortimer Lewis in 1837.

The lively arts

Sydney supports more music and theater with more enthusiasm than a good many cities whose populations exceed its mere three million.

The focal point for both music and theater is, not surprisingly, the Opera House. The Australian Ballet Company, the Sydney Dance Company, and the Sydney Theatre Company all perform here. But the Opera House is only the focal point, as the city boasts other major auditoriums and theaters.

Less formal performances at nightclubs are just as abundant. The center of nightlife is in the neon-lighted King's Cross area, but the purely Australian experience of the league club is worth seeking out too.

Music. Sydney has an appetite for music of every stripe. Fittingly for a city with such an opera house, it has one of the largest per capita opera audiences in the world. Major singers from abroad appear with the regular company and in recital. (One of the visiting performers has been Dame Joan Sutherland.)

The Opera House also is home to the Sydney Symphony Orchestra. Its season is supplemented by visiting orchestras, chamber groups, and recitalists. (Examples include the Warsaw Philharmonic, The Tokyo Quintet, and flautist James Galway.)

Jazz has been healthy in Sydney since the 1940s, and still is. Fans will remember the Australian Jazz Quartet from the 1950s, and genuine veterans may recall Graeme Bell's New Orleans-style band. These days, Sydney boasts many fine jazz bars including Don Burrows Jazz Club at the Regent of Sydney. The annual October Manly Jazz Festival is one of the biggest jazz festivals in the world.

The January Festival of Sydney features operas, pop concerts, and symphony performances.

In addition, there's free entertainment year-round in Sydney. Nearly every Sunday, there are free chamber music concerts at the Opera House, with additional outdoor entertainment on the promenade. There are brass band concerts in Wynyard Park and lunchtime classical music performances at the Conservatorium of Music and St. Stephen's Church on Macquarie Street.

Theater. The city has a dozen permanent theaters in operation including the Ensemble, Elizabeth, and Nimrod theaters.

League clubs. These are the social headquarters (and, to a considerable degree, the financial support) of local football teams. Local residents must be members to enter, but many clubs welcome overseas visitors as guests after telephoned inquiries. The attractions include live entertainment (often big names), poker machines (slot machines to Americans), restaurants, and—not least—a chance to rub elbows with Australians on their own grounds.

Some of these clubs also have swimming pools, saunas or steam rooms, and gymnasiums.

Sydney outdoors

Sydney is blessed with an average of 342 sunny days each year. All this pleasant weather makes for an outdoor city; Sydneysiders flock to nearby golden beaches, a beautiful harbor, golf courses, and tennis courts at every chance. During weekday noon hours downtown workers flee their offices for the pleasure of a stroll in a nearby park. When outdoorsy people aren't getting exercise themselves, they watch spectator sports.

A stroll through the park

The eastern section of Sydney's city center is dominated by three beautiful parks—the Royal Botanic Gardens, The Domain, and Hyde Park. Starting at Farm Cove, this parkland area stretches south to Liverpool Street. In Sydney's eastern suburbs you'll find still another large park—Centennial Park.

The Royal Botanic Gardens. These gardens, sweeping down to the curve of Farm Cove, are renowned for their beauty and design. More than 400 varieties of plants, shrubs, and trees from around the world grow throughout the park's 27 hectares/67 acres. Lawn areas are interspersed with oblong flower beds and dotted with fountains and sculptures. Azalea Walk is in full bloom around mid-September; the rose garden stays fragrant with blossom from early spring into autumn, the Pyramid Glass House features lush tropical varieties. The park is open from 8 A.M. to sunset. (Government House, near Bennelong Point, is in the park, but not open to visit. It is the home of New South Wales's governor.)

The Domain. This open stretch of grassland south of the Royal Botanic Gardens is an ideal place to play a little football or cricket, fly a kite, or give a public speech. On Sundays some of Sydney's orators climb onto their soapboxes (ladders these days) to do just that. They speak on everything from religion to politics, and small crowds gather to listen.

Hyde Park. Stretching from Queen's Square to Liverpool Street, Hyde Park is the most central of the large city parks. Near the city's main shopping district, it provides an excellent resting spot for weary shoppers and a noontime retreat for office workers. The two-block park is graced with tree-lined walks, a multitude of benches, expansive lawns, and beautiful flower gardens.

Hyde Park has several attractions. Archibald Fountain at the park's north end spews forth dramatic streams of water amid striking bronze statuary. The fountain commemorates the French and Australian alliance during World War I. At the other end of the park is another war memorial—The Anzac Memorial.

Centennial Park. This park of ponds, grasslands, and bush in Sydney's eastern suburbs was established during the country's 1888 centennial year. It was also the site of the January 1, 1901 ceremony establishing the Australian Commonwealth.

Today, the park is enjoyed by equestrians and cyclists. Horses are available for hire (phone 39-5314) and bicycles for rent (phone 357-5663 or 398-5027).

The large park also has sports grounds for rugby, soccer, cricket, field hockey, and baseball.

A trip to the zoo

On a north shore promontory overlooking the harbor and downtown Sydney, the Taronga Zoo offers visitors not only an amazing variety of wildlife but also an exceptional view. In fact, *taronga* in Aborigine means "view over the water."

The most pleasant way to visit the zoo is to take a 15-minute ferry ride from Circular Quay (Number 5 Jetty) to the wharf at the base of the zoo area, from where you ride a zoo bus to the top entrance. It's all down hill from there. The zoo's enclosures and gardens stretch downslope to the harbor. You leave the zoo through the bottom entrance, only a few steps from the wharf. At Circular Quay you can buy a package ticket that includes the ferry, bus, and admission.

The zoo has more than 3,000 mammals, birds, reptiles, and fish. Among them are a number of Australia's creatures. In the Platypus House you can watch these elusive monotremes swimming around a water tank from 11 A.M. to noon and from 2 to 3 P.M. In the Nocturnal House, day becomes night so you can see the beautiful cuscus and graceful gliding possums. Strolling through the Rainforest Aviary—a special walk-through wire cage filled with tropical trees and vines—you'll see a number of colorful Australian birds flitting about. Of course there are kangaroos and koalas in the park. There's also an aquarium and a petting zoo for children.

At the zoo's seal show, you might find it hard to concentrate on the performers. From this area of the zoo you have an outstanding view of the harbor and city.

Throughout the zoo, the emphasis is on an open, natural environment for the animals. Instead of cages, there are moated enclosures wherever possible.

The zoo is open daily from 9 A.M. to 5 P.M.

Miles of golden beaches

Sydneysiders claim they have more golden beaches than any of the Pacific islands, and it's true. Within Sydney's city limits are 34 magnificent beaches, most within easy reach of downtown. On summer weekends and holidays, Sydneysiders flock to these beaches to soak up the sun, swim, and catch the big waves on their surfboards. The popular swimming and surfing season is October through March, though a few hardy people use the water the year around.

Most of Sydney's beaches are easily reached by public transportation. Fast hydrofoils as well as more leisurely ferries transport people to Manly. Other beaches can be reached by bus.

Northern ocean beaches. One of the best-known northern beach areas is Manly, at the mouth of Sydney Harbour. With four ocean beaches, this resort area offers a variety of swimming and surfing possibilities. The huge tank at Manly Marineland features all kinds of local sea creatures, including giant turtles, rays, and sharks. Seals perform daily at noon and 2 P.M., with an extra show at 4 P.M. on weekends.

Beyond Manly, the beach world stretches another 40 km/25 miles north to the entrance to the Hawkesbury River. Beaches include North Steyne, Queenscliff, Harbord, Curl Curl, Dee Why, Collaroy, Long Reef, Narrabeen, Warriewood, Mona Vale, Bungan, Newport, Bilgola, Avalon, Whale, and Palm Beach. Favorites among surfing beaches include Dee Why and Collaroy.

Southern ocean beaches. Along the coast south of Sydney Harbour, you'll find about 32 km/20 miles of good beaches. The closest is famous Bondi Beach. Other beaches include Tamarama, Bronte, Clovelly, Coogee, Maroubra, and Cronulla. The best surfing beaches are Bondi, Maroubra, and Cronulla.

Inside the harbor. Within Sydney Harbour, a string of beaches stretches along the southern shore from Rushcutters Bay east to Watson's Bay: Seven Shillings at Double Bay, Rose Bay, Nielson Park and Camp Cove. Along the harbor's northern shores, the well-known beaches are Balmoral, Edwards, Chinaman's, and Clontarf.

A word about sharks. Sharks are found in Sydney's waters. Because of the shark threat, most of the harbor beaches are safeguarded by shark nets. On surf beaches—where nets can't be used—aerial and ground patrols keep a lookout for sharks. It's best to swim only between marker flags at patrolled beaches. If you hear a siren or bell while you are in the water, get ashore immediately; a shark has been spotted.

The harbor, naturally, is not sharkproof outside the netted areas, so don't dive off a boat into the harbor. Unprotected river estuaries also can be dangerous.

One other menace in Sydney's waters is the Portuguese man-o-war, appearing in armada strength every summer in the ocean and estuary waters. Their poisonous sting is itchy and painful.

Other sports to enjoy

In Sydney you can sample a variety of sports—from a number of water sports to those where both feet are on the ground.

Water sports. Besides surfing and swimming, Sydneysiders enjoy other water-oriented activities. Heading the list is boating. Weekend sailors ply the waters of the harbor

Neat geometrical design is consistently repeated in Paddington's rooftops. Sydney's southeastern suburb boasts restaurants, taverns, antique shops, restored Victorian residences, and an art colony.

The Rocks, site of Sydney's beginnings, was once the haunt of sailors and thugs. Today's visitors stroll past art galleries, antique shops, and quaint restaurants.

and nearby rivers. If you want to join them, you can charter boats at many waterfront resorts in Sydney Harbour, at nearby rivers including the Hawkesbury, and at Broken Bay north of Sydney.

There are also snorkeling and scuba diving off the coast of New South Wales. Scuba equipment can be rented at Pro-Diving Services in Maroubra. For more information on scuba diving, contact the New South Wales Government Travel Centre.

Fishing. One of the best places for deep-sea fishing is out of Coff's Harbour, 579 km/360 miles north of Sydney. You'll also find good fishing out of Port Stephens and Bermagui. Deep-sea catches can include marlin, Spanish mackerel, barracuda, and albacore. For boat charter information, contact the Game Fishing Association located in Sydney.

Fresh-water fishers can cast their lines into the rivers and streams of nearby mountain areas, including the Blue Mountains as well as the Hawkesbury River. You'll need an inland angling license, which you can obtain from the Department of Fisheries in Sydney.

Golf. For the golfer, public courses are available and some championship private clubs open their courses to visitors, especially on weekdays. These clubs include the New South Wales Golf Club and The Lakes Golf Club. For more information on Sydney area golf courses, contact the Secretary of the New South Wales Golf Association in Sydney.

Tennis. Sydney has both public courts and private tennis clubs. Club players seeking more information may contact either the New South Wales Lawn Tennis Association or the New South Wales Hardcourt Tennis Association. Public play courts are listed in the telephone book Yellow Pages.

Eating & drinking Australian-style

During your travels around Australia, there's no reason to go hungry or thirsty. Today, Australia offers a pleasant variety of both good food and good beverages.

Culinary specialties. The influx of immigrants from all over the world has had its effect on the cuisine of Australia. Restaurants reflect this international influence, with offerings from Hungarian goulash to coq au vin to beef Wellington on the same menu.

Aside from a number of good international selections, one of Australia's best offerings is seafood. Sydney rock oysters, for instance, are an excellent appetizer. Incidentally, when you're looking for appetizers on a menu in Australia, look at "entrées"—the main course is something separate.

Other good Australian seafoods you'll want to try include Queensland barramundi, John Dory fish, coral trout, Moreton Bay bugs (miniature crustaceans), Queensland mud crab, large king prawns, and large crayfish whose tails are exported to the United States as "Australian lobster tails."

For those who prefer steak, Australian menu offerings include steak and eggs, carpetbag steak (beef stuffed with oysters), and chateaubriand. Also try Australia's roast spring lamb in mint sauce, or perhaps lamb chops.

No matter what you order for a main course in Australia, you'll discover that you get more than enough to eat. In addition to the meat or fish, you'll usually get three vegetables—one of them a potato.

Among Australian staples is the meat pie, particularly popular as a fast-food item. These pies consist of meat and gravy in a crust, and Australians love to pour tomato sauce all over them.

If you go on a bush picnic or an organized cookout with a tour group, you might get to sample damper bread and billy tea. Damper is made from unleavened wheat flour, mixed with water and then kneaded. The dough is placed in a heavy cast-iron pot that is then put in a hole in the ground and covered with hot coals to bake. You wash down the delicious results with billy tea, simply prepared in a tin can over a campfire.

Something to drink. Australia's national drink is beer, and Australians consume it with gusto. There are more than two dozen breweries in Australia producing more than 70 different brands of beer—strong and hearty and with a higher alcohol content than U.S. beers. Some Australian states are currently trying to lower the alcohol content of beers served in their state.

Beer is served in glasses of different sizes that are called by different names—names that vary from state to state. For example, in New South Wales and Western Australia a "middy" is a 10-ounce glass of beer; in other states the term "middy" might not be even used. A "pony" and a "schooner" are among other beer glasses you might hear about.

For a long time Australians didn't drink much wine. Many people order beer with their meals, but wine has become a popular accompaniment to meals as well. The country produces a number of first-rate wines that rival those of California and France. Among Australian wine selections you'll find Moselle, Semillon, Rhine Riesling, Claret, Cabernet Sauvignon, Shiraz (Hermitage), and Pinot Noir, as well as sherries, ports, and champagnes.

Bushwalking. There are a number of walking trails not far from Sydney where hikers can enjoy the out-of-doors. You'll find good trails to the north at Ku-ring-gai Chase National Park, to the west in the Blue Mountains, and to the south in Royal National Park. For more information on bushwalking, contact the New South Wales Federation of Bushwalking Clubs in Sydney.

Horseback riding. From sunrise to sunset, horseback riders exercise in Centennial Park. Horses (and instruction, if desired) are available at a number of riding stables listed in the Yellow Pages.

Sports to watch

In this sports-minded city, you also have a wide variety of spectator sports to choose from.

Racing. Sydneysiders love a good horse race. The city has six race tracks, with Randwick—5 km/3 miles from down-town—the closest and principal track. Randwick's big races are held in the spring and fall, but races are scheduled throughout the year at Canterbury, Rosehill, and Warwick Farm, a little farther from city center.

Trotting races are held Friday nights under the lights at Harold Park, a short distance from the city. Greyhounds race on Saturday nights at Harold Park or Wentworth Park.

Football. Though four codes of football (Australian national code, rugby League, rugby Union, and soccer) are played in Sydney, perhaps the most popular is professional rugby League football. Played throughout New South Wales and Queensland, this game includes international matches between Australian teams and teams from England, France, and New Zealand. Games are played during the winter months (March through September) at the Sydney Sports Ground at Moore Park (south of Paddington) and at other ovals in Sydney.

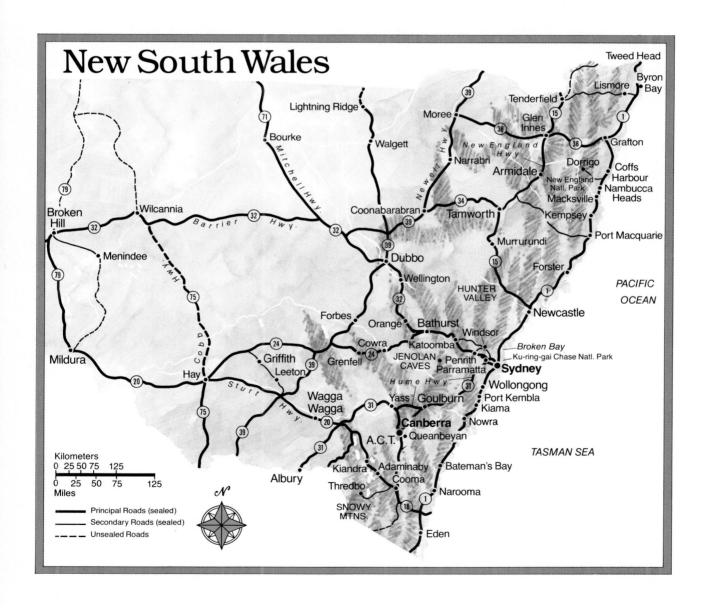

Turreted tops of Three Sisters in the Blue Mountains provide vistas of surrounding countryside. This is a vacation land of plummeting waterfalls, fern-filled gorges, and hidden caves.

Costumed soldiers lounge at ease in Old Sydney Town, a re-creation of Sydney Cove in the late 1700s and early 1800s.

Cricket. Sydney's summer sport is cricket. On Saturday mornings at 11 during the cricket season (October through March), you can watch cricket being played at the Sydney Cricket Ground in Moore Park. Check the newspapers for cricket international test matches between Australian teams and teams from England, New Zealand, India, Pakistan, and the West Indies.

Sailboat racing. Both on weekends and during the week, you'll find the harbor dotted with sailboats, their brightly colored sails catching the breeze. Some are out for a pleasure sail; others are there to race. The yachting season runs from September through May with races and regattas held nearly every weekend. Races that are particularly popular are those between "18-footers." Sailed by a crew of four, these little boats dart back and forth across the harbor at amazing speeds. The 18-footers club is at Double Bay.

Sailors turn out in full force each year for the start of the big Sydney-Hobart Yacht Race, December 26.

There's no need to stand on the sidelines to watch the harbor races—every Saturday during the racing season, you can follow the boats in a spectators' ferry. Catch the ferry at Circular Quay at 2 P.M.

West to the Blue Mountains

Through a dreamlike blue haze, the Blue Mountains rise from the plains just 65 km/40 miles west of Sydney. Part of the Great Dividing Range that runs along Australia's eastern seaboard, these mountains provide a popular, nearby vacation retreat for Sydney residents. There are opportunities for golf, swimming, tennis, horseback riding, rock climbing, and bushwalking, and for people who just want to enjoy the scenery. Vistas include deep fern-filled gorges, wide ravines, steep cliffs, and plummeting waterfalls.

From a variety of good vantage points, you can discover that the mountains do indeed appear blue, an effect caused by the eucalyptus forests that cover the area. Droplets of oil from the gum tree leaves refract the light of the sun, creating a blue haze.

You can get to the Blue Mountains on a 1-day tour out of Sydney. There is also daily train service from Sydney Central Railway Station to Katoomba and Leura, or you can drive yourself. Accommodations in the Blue Mountains include hotels, motels, holiday flats, cottages, cabins, caravan parks, and campgrounds.

The Katoomba resort area

Katoomba, 104 km/65 miles from Sydney, is the main resort center for the Blue Mountains. From here you can visit Echo Point Lookout, where you'll have a good view of forested Jamieson Valley and the massive weathered sandstone formation known as the Three Sisters. From Echo Point, take the Giants' Stairway into the valley. Lookouts and rest stops along the 916-step descent help make the trip a little easier.

Blue Mountain rides. Across from Echo Point, enjoy more of the Blue Mountains on two different rides.

The Scenic Skyway gondola travels on a cable high above the Jamieson Valley floor. From this lofty vantage point, you can see cascading waterfalls, vertical cliff faces, and miles of bushland.

Nearby, you can take another ride whose surprising descent might leave you momentarily white-knuckled. The Scenic Railway—perhaps the steepest railway in the world—drops you 213 meters/700 feet through a tunnel into the valley in a matter of seconds. At the bottom you can leave the rail car and hike to Katoomba Falls or Leura Falls. Like the skyway, the Katoomba Scenic Railway runs on a regular basis from 9 A.M. to 5 P.M. daily.

Still another ride awaits you near Lithgow, about 40 km/25 miles from Katoomba. On weekends the Zig Zag Railway steam train winds through tunnels and along stone viaducts. When it was built in the 1860s, the Z-shaped track, which descends the eastern slopes of the Blue Mountains, was considered an engineering feat.

Tribute to a great artist. In Springwood, 30 km/19 miles from Katoomba, you can tour the home and grounds of Norman Lindsay's estate. Lindsay was one of Australia's best-known artists and writers, and the home—now converted to a museum and gallery—houses some of Lindsay's oil paintings, etchings, manuscripts, and sculptures, as well as a collection of model ships. There are beautiful views of the Blue Mountains from the grounds of the estate. The home is open Friday through Sunday from 11 A.M. to 5 P.M.

Jenolan Caves

Among the Blue Mountains scenic highlights are the Jenolan Caves 77 km/48 miles southwest of Katoomba. Famous for their stalagmites, stalactites, pillars, canopies, and shawls, these limestone caves are among the most spectacular and extensive formations of their type in Australia. Used by Aborigines for centuries, these caves were first discovered by European settlers in 1838 when a stockman tracked a bushranger (highwayman) to his hideout in them.

There are two types of cave formations—great natural archways and underground "dark" caves. You can explore the open archways on your own, but you'll need a guide for the dark caves. Nine of the dark caves have been developed—lighting, pathways, and stairs have been added for easy exploration. Cave inspection tours are held at regular intervals between 10 A.M. and 4 P.M. daily.

Part of the attraction of the Jenolan Caves is their location in a 2,428-hectare/6,000-acre wildlife sanctuary. Aside from exploring the beauty of the caves, you can wander through bushland and perhaps see wallabies scramble about. Along the well-graded trails outside the caverns, many birds can be spotted—among them bright-plumed rosella parrots, satin bowerbirds, Blue Mountain parakeets, kookaburras, and cockatoos. In summer the reserve gains added color as masses of wildflowers come into bloom.

Sydney tour operators include Jenolan Caves on some tours to the Blue Mountains. Daily train service is also available from Central Station in Sydney with a connecting bus tour from Katoomba to Jenolan on certain days. You can stay overnight at Jenolan Caves House.

Three historic towns

If you drive to the Blue Mountains, you can add a bonus to your trip by including a trio of historic old towns: Parramatta, about 24 km/15 miles west of downtown Sydney, and the sister towns of Windsor and Richmond, 21 km/13 miles and 29 km/18 miles northwest of Parramatta. Among Australia's earliest settlements, they contain buildings dating back to the late 18th and early 19th centuries. Most of the historic buildings are open to visitors.

Parramatta. Settled in 1788 less than a year after Sydney's founding, this inland town was Australia's second permanent settlement. At the time of its establishment, many felt the town was located in the wilderness. Today, it is part of the sprawling metropolitan area of Sydney.

Parramatta has a number of historical sites worth looking at. The Old Government House (1799) in Parramatta Park was the country residence of Australia's first governors. This graceful white building with its green shutters and imposing pillars is open Tuesday through Thursday, and Sunday.

The Elizabeth Farm House was constructed in 1793 by John Macarthur, a pioneer of the wool industry. It's a long building with a sloping roof and pillared veranda.

The colonial Georgian Experiment Farm Cottage (1798) marks the site of Sydney's first wheat farm. There's a museum of farm implements in the cottage cellar. Take note of the cottage's courtyard paved in convict-made bricks, and the garden of violas and herbs.

Windsor. Many of Windsor's buildings of the 1800s were designed by convict-architect Francis Greenway. The Georgian-style St. Matthew's Anglican Church, built in 1820, is one of them. Faithfully restored in 1965, the brick church is considered by some to be the finest example of Georgian architecture in the country. Its cemetery has headstones dating from 1810.

Another Greenway creation is the Court House. Built in 1822 by convict labor, this sandstone structure has also been carefully restored. It's a fine example of early-day craftsmanship.

Other interesting Windsor buildings include the Toll House (1814 or 1816), used for the collection of tolls on the Fitzroy Bridge until 1887 and now restored and fitted with period furnishings. You'll find more 19th century furnishings plus farm equipment in the Hawkesbury Museum. John Tebbutt—discoverer of Tebbutt Comet—lived in Windsor and you can visit his home and small garden observatory.

Richmond. Still another town that abounds in old buildings is Richmond. Hobartville (1828) is a Greenway-designed residence. Special features include "bushrangerproof" doors and barred cellars.

Other buildings include Toxana House (1860), now a historical museum; St. Peter's Anglican Church (1837–1841), with a graveyard where many of the area's pioneers are buried; and Woolpack Inn (1830s), which provided lodging for early-day travelers.

Gold rush region

To the west, just beyond the Blue Mountains, is the region known as New South Wales' "Golden West." More than 100 years ago, pioneers and bushrangers flocked to this area in search of gold. Discovery of payable gold in New South Wales occurred not far from Bathurst. Today, the area's riches come mainly from wool, wheat, fruit, and vegetables. But old gold mining settlements like Sofala, Hill End, and Wattle Flat can still be explored, and it's always possible that some gold can be found in the area.

A good center for exploring the gold rush region is Bathurst on the Macquarie River 208 km/129 miles west of Sydney. This sedate settlement of red brick and blue granite is Australia's third oldest city (1815). From Sydney, you can get to Bathurst by train, plane, bus, or on a coach tour.

To the north

A short distance from downtown Sydney are the winding waterways of the Hawkesbury River and the bushlands of Ku-ring-gai Chase National Park. Nearby, Old Sydney Town re-creates the Sydney Cove of the 1800s. The Hunter Valley, an easy day's drive from Sydney, is known for its fine wines.

Farther north are the verdant plateaus of New England and the sweeping North Coast. Several days could easily be spent exploring this area of New South Wales on a circle trip from Sydney or en route to Brisbane.

The Hawkesbury River

The Hawkesbury River flows wide and winding through New South Wales bush and farmland before it empties into Broken Bay 32 km/20 miles north of Sydney. When Sydney was young, the river's course cut through rich alluvial lands where wheat prospered. The river soon became the region's principal waterway to these farmlands. Produce was transported downriver, then across Broken Bay, and south along the coast to Sydney. For many years—beginning in the late 19th century—paddle wheel steamers plied this river on regular runs.

Though the wheat has gone, agriculture is still important to the area, with fruit orchards, market gardens, and farms all along the river; and though paddle wheelers have disappeared, boats—mainly recreational—still ply the river.

Sydney residents and visitors both can enjoy the recreational pleasures of the Hawkesbury River. The area is ideal for cruising—either in your own rented boat or on a tour boat. Dense vegetation edges the river along much of its lower reaches. Palms, ferns, and gum trees grow along the banks. Waterfowl follow its course, and the raucous laughter of the kookaburra (bird) can be heard from the woods along the way. In the Broken Bay estuary, towering headlands overlook the river waters.

One-day tours. Sydney firms offer tours of the North Sydney area that include a short boat ride in the Pittwater and Broken Bay estuaries. Other cruises go up the Hawkesbury River.

Leisurely cruising. If you have several days to cruise on the Hawkesbury, you can rent a boat and explore it on your own. You'll find a selection of small cruisers available at a number of places in the Hawkesbury River area.

Boats sleep four to nine persons, have hot and cold running water, gas stoves, ice boxes, flush toilets, and showers. No boating license is needed. You'll find plenty of overnight anchorages and small refueling/restocking stops along the way. During the peak vacation period (from Christmas holidays through April or May), you must reserve a boat well ahead.

Once on the river, you can set your own pace, stopping at historic old river towns en route. At Ebenezer you can visit the Presbyterian Church. Completed in 1809, it's the oldest church in use by an Australian congregation. A short distance upriver from Ebenezer, Windsor is one of Australia's oldest settlements (see page 40). Some 20 historic buildings, now restored, have been assembled at Wilberforce in the Australiana Folk Village. Also on display are a working ferry and a model of the first train to run from Sydney to the Hawkesbury Valley.

Ku-ring-gai Chase National Park

This vast bushland reserve on the southern banks of the Hawkesbury River, only 24 km/15 miles north of Sydney, offers rugged sandstone plateaus that are rich in native plants and wildlife. Area fauna include swamp wallabies and a small colony of koalas. Between July and November, the area's wildflowers display their colors, and tiny honeyeater birds come to drink the nectar.

In the national park, you can swim, fish, bushwalk, and boat. Boats may be hired at Bobbin Head, Brooklyn, and Terrey Hills.

Several Sydney tour operators include Ku-ring-gai Chase National Park in tours of the northern suburbs, or you can drive there on your own.

Old Sydney Town

About 72 km/45 miles north of Sydney is Old Sydney Town, a re-creation of Sydney Cove as it appeared in the time of Governor Bligh at the beginning of the 19th century.

Built on a hilly, lightly wooded site, the 101-hectare/250-acre park slopes down to a large body of water representing Sydney Cove. Around this cove are unpaved roads and paths dotted with tents, tiny convict gang huts, church, courthouse, jail, and houses of the free settlers and freed convicts. In the cove, the brig *Perseverance* is tied up at Hospital Wharf. Building continues in the park, giving visitors a chance to see the evolution of the township from its beginnings to about 1810.

All the personnel of Old Sydney Town wear the costumes of the period, portraying convicts, soldiers, magistrates, and free settlers. Each day they act out the events of the period. There are speedy court hearings, public floggings, flintlock pistol duels, and street dancing. Craftspeople—blacksmiths, coopers, wheelwrights, seamstresses, candlemakers, and tinsmiths—can be seen at work.

Old Sydney Town is open Wednesday through Sunday from 10:30 A.M. to 5 P.M. Sometimes in the evenings there are special "sound and light" shows that feature a tour of the town and a recounting of the history of the colony's first days.

It's about an hour's drive to Old Sydney Town, or you can take the train from Sydney's Central Station to Gosford—a 1½-hour scenic trip through wooded hills. From the Gosford Railway Station, you can take a bus to the park. The State Rail Authority has a special rail/bus tour from Sydney; there are bus tours from Sydney as well.

Lake Macquarie

About 149 km/90 miles north of Sydney is this pleasant seaboard lake with more than 160 km/100 miles of shoreline. Because of the lake's size, the Royal Australian Air Force was able to use it as a major seaplane base during World War II. Today, it's a popular vacation spot for swimming, water-skiing, fishing, and boating. There also are a golf course, tennis courts, and lawn bowling greens. A guided boat tour from Belmont's main jetty gives you a close look at the lake.

Accommodations in the area include motels, campgrounds, and a caravan park.

Hunter River Valley

It takes only a few hours by car to drive the 208 km/130 miles north from Sydney to the Hunter River Valley, noted for its wineries and vineyards.

The largest wineries in the area are located near Cessnock and Pokolbin, about 32 km/20 miles west of Newcastle. Australia's oldest wine-producing area, the Hunter River Valley combines coal mining with its vineyards. As a result, Cessnock resembles a busy mining center more than a picturesque wine town, but the cellars and winery buildings around Pokolbin have the traditional look of a wine region.

Fine red and white wines are produced here including red shiraz and cabernet and white semillon and chardonnay. Wineries known in other parts of Australia, such as McWilliams and Lindemans, welcome visitors as do most of the smaller local wineries.

There are both motels and hotels at Cessnock and Pokolbin. Some Sydney bus tours include the Hunter River Valley.

The North Coast & New England

The scenery of northeastern New South Wales varies from coastline blessed with golden beaches and banana plantations to tablelands of dairy farms, deep valley gorges, and rain forests.

The North Coast. This narrow strip of land—known as "The Holiday Coast"—extends from Forster (north of Newcastle) 550 km/342 miles to Tweed Heads on the Queensland border. A chain of quiet resorts and tiny fishing villages marks this coast, whose bays, inlets, and beaches offer water sports enthusiasts chances to fish, water-ski, scuba dive, boat, swim, and surf.

At Port Macquarie, 430 km/267 miles north of Sydney, seascapes and beaches are the principal attractions. Pacific Drive offers cliffs, headlands, and pocket beaches for viewing. Sea Acres, a 31-hectare/77-acre sanctuary for flora and fauna located between Pacific Drive and Shelly Beach, 5 km/3 miles south of Port Macquarie, has been preserved as one of the few surviving corners of true primeval rain forest on the New South Wales coast.

(Continued on page 44)

Australia's wonderful wildlife

The first Europeans to explore Australia were amazed at the animal life they saw. Who'd ever heard of a duck-billed mammal with fur that laid eggs, or a bird that could make sounds like a buzz saw, or a hopping creature that carried its young in a pouch? These amazing animals didn't exist in Europe, and it was hard for people back home to believe the explorers' stories. But exist they did and still do, their development the result of Australia's millions of years of isolation from the rest of the world's land masses. In essence, Australia is a living museum of rare and unusual species.

You won't find kangaroos hopping around the streets of Sydney, but you will find them and Australia's other unique creatures in protected areas that provide a natural habitat for the animals. Australia has made an outstanding effort to protect its natural environment and wildlife by establishing more than 200 sanctuaries and national parks. By visiting some of these reserves, you can observe many of the country's 400 kinds of native animals as well as over 1,200 species of birds—half of them unique to Australia.

Check with the government tourist bureau in the capital of each state you visit for a list of the sanctuaries in that area. The following paragraphs tell a little about some of the animals and birds you might have a chance to see.

Marsupials. Animals whose newborn live in their mothers' pouches and nurse for the first 4 or 5 months after birth are marsupials. Australia has more than 170 marsupials, including the kangaroo, koala, wombat, and Tasmanian devil.

Perhaps the most popular of the marsupials is the koala. (Note that it's not a bear.) With woolly fur, big eyes, and a button nose, this animal is considered cuddly and cute. But a word of warning—its claws are sharp. Koalas make their home in gum trees and their diet consists of only a few dozen different types of eucalyptus leaves.

The other well-known Australian marsupial is the kangaroo. This animal has a place of honor—along with the emu—on the Australian coat of arms. There are more than 50 types of kangaroos ranging from great red kangaroos that stand 2 meters/6 feet tall to rat-size quokkas. Both wallaroos and wallabies are also in the kangaroo family. Members of the kangaroo family can be found on grassy plains, in rocky hills, and even in swamps.

The kangaroo has huge hind legs, small forelegs, and a stout, elongated tail it uses as a prop when grazing or standing. When stirred into flight, kangaroos can bound away at great speeds. The red and gray ones have been known to jump more than 6 meters/20 feet and do speeds of up to 48 km/30 miles per hour.

A baby kangaroo is called a "joey." At birth the baby is about an inch long, blind, and furless. By natural instinct the newborn makes its way through the mother's fur into her pouch; the pouch seals itself, and joey stays there until it can hop out to nibble grass and plants. The pouch continues to be used as an emergency shelter—a frightened joey dashes headlong into it, often leaving the long hind legs dangling outside.

Mammals that lay eggs. Monotremes are the lowest order of mammals—unique egg-laying animals whose eggs hatch into mammals. Once hatched, the young are suckled. The combination of laying eggs and nursing the young dumbfounded English and French scientists who studied the first monotremes brought back from Australia in the early 1800s. Australia possesses the only two extant monotremes: the platypus and the echidna.

The adult platypus is less than ½ meter/2 feet in length. This duckbilled, fur-coated, webfooted animal has a large, flat furry tail which is used as a rudder when swimming. The platypus's talents include burrowing, swimming, and diving.

The echidna—really a spiny anteater—resembles a porcupine in size and appearance. Like the platypus, the spiny anteater is an egg-laying mammal of prehistoric vintage; it is the only remaining kin of the platypus.

Though the echidna comes in several varieties, the best known are a short-legged variety living on the Australian mainland, and two long-beaked, densely furred species living in Papua New Guinea. All echidnae are burrowers—masters at disappearing into the sand.

For bird watchers. Australia's birds vary in size from the tiny weebil to the stately emu. There are black swans with scarlet beaks and feet, and a host of brightly plumed parrot family members like lorikeets, cockatoos, ringnecks, rosellas, and budgerigars.

Appearing with the kangaroo on Australia's coat of arms, the emu is considered the most outstanding of the country's unusual birds. The powerfully built, brown-feathered, 2-meter/6-foot bird resembles the ostrich. Though emus can run at high speeds, they can't fly; they graze in flocks on the plains and in wooded country.

The lyrebird lives in the mountain forests of the east coast between Melbourne and Brisbane. He can project his own rich melodious voice up to a quarter of a mile or convincingly mimic birdcalls ranging from a kookaburra's raucous laugh to a thornbill's treble. The bird can even mimic a buzz saw. One of the most outstanding features of the male lyrebird is his spectacular courtship dance.

Also known for its sound is the country's most popular bird—the kookaburra. Because of the bird's rollicking laugh, it has been nicknamed the "laughing jackass." The kookaburra's laugh can be heard everywhere—even in the cities and suburbs.

Ranger introduces *a wombat at Urimbirra Fauna Park near Victor Harbor. This paunchy marsupial is a nocturnal animal that's happy in mud.*

Cuddle a koala *(above) at Lone Pine Koala Sanctuary near Brisbane. Many parks offer opportunities to hug Australia's favorite marsupial.*

Alert red "roo", *Australia's largest marsupial, can leap up to 20 feet and travel 30 miles an hour.*

...Continued from page 41

Banana plantations surround Coff's Harbour, a holiday center for fishing, skin diving, and spear fishing. Northwest of Coff's Harbour is Bruxner Park Flora Reserve, a tropical jungle of vines, ferns, and orchids (blooming in September). Bird watching is good here. Kangaroos, emus, and other Australian animals and birds may be seen at Kumbaingeri Wildlife Sanctuary, 16 km/10 miles north of Coff's Harbour.

Both planes and trains serve several of the area's major towns from Sydney. You'll find accommodations including motels, hotels, caravan parks, and campgrounds all along the coast.

New England. The northern reaches of the Great Dividing Range form an immense tableland—an expansive plateau known as New England. These highlands mix rich farmlands with cattle and sheep holdings. One of the best times to visit New England is in autumn when the landscape is vibrant with fall color, thanks to the first settlers in this area, who planted an array of European deciduous trees including oaks, elms, poplars, and silver birches.

Center for the area's activities is Armidale, 566 km/352 miles north of Sydney. Here you'll find the University of New England, Armidale Teacher's College, a technical college, and several secondary schools. Besides the many schools, Armidale has several cathedrals with noteworthy spires.

A number of motels and caravan parks provide comfortable accommodations in Armidale. The fastest way to reach Armidale from Sydney is by air. It takes about 9 hours by train, 8 hours by car.

Fossicking. Admirers of topaz, diamonds, and sapphires might want to take a side trip to Glen Innes and Tenterfield at the northern end of the New England plateau. Several sapphire reserves have been set aside in the Glen Innes and Invernell areas. Before you begin, you will need to get a fossicker's license from the Department of Mines in Sydney.

New England National Park. About 80 km/50 miles east of Armidale, New England National Park is similar topographically to the Blue Mountains. But it is far less populated and relatively undeveloped.

Some of the best scenery is found along the eastern escarpment, where the tablelands suddenly drop off to the lush subtropical forest below. A trail winds along the edge of the escarpment. Only experienced bushwalkers are advised to descend to the valley floor.

Dorrigo State Park just east of New England National Park gives easy access to the valley rain forest. Here you can take a nature walk through subtropical foliage of huge tree ferns, palms, and orchids. Throughout the area are waterfalls, streams, and cascades.

South of Sydney

South of Sydney, the Princes Highway (1) winds along the coast of New South Wales through the industrial cities of Wollongong and Port Kembla. Then the landscape changes to an area of uncrowded surfing and swimming beaches and miles of rich farm and dairy lands. This is the Illawarra Coast. Here you'll find resort towns and tiny fishing villages, open pastureland, river valleys, and cedar forests. The Princes Highway eventually rounds the southeast corner of the continent, crosses the border into Victoria, and heads westward to Melbourne.

You can see some of the Illawarra on day tours out of Sydney, or you can drive down the coast on your own. There's also air and rail service to Nowra, Wollongong, Bateman's Bay, and Kiama. Along the coast, you'll find motels, hotels, caravan parks, and campgrounds. If you like you can drive from Sydney to Melbourne—a 893-km/555-mile trip. Though the road is paved and well maintained, it does become narrow and winding after Kiama.

Besides the Illawarra Coast, southern New South Wales has another interesting region to explore—the Riverina wine district, an inland, irrigated region that produces some fine wines.

Royal National Park

Only 32 km/20 miles south of Sydney, this national park is a popular retreat for Sydney residents on weekends and holidays. The 14,892 hectares/36,800 acres of bushland include plenty of opportunities for scenic drives and pleasant bushwalks. The park's coast has good surfing beaches. From August through November, wildflowers come into bloom.

Park facilities are not highly developed, but you will find sites for picnicking. There are camping areas at Bonnie Vale and Audley.

The Illawarra coast

South of the Royal National Park, the Princes Highway bends toward the coast. At Sublime Point, 366 meters/1,200 feet above the sea, you get a sweeping view southward along the Illawarra coast as far as Kiama. You'll find another good view point just south of Sublime Point at the top of Bulli Pass.

In the waters off this stretch of coast, half of Australia's fish catch is taken. Salmon fishermen congregate here, and you'll see their net dinghies and power boats anchored offshore and in the little ports along the way.

South of Wollongong, Princes Highway veers inland. For a better coastal view, take the coastside road. You hug the ocean through Port Kembla and see Lake Illawarra—a body of water popular with water-skiers, fishers, and swimmers. The little fishing port of Shellharbour, just south of the lake, is a quiet, pleasant seaside resort with a motel, caravan park, and campgrounds.

Kiama. Lighthouse buffs will be interested in the lighthouse in Kiama, built in 1886 and still in operation. At the foot of the lighthouse, a blowhole funnels a huge jet of spray skyward.

Kiama is situated on the Minnamurra River. About 18 km/11 miles upstream, you can see the river cascading into a deep, rock-strewn gorge. Walking paths provide pleasant opportunities for exploring the subtropical rain forest.

South of Kiama, Princes Highway follows a tortuous route along cliffs and beaches through the little town of Geroa at the mouth of Crooked River; along Seven Mile Beach, famous as the take-off point for Kingsford-Smith's flight across the Tasman Sea in the *Southern Cross*; past the fishing resort of Greenwell Point, Currarong, and Jervis Bay.

Kangaroo Valley. Inland from the Princes Highway, about 22 km/14 miles northwest of Nowra, is an area of pastoral charm. Rain forests, grazing land, and bush offer visitors a variety of scenery to explore. Trails for hiking and horseback riding are well developed. An interesting stone castellated bridge—the Hampden Bridge—crosses the Kangaroo River in the valley. The river, with its chain of pools, is popular with anglers.

Popular recreational pursuits include fishing, canoeing, and swimming. Camping facilities, cottages, and cabins are available in Kangaroo Valley Village.

Nowra. This town on the Shoalhaven River has become popular with vacationers from both Sydney and Canberra. The river follows a rugged course through forest-covered ranges, and the sights include waterfalls, caverns, and interesting rock formations. A sizeable town, Nowra has a good assortment of hotels, motels, cabins, caravan parks, and campgrounds.

Bateman's Bay. This bay, 277 km/172 miles south of Sydney, marks the southern extremity of the Illawarra district. The bay was first sighted by Captain Cook in 1770 and named after Captain Bateman of the sailing ship *Northumberland.*

The small village has an old-world atmosphere and offers beautiful seascapes. Famous for its oysters and crayfish (which can be bought right off the boats), the town is popular with Canberra residents. Favorite area activities include surfing, swimming, fishing, and boating. Motels, a guest house, caravan parks, and campgrounds provide a variety of accommodations.

A wine region

Also south of Sydney, but far inland from the Illawarra Coast, you'll find the productive vineyards of the Riverina District. Nearly 60 percent of New South Wales's wines come from this district located about 644 km/400 miles southwest of Sydney and 322 km/200 miles northeast of Melbourne. The vineyards here thrive on a warm climate and an irrigation system watering some 80,936 hectares/200,000 acres through a canal system fed by the Murrumbidgee River.

The principal town is Griffith, situated on the main irrigation canal. You can reach the area by air, rail, or express bus from Sydney. You'll find hotels, motels, caravan parks, and campgrounds.

McWilliams has three wineries here; Wynn's and Penfold's are the other big names in the area. These contrast with a number of smaller wineries. The area produces both table and fortified wines.

Other trips from Sydney

There are two other side trips you can take from Sydney if you have the time. By air, you can take excursions to the Snowy Mountains southwest of Sydney and to Lightning Ridge northwest of Sydney.

Even though the Snowy Mountains (see page 53) are closer to Canberra, many visitors reach the area from Sydney. Daily flights go into Cooma from Sydney, as do rail, bus, and tour services.

If you want to see what some of the real outback looks like, take a tour to Lightning Ridge. There are both 1 and 3-day tours to this dry, dusty frontier land.

Lightning Ridge is the source of the "black" opal—one of the most valuable opals in Australia. The first of these opals was discovered in 1907, and by 1914, area opal production had reached its peak. Today, fossickers still come to the area to search abandoned mines and sift through heaps in search of opal fortunes. With a fossicker's license, you too can hunt for that elusive fortune.

Lightning Ridge is 772 km/480 miles northwest of Sydney—about 2½ hours by plane.

Visiting a sheep station

Beyond Sydney and its metropolitan area lies the bushland of New South Wales—the "outback." Here sheep roam, and beauty prevails in wide open spaces, rolling pasturelands, and gum trees.

Several tour operators offer day trips to this area. One such tour operator flies you to Dubbo, a rural community of 21,000 on the Macquarie River 402 km/250 miles northwest of Sydney. Beyond the town are the vast open reaches of Australia and the rich farming area of the Macquarie Valley.

During your day's tour of the area, you might see a sheep and lamb auction and visit a sheep station to see sheep shearing, wool grading and packing, and sheep dogs at work. You'll have a barbecued lunch under the shade of the gum trees and learn how to throw a boomerang. A trip to Dubbo's open range zoo is also on the tour itinerary. Here you'll make friends with—and hand-feed—some of Australia's animals.

Still another tour goes to Cowra, a 55-minute flight from Sydney. This day trip also includes a visit to a sheep station and other features like those at Dubbo. Coach tours also leave Sydney to visit sheep properties near the towns of Mittagong, Bowral, and Moss Vale, all southwest of Sydney. In fact, wherever you travel in Australia you'll find sheep stations to visit.

C A N B E R R A

Australia's national capital is one grand design

Australia's national capital was planned for only $3,500. That's right—$3,500.

In the early 1900s, the country's leaders recognized a need for a capital, but neither Sydney nor Melbourne was willing for the other to win this honor. So the Australian Capital Territory (A.C.T.) was created at a compromise location between the two cities, and an international competition was established to plan a capital city. Chicago landscape architect Walter Burley Griffin won the competition and the $3,500 prize money in 1911, when the broad valley that now holds Canberra was little more than a home for grazing sheep.

A planned capital city

Parliament convened for the first time in Canberra in 1927, but it was a sparse place still. In fact, world wars, bureaucratic disagreements, and lack of funds kept development at a crawl until the 1950s. Today, Canberra's population stands at more than a quarter million—but there's still enough space between buildings to make the city seem more like a gigantic college campus than a teeming metropolis.

Like Brasilia and other planned cities, Canberra is of interest to vacationing visitors principally for its monumental architecture, museums, and fine parks.

Canberra is distinct from Australia's other major cities. Planned as the national capital, it was designed and built mainly to hold parliament and the other arms of national government. It's also home to numerous foreign embassies and legations. Unlike Australia's other major cities, Canberra does not border on the ocean—so summers are warm here, winters chilly.

Seeing the grand design

The key to putting Canberra's development into perspective is the Regatta Point Planning Exhibition. This build-

Canberra, the well-planned capital city, borders on Lake Burley Griffin. Water jet commemorates 200th anniversary of Captain Cook's voyage; in background is the National Library.

ing is located in Commonwealth Park, on Lake Burley Griffin's north shore near Commonwealth Avenue Bridge. It houses a collection of models, photos, and diagrams that give you a clear understanding of how this planned city works. The exhibit is open daily from 9 A.M. to 5 P.M.

Of particular interest are color reproductions of Walter Burley Griffin's 1911 plan for his dream city. An excellent audio-visual presentation shows the main events of Canberra's growth. After the presentation step onto the terrace, from where you can see the spacious core of Canberra. Then, to get the big picture, head for the top of Black Mountain or Mount Ainslie.

Canberra's Telecom Tower sits atop Black Mountain. From its viewing platforms and revolving restaurant at 870 meters/2,842 feet, you get a 360-degree sweeping panorama that encompasses Canberra, its three satellite cities, plus distant rivers and valleys with the Brindabella Range as a backdrop. The tower is open daily from 9 A.M. to 10 P.M.

Opposite the Civic Centre sits Mount Ainslie. The view from its summit (842 meters/2,762 feet) offers the best appreciation of Walter Burley Griffin's grand design.

As you look at Canberra along the central axis of the Parliamentary Triangle, immediately below you is the big green dome of the Australian War Memorial. Leading from there to the lake, you see the broad double strip of Anzac Parade. Follow this line across the lake, and you'll see the white facade of the present Parliament House. Immediately behind it is the nearly-completed new Parliament House on Capital Hill, apex of the triangle.

South of the lake

Standing on the lake shore, between the two bridges that form the sides of the Parliamentary Triangle, are the National Gallery, the High Court, the National Library, and the National Science and Technology Centre (scheduled to open in 1988). Behind these are the original Parliament House and the new Parliament House.

Parliament House. Facing Lake Burley Griffin just below Capital Hill, "The House"—as it is known in the capital—is an attractive white building set amid trim lawns, trees, and colorful gardens. But in spite of its established appearance, Parliament House is, and always has been, temporary.

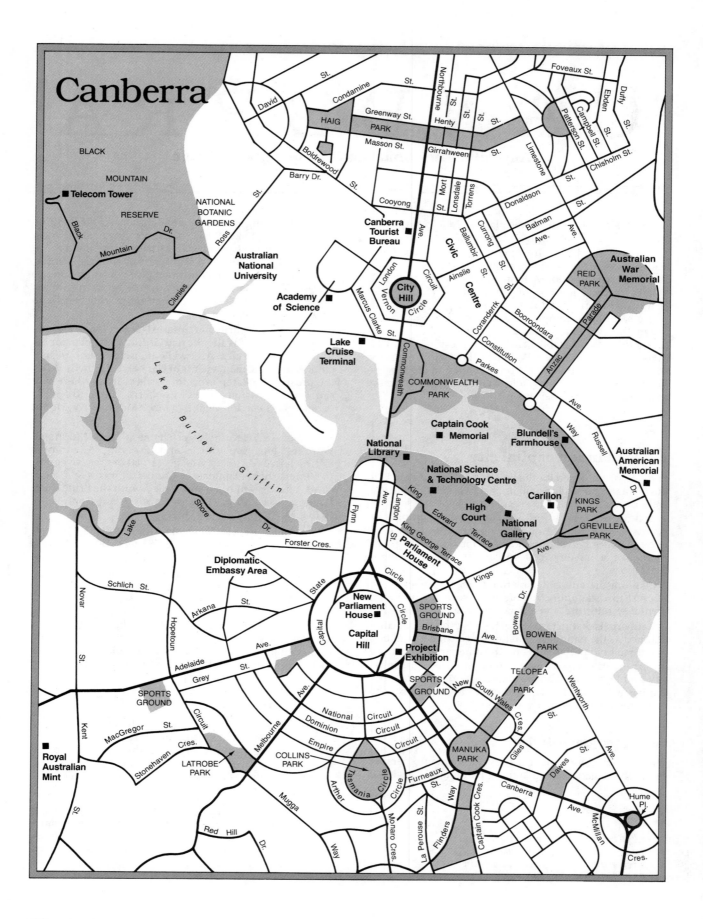

Canberra

When the building was constructed in 1927, city planners intended to use it for only about 50 years. After that a larger building would replace it. The new Parliament House, now structurally complete, is being fitted and furnished in preparation for its opening in 1988, Australia's bicentennial. A nearby project exhibition, open daily from 9 A.M. to 6 P.M., provides information about the new building.

In the meantime, you can stroll through the colonnaded foyer of the current Parliament House. King's Hall has a fascinating collection of paintings and portraits, including a painting depicting the opening of the first Parliament in Canberra. Among the documents preserved there is one of three surviving originals of the Inspeximus Issue of the Magna Carta, dated 1297. This aged parchment document is carefully preserved in a transparent capsule filled with argon and fitted with a filter to reduce fading.

As you enter King's Hall, the Senate chamber is to the right and the House of Representatives to the left. Each chamber has a visitors' gallery where you can watch proceedings when Parliament is in session, normally from March through May and August through November, on Tuesdays, Wednesdays, and Thursdays. In daytime, the Australian flag flies over the chamber that is in session. At night, lights are used: red for the Senate, green for the House.

It is not necessary to get tickets in advance for the Senate visitors' gallery. However, it is recommended for the House. You can pick them up at Parliament House a day or two in advance, or write: Principal Attendant, House of Representatives, Parliament House, Canberra 2600.

Parliament House is open daily from 9 A.M. to 5 P.M. Conducted tours of the building are available when Parliament is in recess.

The National Library. This 5-story building is north of Parliament House and overlooks Lake Burley Griffin. It houses several million books, plus maps, photos, plans, prints, and films. Of particular note are a number of original papers, including Captain Cook's journal for the years 1768 to 1771: a description of his voyage of discovery to Australia on board the *Endeavor*.

The library's exhibition areas—the lower ground floor, the foyer, and the mezzanine—feature changing exhibits of outstanding materials from the library. Don't miss the cannon in the foyer. It's one of the six cannons thrown overboard when Captain Cook's *Endeavor* struck a reef off the coast of Queensland in 1770. An American expedition recovered this bit of history nearly 200 years later.

Leonard French's stained-glass windows add beautiful splashes of color to the foyer. Symbolizing the planets, the windows capture the morning sun in reds, oranges, and golds on the north side, and transform afternoon sun rays into blues, greens, and violets on the south side. (French also created the stained-glass ceiling in the Great Hall at Melbourne's National Gallery.)

The exhibition areas are open Monday through Thursday from 9 A.M. to 10 P.M., and Friday through Sunday from 9 to 4:45.

National Gallery and High Court. These strikingly modern buildings stand side by side on the lake shore just east of the National Library. The two buildings were designed and developed as one project; they're connected by a footbridge.

Inside the gallery, an extensive collection of Australian (including Aboriginal), Southeast Asian, European, and American art fills 11 exhibit areas. A sculpture garden is outdoors. The gallery is open daily from 10 A.M. to 5 P.M.

The High Court building has glass walls that soar to 26 meters/87 feet on the building's north and south sides, exposing angled cornices to sunlight and creating a feeling of light-drenched spaciousness. The courtroom walls (15 meters/50 feet tall) are paneled in red tulip oak brought from a Queensland rain forest. You can visit the High Court between 9:45 A.M. and 4:30 P.M. daily.

Royal Australian Mint. Australia's coins as well as the coins of several other Pacific and Asian countries are produced at the Royal Australian Mint on Denison Street, just off Adelaide Avenue west of Capital Hill.

(Continued on page 50)

The essentials

The information below will help you plan your trip to Canberra.

Getting there. Canberra is served by air, rail, and bus.

Air. Domestic flights by Ansett and Australian Airlines daily from Sydney and Melbourne, with service also from Sydney on East-West Airlines. The airport is 20 minutes from downtown by bus or taxi.

Rail. Direct service from Sydney daily. From Melbourne, rail to Yass, then bus (1 hour ride) to Canberra.

Bus. Direct service from Sydney (4½ hours), Melbourne (9 hours). Bus tours are also available from both cities.

Accommodations. Major hotels include Canberra City Travelodge, Canberra International Motor Inn, Canberra Parkroyal, Canberra Rex, Diplomat International, Hyatt Hotel Canberra, and Noah's Lakeside International.

Food and drink. Local specialties include trout, lamb, and beefsteaks; there's also a wide range of ethnic cuisine available. Several small local wineries produce good-quality red and white table wines.

Getting around. Public buses serve downtown and the suburbs. A day ticket on the Canberra Explorer tourist bus allows unlimited travel with stops at key Canberra attractions. Buses run every 45 minutes to 1 hour. Taxis and rental cars are plentiful.

Tours. Full or half-day bus tours are available. Drive-yourself tours are made easy with five tour routes marked with arrowed signposts.

For more information. The Canberra Tourist Bureau, Jolimont Centre, is open from 8:30 A.M. to 7 P.M. daily. The Visitor Information Centre (Northbourne Avenue near Morphett Street) is open daily (except Christmas) from 8:30 A.M. to 5 P.M.

...*Continued from page 49*

You can take a self-guided tour of the facility and, through windows in the visitors' gallery, see the step-by-step production of the coins. The mint is open Monday through Friday from 9 A.M. to 4 P.M.

Embassies and legations. Seventy countries have diplomatic missions in Canberra. Most embassies are south and west of Capital Hill, scattered through three of the city's suburbs—Red Hill, Forrest, and Yarralumla. Many of the embassy buildings reflect the architecture of their country. For example, the Thai embassy has a golden roof with upswept corners, and the red brick, colonnaded, American embassy is reminiscent of colonial Virginia. Both the Indonesian and Papua New Guinean buildings have exhibit areas open to the public.

Government House. Another impressive building, historic Government House, sits at the end of a tree-lined drive at the southwestern end of the lake. This several-story white building, with beautifully landscaped grounds extending to the lake's edge, was built by early Canberra Valley settlers as Yarralumla Homestead. Later enlarged, it is today the official residence of the governor-general. Neither the grounds nor the residence are open to the public. However, you can get a good view of both from a lookout point off Lady Denman Drive on the western boundary of the grounds.

North of the lake

While Capital Hill and the area south of Lake Burley Griffin are devoted mainly to the working arms of national government, the north side of the lake is where the cultural and social life of the city is centered. Ringing the downtown are monuments, museums, schools, and a diverse array of attractions.

The Civic Centre. Around City Hill is the civic and business heart of Canberra. In Civic Square stands the dramatic Ethos statue symbolizing the spirit of the community. At the head of the square sits the Canberra Theatre complex. Concerts, ballet, opera, and major stage shows are presented in the 1,200-seat Canberra Theatre. Other productions are presented in the more intimate 300-seat playhouse.

Shopping around. Sheepskins, leather goods, opals, and Aboriginal arts and crafts are just a few of the unusual items you can find in Canberra shops. Many of the shops are conveniently located near Civic Square in shopping complexes that include large department stores as well as tiny boutiques and gift shops.

Children (and adults who are young-at-heart) will love Petrie Plaza's colorful merry-go-round. From 1914 to 1974, this delightful ride stood on the Esplanade at Melbourne's St. Kilda beach. Canberra purchased the merry-go-round for more than 10 times the price of its master plan—$40,000.

Canberra's city shops are open Monday through Thursday from 9 A.M. to 5:30 P.M., Friday from 8:30 A.M. to 9 P.M., and Saturday from 8:30 A.M. to noon.

Questacon. Located on Elouera Street near the Civic Centre, this participatory science exhibition features more than 100 working "hands-on" displays. Questacon will double in size when it moves to the new National Science and Technology Centre in 1988. Questacon is open Monday through Friday from 10:30 A.M. to 4:30 P.M.

National Museum of Australia. While the museum itself will not be completed until the 1990s, a Visitor Centre is open. It overlooks the construction site—an 88 hectare/220 acre peninsula at the western end of Lake Burley Griffin. Here, you can view exhibits from the museum's wide-ranging collection as well as models and plans of the museum project. It's open from 10 A.M. to 5 P.M. daily (Mondays from 1 P.M.).

National Film and Sound Archive. The exhibits in this National Trust-classified building focus on Australian movie, radio, and television productions. Located in McCoy Circuit at the edge of the University campus, it's open from 10 A.M. to 4 P.M. daily.

Academy of Science. Some call it The Martian Embassy. This igloo-shaped building, across the street from the National Film and Sound Archive, consists of a copper-sheathed concrete shell, 46 meters/150 feet in diameter, resting on arches set in an encircling pool. It was designed by Sir Roy Grounds, a Melbourne architect. Though not open to the public, it is worth a look for its exterior design.

Australian War Memorial. One of Australia's most popular tourist attractions is the Australian War Memorial at the end of Anzac Parade—a broad boulevard east of City Hill. This handsome building with its huge copper dome serves as a dramatic memorial to Australians who gave their lives in the service of their country, from the Sudan war in 1885 through Vietnam.

Tribute is paid to these war dead in the building's central courtyard. Here, on either side of the Pool of Reflection, are arcaded galleries whose walls contain bronze panels inscribed with a Roll of Honour. At the end of this courtyard is the Hall of Memory with its copper dome, mosaic walls, and beautiful stained-glass windows.

Two floors of exhibition area within the memorial tell the tales of war through paintings, sculptures, photos, and historic relics. Large dioramas vividly depict historic battle scenes. The building houses a massive array of war implements including a Lancaster bomber, a Spitfire fighter plane, tanks, shells, and torpedos. Sections of the museum will be closed for periods during the next 10 years during a major rebuilding and expansion program.

The Australian War Memorial is open daily from 9 A.M. to 4:45 P.M. The building's closing is announced by the sounding of the Last Post.

From the steps of the memorial, you can look down the broad expanses of Anzac Parade and across the lake to Parliament House. Anzac Parade, completed in 1965, honors the cooperation of the armed forces of two nations—Australia and New Zealand.

Australian-American Memorial. Standing at the head of Kings Avenue, this 79-meter/258-foot aluminum spire commemorates the contribution made by the people of the United States to Australia's defense in World War II.

The Royal Military College. In Duntroon, a suburb just east of the Australian-American Memorial, you'll find Australia's West Point. Here the country's regular army officers receive their training.

On ceremonial occasions the college is the scene of

Skiers congregate on the Snowy Mountains. This is Australia's major skiing area, easily reached from Canberra.

Blundell's Farmhouse, one of Canberra's first buildings, was erected in 1858. Across the water in the background stands the original Parliament House.

much pomp and circumstance. Colorful pageantry includes Beating the Retreat in March and October.

The college grounds are open for inspection. At 2:30 P.M. Monday through Friday (except from November through March), you can take a guided tour.

Blundell's Farmhouse. In this city where so many buildings are new, historic Blundell's Farmhouse provides a contrast. It was built in 1858 by pioneer Robert Campbell for his ploughman. The house, still on its original site, sits on Wendouree Drive in Kings Park overlooking Lake Burley Griffin.

Three of the cottage's rooms have been furnished with pieces dating from the mid-1800s. It is open daily from 2 to 4 P.M. and also from 10 A.M. to noon on Wednesday. It's closed Mondays and Wednesdays during winter.

Australian Institute of Sport. This sprawling complex, one of the world's most advanced sport training and competition centers, is located in the satellite city of Belconnen, 10 minutes from Canberra. Here, there are facilities for ten Olympic sports—basketball, gymnastics, volleyball, rowing, soccer, swimming, tennis, track and field, water polo, and weightlifting. Tours begin at the Swimming Hall Saturdays at 2 P.M.

Canberra outdoors

Many of Canberra's outdoor activities are centered around Lake Burley Griffin in the heart of the city. The lake is not only Canberra's major scenic attraction, but also the city's recreational center. Along its 35-km/22-mile shoreline, you can follow lakeside drives and walking paths, picnic in well-developed recreation areas, or stroll across grassy open spaces. The lake itself offers swimming, boating, and fishing. Besides the vast parklands surrounding Lake Burley Griffin, Canberra's open spaces also include large bushland reserves within a short distance of the city.

Seeing the lake. One of the best ways to experience Lake Burley Griffin is to take a cruise on the 11-km/7-mile-long lake. One-hour cruises depart at noon from the Ferry Terminal at West Basin near Marcus Clarke Street, and two-hour cruises depart at 1 P.M. There are also luncheon and dinner cruises.

One memorable feature of the lake is the Captain Cook Memorial Water Jet. Located near Regatta Point just east of the Commonwealth Avenue Bridge, the jet can send up a dramatic water column of more than 137 meters/450 feet. It was installed in 1970 as a memorial to mark the 200th anniversary of Captain Cook's discovery of eastern Australia. The water jet operates daily from 10 A.M. to noon and 2 to 4 P.M., plus summer evenings.

Still another dramatic lake attraction is the carillon on Aspen Island just west of the Kings Avenue Bridge. The 53-bell-carillon and its tower surrounded by graceful white pillars was a gift from the United Kingdom on Canberra's 50th jubilee. The tower's Westminster chimes ring daily every quarter hour from 8 A.M. to 9 P.M., and there are carillon recitals on Wednesdays and Sundays. The tower is open for inspection on weekends.

Parks and gardens. Several interesting parks line the shores of Lake Burley Griffin. Commonwealth Park, along the northeastern shore of the lake, has been land-scaped to include marsh gardens and a children's play area. Thousands of flowering plants add color to the park the year around. Weston Park's adventure playground, on the lake's southwestern shore, features a play area that includes tree houses, a miniature lake with islands and bridges, a maze, and a miniature railway.

The National Botanic Gardens primarily provide a place to enjoy and study plants. Stretching across the lower slopes of Black Mountain, the gardens contain plants from all over Australia grown under conditions similar to their native environment. You can stroll through shady fern glens made humid by artificial misting or enjoy the colorful profusion of acacias in bloom in an area devoted to the growing of this Australian native. On the garden's Aboriginal Trail, you'll learn what plants were used by Aborigines for food, clothing, and weapons. The gardens are open daily from 9 A.M. to 5 P.M. with guided tours Sunday at 10 A.M. and 2 P.M.

Canberra has 105 km/65 miles of paved cycleways and bikes can be rented near the Ferry Terminal at West Basin. Small boats are also available for rent at West Basin.

Two public 18-hole courses lure golfers (Canberra also has several private clubs). For information on tennis, contact the A.C.T. Lawn Tennis Association, P.O. Box 44, Dickson 2602.

Side trips from Canberra

Sheep stations and satellites compete for the attention of visitors looking beyond Canberra for manmade changes of pace from the central city. Then there is always the opportunity to get into the Australian bush at the expense of only a few miles of travel.

Sheep stations

A trip to a sheep station is easier from Canberra than from any other major city in Australia, for the surrounding countryside is still grazing land, just as it was in the early 1900s when the valley was selected as the site of the national capital. Local tour operators offer day visits to sheep stations. These tours include outdoor barbecue lunches, demonstrations of sheep dogs at work, and sheep shearing, and—as an added bit of local color— boomerang throwing.

Stars and space

Students of the stars and deep space will be interested in two nearby attractions.

Mount Stromlo Observatory. Housed in the large silver domes on Mount Stromlo, off Cotter Road 16 km/10 miles west of Canberra, are the telescopes of Australian National University's Department of Astronomy. The visitor center at the 188-cm/74-inch telescope is open daily from 9:30 A.M. to 4 P.M.

Space tracking stations. Two space tracking stations are located about an hour's drive southwest of Canberra. Under the control of the United States' National Aeronautic and Space Administration (NASA), they're part of a worldwide chain of tracking stations.

Of the two, only Tidbinbilla (40 km/25 miles from Canberra) is open to the public. Here, you'll find a visitors' information center with model spacecraft, audio-visual presentations, and photos that tell the story of man's exploration of space. The information center is open daily from 9 to 5.

Nearby bushlands

Several bushland reserves near Canberra offer visitors an opportunity to enjoy some native flora and fauna.

Rehwinkel's Animal Park. Here, just 24 km/15 miles north of Canberra via the Federal Highway, you can meet kangaroos, koalas, and other native fauna in natural surroundings. It's open daily from 10 A.M. to 5 P.M.

Tidbinbilla Nature Reserve. A variety of Australian wildlife dwells in the natural surroundings of this reserve 40 km/25 miles southwest of Canberra, near the Tidbinbilla tracking station. Unspoiled hilly bushland offers a chance for scenic walks on winding trails as well as a number of secluded picnic spots.

In a special enclosure, you can see kangaroos, koalas, and emus close up. The reserve is open daily from 9 A.M. to 6 P.M., and the special enclosure is open daily between 11 and 4.

Cotter Reserve. Canberra's original reservoir (Cotter Dam), 23 km/14 miles west of the city, preserves some bushland, but also has been developed with picnic and campsites. There also is good river swimming nearby in the Cotter and Murrumbidgee rivers.

The Snowy Mountains— An all-year playground

Some of Australia's most rugged and dramatic scenery is found about 161 km/100 miles southwest of Canberra in the Snowy Mountains—the highest range on the continent. In this corner of New South Wales are deep fern gullies and lush hillside forests, snow-capped mountains and flower-dotted alpine meadows, and clear, bubbling streams and deep blue lakes.

Much of the area has been set aside as Kosciusko National Park, making it an ideal spot for both summer and winter vacationers. Besides an abundance of recreational possibilities, the area offers detailed looks at one of the world's most extensive engineering projects—the Snowy Mountains Hydro-Electric Scheme.

Kosciusko National Park. This 6,134 square km/2,368 square mile park is Australia's largest national reserve. Its towering mountain peaks, cascading streams, and majestic forests are enjoyed as a summer and winter playground.

Between June and September, skiers swish down the slopes of towering Mount Kosciusko—at 2,230 meters/7,316 feet the highest peak in Australia. Park resorts shuttle skiers to their favorite runs on chairlifts, T-bars, and Poma lifts. Cross-country skiing is also popular. Summer activities include hiking, fishing, trail riding, tennis, golf, and touring the nearby Snowy Mountains Hydro-Electric Scheme. The park's summer alpine wildflowers—including buttercups, everlasting, and heath—come into brilliant bloom around November.

The Yarrangobilly Caves, in the northern portion of the park about 97 km/60 miles from Cooma, will interest spelunkers. Four large limestone caves have been developed for visitors and contain a variety of stalactites, stalagmites, canopies, and flowstone.

Kosciusko resorts can be found in the southern part of the park at Thredbo Village, Perisher Valley, Smiggin Holes, Mount Kosciusko, Guthega, Digger's Creek, and Wilson's Valley. Resort accommodations include hotels, motels, lodges, and guest houses.

Snowy Mountains Hydro-Electric Scheme. The Snowy Mountains Authority has set up inspection tours for visitors to this vast engineering project that was begun in 1949 and completed in 1973. Sixteen dams have been built and ten power stations installed, some of them buried in the hills. More than 145 km/90 miles of tunnels have been hewn through the mountains, and 97 km/60 miles of aqueducts have been constructed. As a result, water from the abundant Snowy River has been diverted from the unproductive eastern slopes of the mountains into the Murray-Murrumbidgee river system on the west side, thus generating electricity and providing irrigation water for a large amount of productive farmland.

The project has created an additional bonus for sports enthusiasts—a group of lakes, of which the largest, Lake Eucumbene, contains nine times the volume of water in Sydney Harbour. Anglers will be glad to know that Eucumbene, Lake Jindabyne, and Tantangara Reservoir are stocked with trout all year. Other area sport activities include water-skiing, windsurfing, and boating. Accommodations can be found at Jindabyne, Adaminaby, Anglers Reach, Buckenderra, and Braemar.

Seeing the Snowy Mountains. Cooma is the gateway to this mountain country and the area's transportation center. By air, the town is a half-hour from Canberra, about an hour from Sydney or Melbourne. It is easily reached by rail, bus, or car. Situated 106 km/66 miles from Mount Kosciusko, Cooma is an excellent starting point for tours of the national park and the remarkable Snowy Mountains Hydro-Electric Scheme. The town's accommodations include motels, caravan parks, and campgrounds.

In addition to area tours originating in Cooma, several Melbourne and Sydney tour operators feature tours which include the Snowy Mountains; and there are tours from Canberra into the region. The Snowy Mountains Authority has also set up inspection tours of certain installations for visitors.

MELBOURNE

Victoria neatly packages a stately city, fine beaches, snowy peaks

In a country where distances are measured in the thousands as often as the hundreds, where Texas would be a middle-sized sort of state, Victoria is small. In fact, it is almost 10,000 square miles smaller than Oregon.

Size is no handicap, though, for this is one of those happily compact regions where a great city—Melbourne—is flanked on one side by warm ocean waters and on the other by beautiful mountains. The history of the place encompasses a greater gold rush than California's. On Victoria's innermost border is a river big enough to carry steamboats. The state has deserts, named, forthrightly, Big Desert and Little Desert. (It also has a region we cannot resist mentioning, Sunset Country.) Between river and deserts, it has wine valleys.

And for all of this, Victoria is purely Australian, full of tree ferns, eucalyptus forests, koalas, lyrebirds, and all the other exotics that come to mind.

Melbourne—A dignified capital

Instead of the frenetic tempo usually associated with a metropolis, Melbourne has a quiet dignity. There's a sense of culture, graciousness, beauty, and unhurried growth and prosperity. In spite of the city's position as Australia's financial hub, there still exists a sedate charm. Broad avenues are lined with beautiful deciduous trees, and intermingled with today's glass and steel are elegant Victorian-era buildings.

Don't let Melbourne's conservative appearance fool you. The city does hum.

Fine theater productions and concerts are staged the year around. In addition, Melbourne is a mecca for the fashion-minded because it is Australia's major fashion center. The boutiques and department stores reflect this.

Melbourne is also perhaps the most sports-minded city in Australia. Tens of thousands flock to Australian Rules football games, as well as horse races and cricket matches.

The activity-oriented spirit of Melbourne is perhaps best revealed during the annual Moomba Festival. Each March, as summer yields to autumn, the city kicks up its heels in the 10-day Moomba, a zesty celebration of the arts, sports, and sheer fun in living.

The Royal Botanic Gardens, one of the city's many parklands, is considered one of the best in Australia. Within a half-hour's drive south of downtown are a host of good beaches for water sports enthusiasts, and to the east the lush Dandenong Ranges offer hikers and picnickers a number of pleasant spots.

What Melbourne is, above all else, is big. The city and its suburbs spread far inland from Port Phillip Bay and the mouth of the Yarra River, as far as the lush Dandenong Ranges. A population of 2.8 million lives in 59 separately named communities within the 1,852 square km/715 square miles of Melbourne.

The heart of the city

Melbourne is a city for strolling.

In spite of extensive redevelopment, its compact center retains an old-world, 19th century character. Amid today's skyscrapers, many of its early Victorian-style buildings still stand, reminders of the city's history and tributes to gold rush boom times.

Even downtown, wide, tree-lined boulevards capture the essence of the city—spaciousness and greenery—before they plunge into a luxurious greenbelt of parklands rare by any standard for their generous proportions. Some of these parks are so close to offices that they are favorite lunchtime retreats for workers, offering instant respite from urban pressures.

The heart of the inner city, called the Golden Mile, contains the government and commercial hub of Melbourne, its chief shopping street, and the main hotels and theaters. The perimeters are the Yarra River on the south, Spencer Street on the west, LaTrobe Street on the north, and Spring Street on the east.

For a bird's-eye view of downtown Melbourne, go to the observation deck of the AMP Building at the corner of Bourke and Williams streets. Viewings, restricted to once daily Monday through Friday at 1:40 P.M., can be arranged through the security guard. The top of the Shrine of Remembrance (see page 57) on St. Kilda Road provides good views of the downtown skyline and parklands.

Broad, tree-lined boulevards like Collins Street typify Melbourne's famed Golden Mile. Electric trams make city-exploring enjoyable and inexpensive.

Landmarks. The greatest of Melbourne's public buildings are in or adjacent to the Golden Mile, all within walking distance of each other.

Victoria's legislature meets at State Parliament House, on Spring Street opposite the end of Bourke Street. Between 1901 and 1927 the Federal Parliament also met here. This neoclassic building with its Doric columns was begun in 1856; it's still considered unfinished today. A simple rectangle, it lacks the north and south wings and imposing dome included in the architect's original drawings. Weekdays there are guided tours of the building.

From the steps of State Parliament House, you have a clear view of the Princess Theatre on Spring Street. This elaborately decorated structure was built in 1887 for Queen Victoria's Jubilee, and still is being used for legitimate theater.

South on Spring Street, the Old Treasury Building borders on Treasury Gardens. Built between 1859 and 1862, it is considered an excellent example of Italian Renaissance. At one time its underground vaults held £100,000,000 in gold from the fields at Ballarat and farther north. (Today the building houses many state government offices.)

At the corner of Flinders and Swanston streets stands the Flinders Street Railway Station. Built in the 19th century, the French Renaissance building with its two clock towers and copper dome is one of the busiest railway stations in the world. Suburban commuters rush through it daily. Clocks telling departure times of suburban trains line the facade above the main entrance.

One of Melbourne's finest examples of 19th century Gothic Revival architecture is just a few blocks northeast

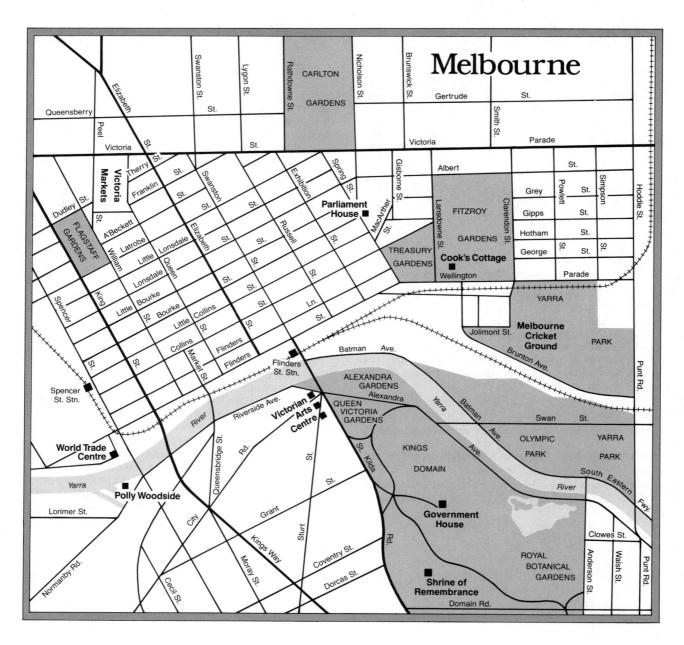

of the State Parliament House. The triple spires of St. Patrick's Roman Catholic Cathedral rise from a spot at the corner of Gisborne and Albert streets. Construction on the cathedral began in 1863. The west portal and spires were added in 1939.

You'll find another impressive cathedral across from the Flinders Street Railway Station. Designed by William Butterfield, the church is another good example of post-Gothic Revival architecture. It was the second Anglican cathedral—it replaced St. James Old Cathedral in 1891.

St. James Old Cathedral, once located on Little Collins Street, was moved to its present location at the corner of King and Batman streets in 1914. Completed in 1842, it served as Melbourne's Anglican cathedral for a half-century. This historic church retains its original box pews and furnishings, including a baptismal font donated by Queen Victoria.

Though LaTrobe's Cottage—the first Government House—may be beyond casual strolling range, it still belongs in a tour of landmark buildings as a reminder of the beginnings. It is located in King's Domain park.

LaTrobe's Cottage was shipped prefabricated from England in the late 1830s and erected on a site near what is now Melbourne Cricket Ground. The small, weatherboard building served as home for Lt. Gov. Charles LaTrobe during his term of office, 1839 to 1854. The cottage was moved to its present site and restored by the National Trust. Open daily from 10 A.M. to 4:30 P.M., the house still has many of its original furnishings.

Also in King's Domain is the Shrine of Remembrance, an impressive memorial to Victoria's war dead. It was designed so that a ray of sunlight falls on the Rock of Remembrance at the 11th hour of the 11th day of the 11th month, the exact moment of the armistice ending World War I.

For serious shoppers. Melbourne is Australia's major fashion center. Tree-shaded Collins and Bourke streets are noted for department stores and boutiques.

Two of the city's major department stores—David Jones and G.J. Coles—are located on Bourke Street. The huge Myer department store on the Bourke Street Mall (between Elizabeth and Swanston streets) is the largest department store in the Southern Hemisphere. The mall, a one-block section of Bourke Street, is closed to all vehicular traffic except trams.

At the top end of Collins Street, between Spring and Swanston streets, some of Melbourne's most exclusive (and expensive) fashionable boutiques specialize in imported designer clothes. Georges—an exclusive department store on Collins Street—has fine women's and men's wear and household goods. The nearby Figgins Diorama features 40 boutiques in a restored Victorian building.

A dozen arcades—filled with tiny shops offering a surprising array of merchandise—branch off from the city's main shopping streets. The oldest, Royal Arcade, dates from 1870. Other arcades include Block Arcade with entrances on Collins, Little Collins, and Elizabeth streets; and the Australian Arcade under the Hotel Australia.

Most of Melbourne's stores are open from 9 A.M. to 5 P.M. Monday through Thursday, 9 to 9 on Friday, and 9 to noon on Saturday.

(Continued on page 58)

The essentials

The capsule version below is what you need to know about getting to and around Melbourne, and enjoying your stay there.

Getting there. Melbourne is served by air, sea, rail, and bus.

Air. International service by Qantas and foreign carriers. Domestic flights by Ansett, Australian, East-West, and Kendell airlines. Tullamarine Airport is 23 km/14 miles from downtown by bus or taxi.

Sea. International cruise ships put in at Port Melbourne. A suburban train takes you from piers to city center.

Rail. Interstate trains provide regular service to and from other state capitals. Spencer Street Station adjoins downtown area.

Bus. Ansett Pioneer, Greyhound, Deluxe, and VIP journey between Melbourne and other state capitals.

Accommodations. Major hotels in the downtown area include the Melbourne Hilton International, Rockman's Regency Hotel, Noah's Hotel Melbourne, Regent of Melbourne, Menzies Rialto, Hyatt on Collins, Windsor Hotel, and Southern Cross. A short tram ride up St. Kilda Road are the Travelodge and Parkroyal. *Note:* You may find it hard to obtain reservations during Australian Rules finals (late September), Melbourne Cup Week (early November), and Moomba Festival (March).

Food and drink. Local specialties are led by the whiting, a white-fleshed saltwater fish, followed by other seafoods such as prawns, lobsters, and oysters. A wide range of ethnic cuisine is available. For an unusual dining experience with gourmet food plus a city tour, try the Colonial Tramcar Restaurant.

Local beers include Carlton Crown Lager, Crest Lager, Fosters, and Victoria Bitter. Wines of note come from Best's, Brown Bros., Bullers, Chateau Tahbilk, and Seppelt. To sample some of these wines, visit the Wine Industry House in the Banana Alley complex.

Getting around. Local transportation includes an extensive tram system, an underground train loop, and bus service. There's also an extensive suburban train system operating from Flinders Street Railway Station. Bargain (2-hour, daily, weekly) local and multi-neighborhood travel tickets are available. The City Explorer Bus does a circular tour of Melbourne, stopping at city attractions.

Tours. Several full or half-day tours of city available. Regional tours to Dandenongs (page 64), Phillip Island (page 73), Wilson's Promontory (page 67), Lorne and Great Ocean Road (page 68), and Ballarat and Sovereign Hill (page 60). Also available: spring wildflower tours into the Grampians (page 69), winter ski tours (page 69), and 1 and 2-day weekend excursions into Victoria on a restored, vintage steam train, *The Melbourne Limited*.

For more information. Victour, 230 Collins Street, Melbourne 3000.

...Continued from page 57

For an uncommon shopping experience, stroll through Queen Victoria Market, a few blocks north of the Golden Mile via Elizabeth Street. Tuesdays, Thursdays, Fridays, and Saturdays, the century-old market has everything—fruits, vegetables, fish, meat, clothing, and much more. On Sundays it becomes a craft market. Additional craft items are featured at the Meat Market Craft Centre in North Melbourne.

Beyond the city center, inner suburbs like South Yarra, Prahan, Camberwell, and Toorak have shops specializing in antiques. South Yarra's and Toorak's boutiques sell trendy fashions.

Victorian Arts Centre

This complex of three buildings, located on St. Kilda Road across from Queen Victoria Gardens, is the focal point for many of Melbourne's cultural events (see page 62). Included in the complex are the Melbourne Concert Hall, Theatres Building, and the National Gallery.

The circular-shaped, 2,600-seat Concert Hall lies closest to the Yarra River with a riverside promenade along one border. The hall's interior reflects the colors and textures of Australia: wool for carpeting and seat covers, leather for lining the foyers, and native woods for the stage, wings, and floors. Works by famous Australian artists decorate the entrance walls, and a gigantic light sculpture of brass and steel reflects light from spotlights scattered through all five floors of the complex. The Concert Hall building is also home to the Performing Arts Museum and its changing exhibits.

The Theatres Building, set between the Concert Hall and the National Gallery, is topped by a 115-metre/377-foot spire. Inside are three theaters—the 2,000-seat State Theatre, the 880-seat Playhouse, and the versatile 420-seat Studio.

Guided 1-hour tours of the Concert Hall and Theatres Building are offered daily between 10 A.M. and 5 P.M.

You approach the National Gallery by crossing a bridged moat. The front window is highly unusual: two sheets of glass with a water curtain flowing between them. More surprises await you inside the gallery. The soaring stained-glass ceiling is a breathtaking sight; designed by Leonard French, it took 6 years and 10,000 pieces of glass to complete.

Museums in Melbourne

The story of Melbourne and Victoria's past is told through exhibits in several Melbourne museums.

The Old Melbourne Gaol and Penal Museum, at the corner of Russell and LaTrobe streets, provides an excellent opportunity to discover what imprisonment was like in 19th century Melbourne.

It was here that the infamous bushranger, Ned Kelly, was hung in November 1880. (Kelly and a band of fellow highwaymen terrorized the countryside during gold rush days, ambushing gold escorts and robbing banks.) The hangman's scaffold and Kelly's bullet-dented armor are on display, gruesome reminders of rough and tumble times during Victoria's early days. The Old Gaol, now open to visitors daily from 10 A.M. to 5 P.M., has been carefully renovated.

The National Museum on Russell Street offers special insights into things uniquely Australian—Aboriginal weapons, domestic articles, and ceremonial objects, as well as mammals, birds, reptiles, and minerals. To most Australians the museum's prime exhibit is Phar Lap, the Australian chestnut gelding who—before meeting a taxidermist—won 37 races in the 1930s. The museum is open from 10 A.M. to 5 P.M. Monday through Saturday, and 2 to 5 P.M. on Sunday.

Museum of Chinese Australian History. Located in Chinatown, on Cohen Place, the exhibits trace the history of the Chinese in Australia from the gold rush of the 1850s onward. The museum is open weekdays (except Tuesdays) from 10 A.M. to 4:30 P.M., and weekends from noon to 4:30 P.M.

Melbourne Maritime Museum. The showpiece of this museum is the restored barque *Polly Woodside*, a square-rigged ship built in the 1880s. The museum is located at the corner of Normanby Road and Phayer Street in South Melbourne. Open weekdays from 10 A.M. to 4 P.M., and weekends from noon to 5 P.M.

A short trip away

Not all of Melbourne's great landmarks and points of interest nestle into the downtown. The suburbs contain a fine zoo, the University of Melbourne campus, and some extraordinary houses.

An elegant age. Como House, off Williams Road in South Yarra, reflects the elegant prosperity of the Victorian era in Melbourne. Overlooking the Yarra River, this stately mansion is one of Melbourne's oldest residences and one of the few remaining, unspoiled historic mansions. It was home for the Armytage family for nearly a century before it was sold to the National Trust in 1959. Much of the original furniture remains.

The gardens, laid out following suggestions of the famous botanist Baron von Mueller, were once the scene of annual cherry picking parties. If the trees didn't produce a sufficient crop, the boughs were hung with ripe cherries purchased for the event.

Two other historic homes worth a visit are Rippon Lea in Elsternwick and Werribee Park Estate in Werribee. Rippon Lea, a polychrome brick mansion built in the 1860s, is surrounded by beautifully landscaped gardens.

The expansive grounds of Werribee Park Estate include a golf course, picnic grounds, children's playground, zoological park, equestrian center, and large formal garden. The estate's 60-room Italianate mansion, built in the 1870s, features lavish furnishings.

Como House and Rippon Lea are open daily from 10 A.M. to 5 P.M. Werribee Park Estate is open Friday through Tuesday from 10 A.M. to 5 P.M.

Zoological Gardens. You'll find grounds beautifully landscaped with Australian flora as backdrops to koalas, kangaroos, wombats, echidnae, emus, and fairy penguins at the Zoological Gardens located in the corner of Royal Park near the University of Melbourne.

The emphasis at this zoo is to preserve a natural environment for the animals. At the Lion Park you can watch lions stalking the savanna below from the safety of an enclosed bridge. The orangutans and chimpanzees at the

(Continued on page 62)

Sky-piercing spire tops the Theatres Building at the Victorian Arts Centre, venue for Melbourne cultural events.

Gog and Magog preside over the Royal Shopping Arcade in Melbourne's Golden Mile. Ornate ironwork adorns the arcade's arched dome; glossy boutiques and gift stores fill the mall.

Australia's golden bonanza

The story of Australia's gold rush begins on the banks of California's Sacramento River in 1849. An Englishman, out to gain his fortune in the California gold fields, recognized the similarity of the Mother Lode terrain to a valley in the mountains behind Bathurst, New South Wales. Though 18 years had passed since Edward Hargreaves had seen that valley, he returned to Australia, struck out across the Blue Mountains, and immediately found gold beside Summer Hill Creek.

News of the discovery soon emptied Australia's cities. Melbourne, drained of its citizens, offered a £200 reward to the first person to find a gold field within 100 miles of town. In July 1851, gold was discovered at Clunes, and in August, at Ballarat—the richest alluvial gold field the world has ever known. Discoveries at Bendigo and Mount Alexander followed soon after.

The gold was easily won. So rich were the alluvial deposits that the output of Bendigo and Ballarat alone nearly equaled that of all the California fields. By the middle of 1852, adventurers from all over the world were pouring into Melbourne and fanning out across Victorian bush—"forty-niners" from California, New Englanders, Texans, Irish, English, Europeans, and Chinese—100,000 in one year alone. Port Phillip Bay became a forest of masts—at one time about 500 ships were anchored in Sandridge. Many of these were empty, deserted by their crews who set off to seek their fortunes in the fields. (Shanghaiing became a popular form of obtaining a new ship's crew.)

Almost overnight, towns sprang up in the bush, at first just canvas and clapboard cities, but soon replaced by ornate neoclassic stone structures that reflected the area's new-found wealth.

Australia's bushrangers (highwaymen) also joined the rush to the gold fields. But their method of obtaining riches was far different from that of the hard-working digger. Bands of bushrangers swept the countryside, ambushing gold escorts and robbing banks. Many of the country people admired these dapper individuals and their deeds soon were immortalized in Australian folk ballads.

Today you can easily reach this colorful, historic area of Victoria from Melbourne by daily coach or rail service. There are also full-day coach tours to Ballarat and Sovereign Hill as well as Bendigo.

Ballarat. Located in hilly country 113 km/70 miles west of Melbourne, Ballarat was a small farming community until Thomas Hiscock found gold near Buninyong cemetery in 1851. The area's alluvial gold fields turned out to be the richest in the world.

In 1854, Ballarat witnessed Australia's only civil war—the Eureka Stockade rebellion. At this time, the Crown technically owned all the land and claimed the gold mines as property of the government. However, the Crown didn't lay claim to the gold found on the land. Instead, they required diggers to have a license which cost 30 shillings per month. Many diggers—unlucky in their search for gold—couldn't afford this amount and didn't pay it. Soon the police were stopping everyone, demanding to be shown licenses. Harrassment and corruption became common. A group of 150 diggers, angered by oppressive government policies and the arrogance of the police, declared themselves independent. Though they were overwhelmingly defeated, the rebellion of the diggers resulted in sweeping reforms.

Ballarat retains much of its Victorian atmosphere, with 1860s stone buildings and churches bordering tree-lined avenues. Among interesting places to visit are the Eureka Stockade Memorial, site of the original stockade; Adam Lindsay Gordon's Cottage; the Botanic Gardens, containing the famous Begonia House (center of the annual March begonia festival); and "Ercildoone," a pioneer homestead built by the Learmonth brothers around 1859.

Of particular note is the Gold Museum located a short distance southeast of Ballarat across from Sovereign Hill Goldmining Township. Through a variety of well-done displays and graphics, the museum tells the story of gold and the part it has played in the history of mankind.

There are displays showing precoinage of valuable gold items from ancient civilizations. Gold coins from around the world, including coins from Australia, Great Britain, Europe, the Middle East, the Americas, India, and Africa, are presented—accompanied by graphics describing historical facts, and relating interesting anecdotes about the country's gold coins. Modern uses of gold in today's industries are also illustrated.

In a special section of the museum you can study a bas-relief map that shows the location of places where gold was discovered in the Ballarat area, plus the types of nuggets found at each site.

More than 20 hotels and motels, as well as guest houses, caravan parks, and campgrounds provide comfortable accommodations for visitors.

Sovereign Hill Goldmining Township. This historical park, a short distance southeast of Ballarat, evokes memories of the gold rush period. Set near land once mined by the diggers, the park re-creates the town of Ballarat during its first 10 years of development following the discovery of gold in the area in 1851.

Many aspects of mining life are exemplified, from the first gold diggings through the development of an established town. In Red Hill Gully Diggings you'll see windlasses, shafts, whims, and the tents in which early diggers lived. At the Gold Commissioner's tent, you can buy a "miner's right" to pan for gold in the nearby creek.

A fascinating array of buildings—re-created from drawings and photographs of the time—line the township's main street. Strolling its wooden sidewalks, you can stop in the confectionary shop for a "lolly," get your name printed on a "wanted" bulletin at the *Ballarat Times* office, or attend a production at the Victoria Theatre.

At the far end of town is a reconstructed quartz mine. Descending to its depths, you'll learn of mining techniques used between 1860 and 1918.

Eating establishments at Sovereign Hill include the New York Bakery and the United States Hotel. Sovereign Hill's Government Camp has family, bunk-bed accommodations and is also an associated youth hostel.

Bendigo. About 153 km/95 miles northwest of Melbourne, Bendigo ranked second to Ballarat in gold production. Its record year was 1856, when 661,749 ounces were taken from the fields. Today, Bendigo is a prosperous agricultural center, with the third largest sheep market in the country.

As in Ballarat, the wealth of the gold fields found its way into the construction of many ornate, neoclassic public and commercial buildings. Some of Australia's finest examples of Victorian architecture line the city's streets. A number of them have been classified by the National Trust as notable buildings. Included among noteworthy structures are the Town Hall, the Post Office, the Law Courts, several banks, a couple of churches, the old police barracks, the Shamrock Hotel, and the Temperance Hall. The Fortuna Villa is an outstanding example of a Victorian mansion.

One of the town's main attractions is the Central Deborah Gold Mine, which has been restored to working condition with a boiler, compressor, poppet legs, winding equipment, and blacksmith's shop. The Central Deborah Gold Mine was the last deep reef mine to close on the Bendigo gold fields. When it closed, the mine's main shaft extended through 17 levels and was 396 meters/1,299 feet long. There are guided tours of the mine daily between 10 A.M. and 5 P.M.

A good way to take a brief tour of the town is on the "Talking Tram" from the Central Deborah Gold Mine. The trip takes you on an 8-km/5-mile ride through town, to the Tramways Museum, and out to the Chinese Joss House at Emu Point before it returns to its starting point. The running dialogue covers many of Bendigo's historical sights.

Other town highlights include the Bendigo Art Gallery where you can enjoy a fine collection of Australian and French impressionist paintings. The new Bendigo Steam and Oil Engines Museum (open the last Sunday of each month) has a number of working models.

On the outskirts of town is an interesting pottery factory —one of Australia's oldest, established in 1857. Here you can buy famous Epsom stoneware that has been salt-glazed in vintage kilns heated by wood and coal.

If you decide to stay in the area, you can choose from 25 hotels and motels, several caravan parks, and campgrounds.

Castlemaine. This small gold mining town is located south of Bendigo.

During gold rush days, Castlemaine played an important role as the gold fields market center for the gardens and or-

chards in the area. The Castlemaine Market, built in 1862, stands as a reminder of this era. Renovated in 1974, the building now houses a museum of old photos of gold rush days. These photos feature the gold fields and show what living conditions were like for the diggers. They are the work of Antoine Foucherie, a French photographer who visited Castlemaine in 1857–58. Also included in the market/museum are early maps and plans of the area and other gold mining memorabilia.

At Pennyweight Flat, on the outskirts of town, tombstones tell of the harshness of life on the gold fields. Many diggers and members of their families went to early graves, the victims of numerous diseases that ravaged the crowded gold camps.

You'll find hotels, motels, and caravan parks in the area.

Maldon. Still another historic town lies south of Bendigo not far from Castlemaine. Located on the slopes of Mount Tarrangower, Maldon is a well-preserved town of the gold mining era. It is the only town entirely protected by the National Trust of Victoria. Maldon's main street is lined with an interesting assortment of shops with wide front verandas. Included among noteworthy buildings are the Holy Trinity Church, the Court House and Police Lock-up, and the Maldon Hospital. The Folk Museum, housed in the old Council Offices, contains a wealth of interesting gold rush items.

Just outside of town, you can see evidence of gold mining days—grass-covered mounds, the tailings of early diggings. You can also tour Carmen's Tunnel, a 468-meter/1,535-foot tube carved out of solid bluestone, and view the Beehive Mine Company chimney.

The area around Maldon is known for unusual rock formations with such descriptive names as The Sphinx, The Judge, and Witch's Head. In spring, the hills are ablaze with wildflowers.

Area accommodations include hotels, motels, and caravan parks.

Beechworth. This old mining town—about 241 km/150 miles northeast of Melbourne (via the Hume Highway to Wangaratta)—had a role in the saga of Australia's notorious bushranger, Ned Kelly. This is "Kelly Country." Ned and his gang roamed the hills around the town and Kelly was imprisoned in Beechworth's jail in 1881.

Established in 1852, Beechworth has an excellent collection of well-preserved historic buildings including the historic jail and several stone churches. The powder magazine, built in 1859, tells of the time when large amounts of blasting powder were necessary for nearby gold mining operations. The town's museum contains an interesting collection of pioneer relics.

Just outside of town are abandoned gold mines. If you like, you can do a little gold panning in nearby streams. There's also a trout farm where you can sink a line to catch your dinner.

Area accommodations include hotels, motels, and caravan parks.

Wild ducks and black swans *gather for a handout at Royal Botanic Gardens, one of Melbourne's popular parks.*

...*Continued from page 58*

Ape Complex swing and play in freedom in open-air, moated enclosures.

The zoo, open daily from 9 A.M. to 5 P.M., has both a souvenir shop and snack bar.

University of Melbourne. Founded in 1854, this was Australia's second university—but the first to admit women. It's located in Parkville, about 3 km/2 miles from the city. The avenue of palms leading to the main entrance was planted with seedlings brought back from the Middle East by Australian soldiers after World War I. As you stroll around the campus, you'll discover the Percy Grainger Museum, displaying the personal effects of the noted composer-pianist, and some striking murals by Douglas Annand.

The lively arts

Melbourne's entertainment scene is highly varied, ranging from concerts and opera to night clubs and discotheques.

Primary venue for many cultural events is the Victorian Arts Centre (see page 58). The Melbourne Theatre Company stages a variety of plays in the Playhouse, and the Playbox Theatre performs in the adjacent Studio. The State Theatre, also in the Theatres Building, is home to the Australian Ballet, Australian Opera, and Victorian State Opera. Performances are staged throughout the year.

Between April and October, the Melbourne Symphony Orchestra performs in the Melbourne Concert Hall.

The peak month for theater and almost every other kind of performance is March, during the great festival called Moomba (pronounced Moo-mba). Along with theater and music for every taste, the festival includes an open-air art show in Treasury Gardens, an international book fair, water-ski competitions and sailing regattas on the Yarra, horse shows and horse races, a Queen of the Pacific contest, parades, carnival rides, and, as the grand finale, a fireworks spectacular.

If you're visiting Melbourne between November and April, take advantage of free outdoor concerts—symphony, pop groups, ballet—at the Sidney Myer Music Bowl. The bowl, in the King's Domain on St. Kilda Road, has a tentlike roof of aluminum and steel housing the sound shell and stage. During the winter, the music bowl's stage area becomes an ice-skating rink.

Other free entertainment is also held throughout the city in gardens and squares between November and April. There are free Sunday concerts the year around in the National Gallery's Great Hall on St. Kilda Road and in the Melbourne Town Hall on Swanston Street.

A swinging night life hasn't been part of the Melbourne scene since the boom days of the Australian gold rush, when Lola Montez entertained the diggers. Today, though, you'll find night clubs as well as theater restaurants and a growing number of discotheques. Rock and jazz music livens the scene at some pubs and wine bars in the city and its suburbs.

For more information on Melbourne's lively arts, pick up a copy of *This Week in Melbourne* from the Victour office.

Sports to watch

If you want to watch Melbournians cast aside their Victorian reserve, any major sports event will do, but football and horse racing are the surest bets.

The phenomenon known as Australian Rules football is at its best in Melbourne. The 12 professional teams in the Victorian Football League represent district clubs throughout the Melbourne area, and some of the rivalries are fierce. Six matches are held each Saturday during the April to September season. The finals pit the two top teams at the Melbourne Cricket Ground before Super Bowl-sized crowds of 100,000. (See page 12 for more on the game of Australian Rules football.)

Just as fervently followed is horse racing, held the year around both midweek and Saturdays at Flemington, Caulfield, Moonee Valley, and Sandown race tracks.

Flemington is the home of the Melbourne Cup, an internationally famous racing event held on the first Tuesday in November. On this special day the entire nation comes to a halt to hear the race on radio, or see it on television. Meanwhile, all Melbourne is at the track, when huge amounts of champagne and betting money flow. On this occasion, gentlemen wear gray top hats and dark morning suits, and ladies splash color through the stands with wacky, wonderful hats. The Melbourne Cup is part of the Spring Racing Carnival which includes a line-up of important horse races.

Harness racing meets are held the year around at the Moonee Valley Racecourse.

Greyhounds race at Olympic Park on Batman Avenue in East Melbourne, and at Sandown Park in Springvale.

Soccer adds to the excitement of the summer sports season. The highest level is found at Ampol Cup contests on January and February nights.

December through February is the season for international test cricket matches, played at the Melbourne Cricket Ground.

Fun in the sun

For those who'd rather play than watch, Melbourne provides plenty of opportunities.

The city beaches. During the summer months, Port Phillip Bay comes alive with summer sports activities. Sunbathers and swimmers will enjoy beaches around the bay. St. Kilda, Elwood, Brighton, and Sandringham are some of the best, and they are all within a half-hour of downtown by car or train. You'll find good boating and sailing at Sandringham, Black Rock, Mordialloc, and Frankston, as well as near town at Albert Park Lake. Water-skiing is also popular on the bay.

For more information on sailing, contact the Royal Melbourne Yacht Squadron on the Lower Esplanade in St. Kilda. Water-skiers can get additional information from the Victoria Water-Ski Association in Elwood. Boats and water-skis are available for rent around the bay at beach resorts.

Closer to town is the Yarra River, a good place for paddling a hired canoe or dinghy. There are also boats for hire at Albert Park Lake. The less ambitious might want to take a riverboat cruise on the Yarra, departing from Princes Walk near Princes Bridge.

There's good deep-sea fishing at Westernport Bay and Lakes Entrance. The major catch is the bluefin tuna. Freshwater anglers should contact the Victour office on Collins Street for more information on inland lake fishing.

Tennis. Players will find both grass and hard courts in Melbourne. The Secretary of the Lawn Tennis Association (50 Commercial Road, South Yarra) has information on private clubs offering guest privileges. Public tennis courts for hire are listed in the phone book's Yellow Pages. Melbourne hosts the Australian Open Tennis Championship each year in January.

Golf. There are about 3 dozen public courses in the Melbourne area. Private clubs will usually grant guest privileges if you can arrange for an introduction by a member or if arrangements are made through your home club. Royal Melbourne Golf Club heads the list of private clubs. It's considered one of the best courses in Australia and is well-known for its sand traps. Melbourne hosts the Australian Open Golf Championship each year in November.

Jogging and cycling. A 4-km/2-mile jogging trail runs along Alexandra Avenue near the Royal Botanic Gardens and King's Domain. Bikes are available for rent near Princes Bridge and opposite the Royal Botanic Gardens on the south side of the Yarra.

Parks and gardens

Melbourne enjoys a wealth of beautiful parklands beginning literally at the heart of the city and fanning out through the farthest suburbs.

King's Domain, capstone of the system, is just across the Yarra River from Flinders Street Railway Station via the Princes Bridge.

The park rises gently from the banks of the Yarra alongside St. Kilda Road. It merges with the Royal Botanic, Alexandra, and Queen Victoria gardens to form a huge parkland of more than 214 hectares/530 acres of beautiful gardens, expansive lawns, and recreation grounds.

The Royal Botanic Gardens, south of King's Domain, is one of Melbourne's oldest and most beautiful parks. The site was selected in 1845.

(Continued on page 64)

...Continued from page 63

Stroll through its glades of majestic, venerable trees—some planted by such famous personalities as Prince Albert, Dame Nellie Melba, Alfred Lord Tennyson, and the Duke of Edinburgh. A plaque on a gum tree proclaims the spot where Melbournians celebrated their "separation" from New South Wales in 1851.

The beautiful landscaped gardens include manicured lawns, colorful flower beds, and three lakes where wild ducks and black swans congregate. The park's plantings include Norfolk pines, Japanese cedars, magnolia and oak trees, ferns, camellias, rhododendrons, azaleas, and cacti and succulents. In the southwest corner, the Tropical Plants Glasshouse contains exotic plants.

Alexandra Gardens, a section of the park directly next to the Yarra, is a popular lunchtime retreat for downtown office workers. Next to it, Queen Victoria Gardens has a 10,000-plant floral clock as its focal point.

Still more gardens await exploration. At the east end of Collins Street are Fitzroy Gardens and the adjacent Treasury Gardens. Magnificent elms shade these plots laid out in the late 1850s. Broad open lawns provide places for pleasant picnic lunches. There are also several pond areas trimmed in lush flowering bushes and flanked by an occasional bench for quiet contemplation.

Here, amid lawns and flowers, you can see whimsical Fairy Tree—carved by the late Australian sculptress, Ola Cohn—and a miniature Tudor village that delights children of all ages. Nearby, a conservatory displaying seasonal flowers is open daily from 10 A.M. to 4:45 P.M.

In the Fitzroy Gardens, surrounded by lawns and covered with ivy brought from England, is one of Melbourne's historic monuments—Captain Cook's Cottage. It was brought to Melbourne from England in 1934 to commemorate Melbourne's first centennial the following year. The cottage was probably built by Cook's father around 1755. Though it can't be verified that James Cook ever lived in the house, it's assumed he must have returned often to visit his father. Be sure to explore the tiny 18th century cottage garden with herbs such as rosemary and thyme, old-fashioned rose bushes, red and black currant bushes, and a hawthorn hedge.

Carlton Gardens, a 24-hectare/60-acre park of lawns and flowers, also contains Exhibition Building. Topped by an exotic dome and minarets, it was constructed for the International Exhibition of 1880, and still is used for trade shows. Another Melbourne park of great charm is Flagstaff Gardens on King Street opposite St. James Old Cathedral.

Nearby mountain retreats

The mountains just east and north of Melbourne provide a pleasant respite from the city's bustle. There are fern-filled forests, a wildlife sanctuary, resort towns, and an antique steam train ride.

Dandenong delights

In less than an hour, you can leave downtown Melbourne behind and travel to the deep fern gullies and forested hills of the Dandenong Ranges. These gray green hills provide a pleasant topographical backdrop to the city's northern and eastern suburbs as well as a nearby, quiet retreat for city dwellers.

Many Melbournians have built homes in the seclusion of the wooded hills, their own touches of trees and shrubs adding color to the natural landscape. Nearly every season has something special to offer—camellias in spring, tulips and rhododendrons in summer, and red and gold leaves in autumn.

Throughout the Dandenongs are a number of pleasant walks, drives, and picnic spots. Good roads wind through the area, making it a fine day's outing from Melbourne. Suburban electric trains as well as coach tours also journey into the Dandenongs. The following are a few places you'll want to see during your Dandenong excursion.

Ferntree Gully National Park. Heading into the Dandenongs on the Burwood Highway (Route 26), you stop first at Ferntree Gully National Park, located 34 km/21 miles east of Melbourne. This park has magnificent tree ferns and tall gum trees, and you'll stroll through cool, fragrant valleys where ferns grow over the pathway creating a delicate green tunnel. Wildlife in the area includes swamp wallabies, platypuses, echidnae, lyrebirds, and whipbirds.

Puffing Billy. Children and adults alike will enjoy a ride on this famous old narrow-gauge steam train that chugs through wooded hills, fern gullies, and flower farms between Belgrave and Emerald. Some trips continue on to Lakeside. You can hop aboard at Belgrave just a short distance from Ferntree Gully National Park. The trip generally operates weekends, public holidays, and special school holidays. Menzies Creek—one of the stops on the line—has an interesting Steam Museum featuring locomotives and early narrow-gauge rolling stock.

Sherbrooke Forest. Just 8 km/5 miles north from Belgrave on Monbulk Road, you'll come to one of the gems of the Dandenongs—Sherbrooke Forest. A favorite with bush ramblers, it's also one of the best places in Australia to observe lyrebirds. You'll hear their mimic calls and perhaps see them on forest trails. The male on occasion displays his beautiful tail in a courtship ritual. Road signs remind you to watch: "Drive Carefully—Lyrebirds Cross Here."

William Ricketts Sanctuary. Still farther north you'll discover a world of eerie beauty at the William Ricketts Sanctuary. As you walk along trails between giant ferns, the sculpted clay forms of Aborigines—carved by Ricketts—seem almost alive in the filtered green light of the rain forest. The sculptor has spent most of his life depicting the faces and legends of Australian Aborigines.

Mount Dandenong. Nearby Mount Dandenong is the highest point in the ranges—633 meters/2,077 feet. From the lookout, you can see Port Phillip Bay and Melbourne across patches of farmland and forested slopes. At the summit a restaurant takes full advantage of the view.

Beyond the Dandenongs

The foothills of the Great Dividing Range—just north of the Dandenongs and a few hours from Melbourne—have both charming towns and one of Australia's most attractive wildlife sanctuaries.

Sir Colin MacKenzie Wildlife Sanctuary. This fascinating natural refuge is near Healesville, 63 km/39 miles northeast of Melbourne. Here koalas, kangaroos, wombats, and a variety of birds live in conditions closely resembling their native habitat.

Also known as the Healesville Sanctuary, this wildlife park began as a research station and is home to the first platypus bred in captivity. The sanctuary houses some of these elusive duck-billed creatures in a glass tank where you'll see them swimming about.

Half-day coach tours travel from Melbourne to the sanctuary, which is open daily from 9 A.M. to 5 P.M.

Mountain resorts. Mountain air, unspoiled bushland, lakes, streams, and plentiful wildlife lure vacationers to resort towns like Healesville, Marysville, and Warburton. Activities in these mountain towns include trail riding, fishing, golf, and tennis. Bushwalkers enjoy short tracks leading through forests to waterfalls. Nearby Mount Donna Buang is Melbourne's closest snowfield for winter skiing.

Kinglake National Park. Waterfalls and magnificent mountain ash trees are highlights of this park on the southern slopes of the Great Dividing Range. It's located 20 km/12 miles northwest of Healesville and 64 km/40 miles north of Melbourne. From the summit of Bald Hill within the park, visitors have wonderful views across the forest and fern gullies toward Melbourne and Port Phillip Bay. Kangaroos, wallabies, lyrebirds, and many other species of birds unique to Australia make their home in the park.

Natural bridges carved by wave action
are part of a scenic stretch of coastline
preserved in Port Campbell National Park
along Great Ocean Road.

It's wool harvesting time at a Victoria
sheep station. Guests can watch or shear;
secret is to keep sheep relaxed.

By the beautiful sea

Somewhere close to Melbourne is the kind of salt-water shoreline you want. Within a few hours of the city are two great, sheltered bays, miles of straight-edged sand facing open ocean, and a whole series of gloriously rugged headlands, and you can have any one of the lot populated either thickly or hardly at all.

Port Phillip Bay stretches away from Melbourne, a broad, open expanse of water 61 km/38 miles long, and just as wide. Westernport Bay, its neighbor to the east, is the opposite—a narrow circle of water between the mainland and, in its center, French Island.

The greatest and most rugged of the headlands, Wilson's Promontory, has been preserved as a national park. The sea has pounded against the shore here for centuries, whittling the rocks into curious shapes. Just upcoast is the sparsely populated Gippsland Lakes region; its one beach stretches for 144 km/90 miles. Popular pastimes are boating, fishing, strolling, and hiking.

The surfing and sunning beaches run westward from the mouth of Port Phillip Bay, facing Tasmania across Bass Strait. Still farther to the west are the warm-water beaches collectively known as the Australian Riviera.

Mornington Peninsula

The beaches of Mornington Peninsula—a boot-shaped promontory separating Port Phillip Bay from Westernport Bay—are a playground for residents of Melbourne and its suburbs.

Easily reached by electric train and shoreline highway, these beaches offer a diverse assortment of water sports opportunities. The calmer waters of bayside resorts bordering protected Port Phillip Bay provide good opportunities for swimming, water-skiing, sailing, and surf sailing (wind surfing).

On the opposite side of the peninsula, ocean "back" beaches facing Bass Strait—Portsea Surf Beach, Sorrento Ocean Beach, Rye Ocean Beach, and Gunnamatta Surf Beach—offer fantastic surfing possibilities.

Resort areas like Flinders and Shoreham on Westernport Bay feature surfing as well as fishing and scuba diving. Water sports equipment including boats for hire for sailing and fishing are available at many of the resorts.

Collins Bay, at Sorrento, is a good spot for picnicking and shell collecting, and rock hounds can hunt for gemstones in outcroppings along the beach near Shoreham on Westernport Bay. You'll find golf and tennis are readily available.

Points of interest. At Arthur's Seat, near Dromana, a chairlift transports sightseers to the summit for panoramic views of both bays, Phillip Island, and the orchards and small farms of the peninsula itself.

The fashionable resort of Sorrento, near the peninsula's tip, is the site of a part in Victoria's history. In October 1803, Lt. Col. David Collins landed here and attempted to establish a colony—the first in Victoria. However, the colony's success was short-lived, and it was abandoned in 1804. The area became popular in the late 1800s when a resort was built, and paddle steamers were employed to transport vacationing Melbourne residents to Sorrento. Today, you can zoom across Port Phillip Bay on a wave-piercing catamaran, the *Spirit of Victoria*, which stops at bayside towns, including Sorrento. It leaves from Melbourne's Station Pier, Friday through Sunday.

Accommodations. The Mornington Peninsula has a variety of accommodations from hotels to caravan parks.

Wilson's Promontory National Park

Jutting into Bass Strait—223 km/139 miles southeast of Melbourne—this mountainous and windswept peninsula is one of Victoria's most popular national parks.

"The Prom," as it is affectionately known, possesses a grand beauty. Heavily wooded mountains descend to the edge of white sand beaches and massive granite headlands. Deep gullies shelter pockets of luxuriant rain forest, and open heaths come alive with colorful wildflowers in spring and summer. Wildlife, including wombats and wallabies, roam the forests and heathlands. You may be fortunate enough to spy one or two.

Holiday lodges and caravan and camping areas at Tidal River Camp provide accommodations for leisurely enjoyment of this wildly beautiful place. Out of Melbourne, there are 1-day excursions into the area by coach.

Gippsland Lakes region

Good highways lead from Melbourne to Gippsland, a popular resort district in southeastern Victoria. It's known for rich farmlands, coal and oil fields, forests, rivers, an extensive stretch of beach, and large navigable lakes.

Ninety Mile Beach. East of Wilson's Promontory is an unbroken stretch of beach extending northeast in an almost straight line for nearly 145 km/90 miles. Named for its length, Ninety Mile Beach is relatively undeveloped, making it ideal for surfing, surf fishing, and undisturbed beach walking. Fishers try for salmon, trout, snappers, greybacks, tiger flatheads, and flounder. Good spots to explore this area from include Bairnsdale, Lakes Entrance, Paynesville, and Metung.

The lakes. Inland from Ninety Mile Beach, the Gippsland Lakes run parallel to the shoreline for more than 80 km/50 miles. In some places these waterways are separated from the ocean by only a narrow ribbon of land.

Because the lakes are connected, they are ideal for long leisurely days of cruising. You can take organized launch trips from Paynesville or Metung or rent your own boat to sail. Nearly every type of craft is available for hire, including well-equipped four and six-berth cruisers. You can book craft through the Victour office on Collins Street in Melbourne.

Swimming and fishing are excellent. In the tidal waters you'll find bream, perch, mullet, and skipjack; lakes and streams abound with blackfish, perch, and bream. From many of the lakes you can hike over extensive dunes to Ninety Mile Beach.

Lakes National Park on Spermwhale Head is ideal for picnics. Flowering wattles, tea trees, and ground orchids add patches of brilliant color to the park in winter and spring.

Getting to the lakes. The Gippsland Lakes region is easily accessible from Melbourne by car, or you can take a train as far as Bairnsdale and then a bus. There are also coach and rail tours from Melbourne. Some coach tours traveling between Melbourne and Sydney include the lakes area in their itineraries.

Accommodations. Lakes area resort towns have a variety of modest accommodations in small hotels, motels, guest houses, holiday flats, and caravan and camping parks.

Southwest Riviera

Route 1—the Princes Highway—and fast rail service connect Melbourne with Geelong, 72 km/45 miles southwest of Melbourne. From Geelong—Victoria's largest provincial city—you can reach sheltered beaches on the nearby Bellarine Peninsula or head southwest along the Great Ocean Road to the popular ocean beaches of the Southwest Riviera.

Though basically a regional commercial center—wool-selling headquarters and busy port—Geelong itself is an attractive city with extensive parklands. Geelong has a large number of hotels, motels, and caravan and camping grounds.

Bellarine Peninsula. There are several pleasant holiday resorts along the shores of this peninsula not far from Geelong. The area offers sheltered swimming beaches, boating facilities, and good fishing grounds, as well as opportunities to play tennis and golf. Surfing is best on the southern beaches below Point Lonsdale.

You'll find comfortable accommodations in hotels, guest houses, and motels in the Portarlington area (inside Port Phillip Bay), Queenscliff-Point Lonsdale (on the headland at the entrance to the bay), and in Ocean Grove and Barwon Heads (both on the ocean side of the peninsula). Campers will find well-equipped parks in most local peninsula towns.

The Great Ocean Road. One of Victoria's most scenic routes is along the Great Ocean Road, which follows the coast southwest of Melbourne for nearly 322 km/200 miles. The highway begins just south of Geelong at Torquay and winds south and west to Warrnambool. It skirts sheer cliffs, parallels golden sand beaches, and traverses the forested slopes of the Otway Ranges.

Along the way, at seaside towns like Torquay, Anglesea, Airey's Inlet, Lorne, and Wye River, visitors will find swimming, surfing, boating, fishing, tennis, and golf. At Anglesea's golf course, you'll have to share the green with grazing kangaroos.

The Otway Ranges meet the ocean at Lorne. You can bushwalk through groves of giant eucalyptus and fern-filled valleys, surfcast, or laze away the days on a wide, golden strand of beach.

Beyond Apollo Bay, the road turns inland, crossing the Otway Ranges, and then returns to the ocean west of Port Campbell. Here, brown, yellow, and orange cliffs have eroded into a series of natural bridges and rock stacks. Particularly interesting are the rock formations named the Twelve Apostles: a dozen rock stacks of varying sizes. Port Campbell National Park comprises a 30-km/19-mile stretch of this spectacularly beautiful coastline. Offshore islands in the area support many birds. Mutton Bird Is-

land, just offshore near the mouth of the Sherbrooke River, is the nesting ground for a large number of mutton birds. At sunset, you'll see the adults returning to their young with food.

At the resort town of Warrnambool in the center of rich dairy farming country, you can rejoin Princes Highway and return to Melbourne along the inland route. Or you can continue along the coast to the old whaling town of Port Fairy and then on to Portland, another whaling town with numerous historic sites.

Resort towns all along the Great Ocean Road offer visitors a choice of accommodations—hotels, motels, and caravan and camping parks.

Victoria's rugged west

West and northwest of Melbourne the countryside varies from rolling farm and grazing lands to rugged hills and forested mountains. You can sample vast sheep stations, wild Australian bushland, and gold rush boom towns. (To learn more about Ballarat and other gold rush towns see page 60.)

Visiting a sheep station

It is said that much of Australia's wealth has been shorn from the backs of sheep. Traveling west from Melbourne, you'll pass through Victoria's rich grazing land—rolling, pastoral fields edged with stands of pines and gum trees. A number of working sheep properties welcome visitors. Here, discover what it's like to live on a station today, as well as learn what it was like to be a pioneer settler homesteading this area in the mid-1800s.

Naringal. At this historic working station near Cape Clear (161 km/100 miles west of Melbourne), you can watch the Australian pastoralist at work and, if you like, participate in the duties of the station yourself. As a guest you'll be able to watch sheep mustering and shearing and learn how wool is graded. Naringal, established before 1845, is still owned by descendants of the founding family. You can also visit the family's original slab timber hut and see the private cemetery. Both are reminders of the hardships endured by Victoria's pioneer settlers.

At Naringal, you can enjoy gracious living in the family's beautiful homestead or stay in a self-contained cottage or in dormitory-style accommodations. It's an easy drive from Melbourne via Ballarat.

Glenisla Homestead. Founded more than 140 years ago, this property (305 km/190 miles west of Melbourne) also ranks among Victoria's oldest.

The historic homestead complex was built in 1873 by a great-grandfather of the current owners. Constructed of local sandstone, the site is listed with the Australian National Trust. Guest accommodations are in the main house and adjacent courtyard buildings.

In addition to sheep station activities, there are guided tours from Glenisla to the Grampian Mountains to see the diversity of plant and animal life (see page 69). Glenisla can be reached by car, bus, and plane.

Other stations. Farm stays are available at other stations throughout Victoria. Accommodations and activities vary. In some cases, guests may have to bring food and linens. For information on farm stays, contact the Victour office.

Victoria's Farm Shed. This indoor farm animal display center, on the Princes Highway an hour's drive east of Melbourne, provides a quick look at Australia's livestock and farm activities. There are twice-daily shows featuring livestock identification, sheep shearing, cow milking, and sheep dogs working. It's open daily from 9 A.M. to 5 P.M.

The Grampians

The stark, sandstone ridges of the western edge of the Great Dividing Range rise from the surrounding plains some 266 km/165 miles west of Melbourne. Over the centuries, wind and water have eroded the Grampians' red bulk into weird and unusual shapes with descriptive names like The Lady's Hat, Mushroom Rock, and The Fallen Giant.

For thousands of years, Aborigines occupied the Grampians. Many sacred ceremonies and initiation rites were performed here. The stories of these early residents are told in the interesting rock paintings of Grampian mountain caves.

Bushwalkers traversing the area on short or long hikes can enjoy cascading waterfalls, awesome lookout points, and plentiful wildlife such as kangaroos, emus, echidnae, koalas, and platypuses. The towering cliffs and craggy rock faces offer some stiff challenges to rock climbers. Anglers can work well-stocked lakes.

During the spring and early summer months (August to December) the Grampians are colorfully carpeted with wildflowers—wild fuchsias, ground orchids, wattle, and flowering peas. There are nearly 1,000 native plant species.

During wildflower season, all-day tours from Melbourne give visitors a good opportunity to enjoy the region's wildflowers, scenery, and wildlife. If you want to linger awhile longer, you'll find comfortable accommodations in Hall's Gap in the heart of the Grampians and in Ararat, Horsham, and Stawell.

Ski country

Melbourne residents enjoy the ski areas of the Snowy Mountains (see page 53), but Victoria also has its own ski country in the Southern Alps, stretching south and west from the Snowy Mountains. Here the terrain is gentle, with long, hazard-free runs—ideal for ski touring. The best skiing comes during the latter part of the season (late August and September) when the snow has been compacted. Skiers will find that powder snow is virtually unknown in the area.

Occasional years of light snowfall make some of Victoria's resorts chancy—but you can generally count on good snow conditions from mid-June to mid-September at Mount Buller, Mount Buffalo, Mount Hotham, and Falls Creek.

Winter isn't the only season to enjoy Victoria's mountain playgrounds. Most of the area's resorts operate the year around. In spring, the mountains are a patchwork of alpine flowers. Summer activities include camping, trout fishing, horseback riding, bushwalking, and mountain climbing.

From Melbourne you can reach the area by car or by flying to Albury and going the rest of the way by coach.

Mount Buller

Victoria's busiest ski resort is Mount Buller (1,800-meter/5,907-foot elevation), only 241 km/150 miles by road from Melbourne. Ski runs descend three sides of the mountain peak. Providing transportation to the top are ten Poma lifts, seven T-bars, and three chairlifts.

Accommodations include a chalet, a motel, a pension, and a lodge.

Mount Hotham

The most reliable snowfall in the entire region occurs at Mount Hotham (1,862-meter/6,109-foot elevation). But this is also the most difficult of the four resorts to reach because of road and weather conditions. Distance from Melbourne is 373 km/232 miles. Mount Hotham is close enough to the Mount Buffalo ski area (both are off the same road) that you can stay at one resort and enjoy skiing at both.

Used primarily by intermediate and experienced skiers, the area has four Poma lifts, a chairlift, and two T-bars. Hotham Heights, on the slopes of the mountain, has two lodges, one chalet, and a few apartments.

Mount Buffalo

With an elevation of 1,723 meters/5,654 feet, Mount Buffalo presents snow conditions less predictable than those at the other three major resorts. For skiers there are three Poma lifts and a chairlift.

The area is not only a winter vacation spot, though. Mount Buffalo National Park, 322 km/200 miles from Melbourne, is a year-round resort with good opportunities for swimming, boating, fishing, horseback riding, and bushwalking. The massive rock face of Mount Buffalo is popular with mountain climbers.

The area has two hotels and several smaller commercial chalets.

Falls Creek

The ski village at Falls Creek nestles in a natural bowl deep in the heart of the Bogong High Plains, 380 km/236 miles from Melbourne. The bowl not only forms a natural trap for sunshine (promoting spring skiing) but also provides excellent beginners' slopes. The resort's international-standard runs are the site of an annual international race, the Ross Milne Memorial Slalom, held in July or August.

The area offers skiers a chairlift, six Poma lifts, and four T-bars in a carefully integrated system that can lift 5,500 skiers per hour. Accommodations are available in about a dozen lodges.

Mother Nature shows off in full flower

Artists glorify it in their paintings, writers dramatize it in their prose, and Australian suburbanites escape to it on their vacations. "It" is the Australian bush, less than a day's drive from most of Australia's major metropolitan areas.

The term "bush" applies to rain forests, tropical jungle, rolling hills covered with scrub, forests of gums or conifers, and even grasslands. Much of this bush boasts a profusion of colorful blossoms and pervading fragrance. Sailors say they can smell the sharp, medicinal scent of gum trees (eucalyptus) far out to sea.

Gum trees. Perhaps the most prolific of Australia's native plants is the eucalyptus—commonly called gum tree. It's as Australian as the kangaroo. More than 700 different species have been identified, and many have colorful pungent blossoms—scarlet, coral, white.

The prolific gum tree comes in a variety of shapes and sizes, and grows in nearly all parts of Australia. The eerie white ghost gum sinks its roots into the dry earth of outback regions around Alice Springs, while the twisted snow gum survives the frigid winters of the alpine highlands. In the mountains of eastern Victoria, in parts of Tasmania, and in southwestern areas of Western Australia, stand dense forests of giant gums, some 91 meters/300 feet tall. Smaller varieties of gum trees are found in the drier woodlands. These trees, having an open structure and small leaves, attain a height of only about 6 meters/20 feet. Still other vinelike, crawling varieties of gum trees exist along the fringes of the country's desert areas.

Like Australia's other flora and fauna, the gum trees have been separated by ocean from the rest of the world since prehistoric times. But this doesn't mean they're unknown. In fact gums are among the most transplanted trees in the world. They were first planted in California for windbreaks more than 100 years ago, and now more than 150 varieties grow in California and Arizona. Other countries that have imported and planted gum trees include Italy, Russia, India, and China. In total, they're found in 73 countries.

A profusion of wildflowers. Many of Australia's native plants are found nowhere else in the world. Sturt desert peas stretch like a red carpet across vast tracts of inland desert; dainty white snow daisies brighten the slopes of the Australian Alps; and more than 600 varieties of orchids lend their beauty to the steamy rain forests of the north.

Western Australia alone grows more than 7,000 species of wildflowers and flowering shrubs and trees, many found nowhere else. For eons, the southwestern corner of Australia was virtually a floral island, isolated from the rest of the continent and other land masses by the Indian Ocean on the west and south and by the desert areas to the east and north. Because of this isolation, unique and unusual plants developed.

Among the most colorful of Western Australia's plants are the unusually shaped kangaroo paw in vivid green and red, the Geraldton wax flower with either white or deep rose flowers, the *Banksia coccinea* with its scarlet conelike flowers, and pine grevillea, its big spikes of deep orange flowers crowning plants growing 6 meters/20 feet high. There are also gray smokebush and blue leschenaultia.

For a strange shape there is the blackboy with its spear-shaped blossom. Related to the lily, it grows about 1½ meters/5 feet tall, and the "spear" can add another 2 meters/6 feet to its height. The bush blossoms along its spear, bearing hundreds of tiny flowers.

Two native plants are carnivorous—the pitcher plant and the rainbow plant, both designed to attract insects. The pitcher plant's lure is a pitcherlike flower full of sweet nectar, and the rainbow plant attracts with rainbow-colored, threadlike leaves.

Other interesting plants. The acacia, found in some variety over most of the continent, has gained national fame. It appears on Australia's coat-of-arms. In early days, colonists used acacia branches to make "wattle and daub" huts, resulting in the name "wattle" becoming attached to the acacia. More than 600 species are found in Australian gardens, parks, and street plantings, and as part of the bush.

Perhaps not as prolific but equally interesting is the baobab tree. Found mainly in northwest Australia, this tree possesses an unusual shape—a bulging base that can have a circumference of 18 meters/60 feet. The water collected in this base helps the tree survive during long periods of drought. Some baobab trees are probably 2,000 years old. Hollowed-out baobab bases have even been used as temporary, overnight jails for prisoners being transported to town. One such prison tree can be found near Derby in Western Australia. Although the tree has been hollowed out, it goes on living.

Still other Australian plants include bottle brush, cycads, and coral trees. In the country's tropical north, you'll find flame, pawpaw, and Davidson's Plum trees. Although the growing of macadamia nuts is a big industry in Hawaii, the macadamia nut tree's native home is Queensland, Australia.

Ghost gum gleams in sunshine, its far-flung branches rising high above bushwalkers' heads. Rich green leaves make a strong contrast to stark white bark.

Fluffy Golden Wattle , an acacia that blooms profusely throughout the country, is Australia's national flower.

Regal Waratah was chosen for New South Wales's floral emblem. This flower is one of more than 6,000 species of wildflowers, flowering shrubs, and trees in Australia.

Murray River country

Australia's most important waterway—the Murray River—flows westward from the mountains of northeast Victoria through the state's quiet pastoral land of orange groves and farmsteads. Its meandering path delineates Victoria's border with New South Wales.

The river was once a great trade route providing access to hard-to-reach inland towns. Hundreds of paddle steamers plied the Murray's length, bringing in supplies and taking wool bales out to market. Today, the Murray River's waters provide irrigation and hydroelectric power for New South Wales, South Australia, and Victoria.

You can drive along the river on the Murray Valley Highway, which parallels the water from Albury northwest to Mildura, near the South Australia border. Or you may prefer a leisurely cruise on the river out of Echuca, Swan Hill, or Mildura. These main river towns can be reached by rail from Melbourne. There's also air service to Mildura and Swan Hill, and Melbourne tour operators have coach tours of the valley that include these towns.

All three areas have accommodations—hotels, motels, and caravan and camping parks. The best times to visit the Murray River region are spring, autumn, and winter; summers can be very hot.

Echuca, a river port town

Once a roistering river port, Echuca sits at the junction of the Murray, Campaspe, and Goulburn rivers—206 km/128 miles north of Melbourne. In the 1800s more than 200 boats docked here annually to unload and load goods. Echuca was considered Victoria's second largest port and the largest inland port in Australia.

The restored Port of Echuca, major setting for the television mini-series "All the Rivers Run," recreates these early days. Moored at the red-gum wharf are two historic paddle steamers, the *Adelaide* and the *Pevensey*. A diorama in the wharf's cargo shed depicts wharf activities over 100 years ago. Nearby restored buildings include the Bridge Hotel, built in 1858, and the Star Hotel, built in 1867.

From Echuca, you can take 1-hour river cruises on the P.S. *Canberra* and the P.S. *Pride of the Murray*. Two-night cruises are available on the P.S. *Emmylou*.

Neighboring marshes provide good fishing and duck hunting possibilities. Barmah State Forest, a well-known bird watching territory, lies only 32 km/20 miles northeast of Echuca.

Swan Hill's Pioneer Settlement

One of Australia's most interesting outdoor folk museum villages sits on the banks of the Murray River at Swan Hill 338 km/210 miles northwest of Melbourne.

Visitors enter the Pioneer Settlement by strolling through the paddle steamer *Gem*, once queen of the Murray. On the other side of the ship's gangplank is a re-creation of a 19th century Australian inland river town complete with general store, print shop, stereoscopic theater, saddler's shop, stagecoach office, fire station,

and pioneer log cabin. Tradesmen, dressed in period costume, demonstrate skills such as blacksmithing and wood turning. At Jimmy Long's Bakery, hunger pains can be quieted with freshly baked bread.

There are steam engines that work and horse-drawn vehicles to take you for a ride through town. Throughout the settlement are everyday household and agricultural items used by the pioneers, including farm implements and windmills.

A highlight of a visit to the Pioneer Settlement is a cruise on the Murray River on the paddle steamer *Pyap*. Several trips leave the settlement's wharf daily. The boat sails leisurely around the river's sweeping bends, beneath overhanging red gums, and past old historic homesteads.

Other Pioneer Settlement attractions include an art gallery and restaurant, both located on the paddle steamer *Gem*. The restaurant features such local delicacies as wichety grub soup and yabbies (freshwater crayfish) caught nearby. You might want to follow a dinner on the *Gem* with a special evening sound-and-light tour through the settlement. A daytime tour takes you by bus to Murray Downs Station, an historic sheep property; you return on board the paddle steamer *Pyap*. Reservations are recommended for both these tours. The Pioneer Settlement is open daily from 8:30 A.M. to 5 P.M.

Other Swan Hill attractions

While in the Swan Hill area, you'll want to explore a number of other attractions, including a museum, a homestead, and a bird sanctuary.

Military museum. This museum, in downtown Swan Hill, houses memorabilia from every war in which Australians have fought, from the Crimean War to Vietnam. Museum items include arms, uniforms, documents, and letters.

Tyntynder Homestead. Just 17 km/11 miles north of Swan Hill is the pioneer Tyntynder Homestead. Built in 1846, it evokes the gracious living of an era when paddle steamers plied the Murray and the homestead was the area's social center. Items of interest include an old wine cellar, costume museum, station store, and furnishing and implements of the time.

Kerang. About 60 km/37 miles southeast of Swan Hill (between Swan Hill and Echuca) is a spot of special interest to bird watchers. The town of Kerang, located on the Loddon River at the junction of the Murray and Loddon highways, is surrounded by marshlands. Here enormous flocks of ibis make their home. In fact, Reedy Lake is thought to be the world's largest ibis rookery. Over 130 species of birds have been identified in the area where blinds have been set up for bird watching.

Mildura, an inland resort

This prosperous small city is the center of an irrigated fruit growing area 557 km/346 miles northwest of Melbourne. Its warm, mild winter climate makes it an inland holiday resort during Victoria's colder months.

The city is home port for the 1912 paddle steamer *Melbourne*. This historic boat plies the waters of the Murray on 2-hour morning and afternoon cruises, departing Mildura's wharf daily except Saturday. A 2-hour lunch cruise is offered daily on the paddle steamer *Avoca,* with 4-hour dinner cruises on Wednesday, Friday, and Saturday nights. A 5-day Murray River cruise on the paddle steamer *Coonawarra* departs Monday mornings and includes accommodations and meals. You can book passage for this trip through the Victour office in Melbourne.

Besides an exciting collection of river vessels, Mildura also lays claim to the longest bar in the world: 87 meters/285 feet of drinking space. It's a claim you can verify for yourself at the Working Men's Club. Other attractions include Rio Vista, a stately home that serves as a museum of local history as well as an art gallery featuring more than 200 paintings. In adjacent Rio Vista Park, you'll see a display of pioneering machinery including an engine used to pump water from the Murray River into Mildura's irrigation channels.

Houseboats are available for rent in the Mildura area, and there is good fishing in nearby backwaters of the Murray River. A colony of koalas inhabits nearby Lock Island.

Hattah Lakes National Park, 80 km/50 miles south of Mildura, is the home of many varieties of water birds, including large nesting colonies of ibis. In the spring, you'll find a profusion of wildflowers too.

Victoria's wine country

The state of Victoria was once Australia's major wine producer. Then, at the close of the 19th century, the plant louse *phylloxera* (which earlier had played havoc with French and California vineyards) found its way to Victo-ria. The devastating *phylloxera* infestation was finally contained and several of Victoria's wine regions are again producing wines.

Rutherglen

This region of vineyards, about 278 km/173 miles northeast of Melbourne near the Murray River, has staged one of the state's strongest recoveries. It is considered one of the oldest winegrowing regions in Australia, the first plantings having taken place in 1851. Almost wiped out in 1899 by the vine disease, it was among the first areas to plant resistant strains.

Today the Shiraz grape does particularly well, and each winery treats it a bit differently. This region also produces some delicate white wines, sherry, and dessert wines that have a good reputation.

A number of wineries in the area are worth a visit. Among them are Campbell's, Bullers, Rosewood, All Saints, Pat Morris, Stanton and Killeen, Jones, St. Leonards, Mt. Prior, and Fairfield.

Great Western district

Another important Victorian wine area is near the town of Ararat, 203 km/126 miles northwest of Melbourne along the foothills of the Grampians. The first vines were planted here by French immigrants in 1863; today, most of the vineyards are owned by the big Seppelt winery. Known primarily for its champagne, the area also produces some fine dry red wines.

You can tour Seppelt's winery and underground champagne cellar, located 16 km/10 miles west of Ararat. Other area wineries include Best's, Boroka, and Montara.

Penguins on parade

One of the most enjoyable tours out of Melbourne is the excursion to Phillip Island, 145 km/90 miles south of the city at the entrance to Westernport Bay. Every night, the year around, tiny fairy penguins stumble ashore at Summerland Beach and parade in squadrons up the beach to their burrows.

The show begins at dusk and lasts about a half-hour to an hour. Spotlights play across the sand, picking up one dark form, then another, and another, as up from the surf they strut, undaunted by the nearness of humans. For them the day's hunt for food is over and they can return to their rookeries to feed their young and rest.

Eudyptula minor is the world's smallest penguin—less than a foot tall. Though several penguin species visit the Australian coast, the fairy penguin is the only one to breed there, nesting amid grass tussocks, in crevices, and in burrows—as many as 200 penguins to the acre.

Besides penguins, Phillip Island offers visitors a variety of other wildlife. You can see one of Victoria's largest fur seal colonies off the westernmost tip of the island, and the island has a thriving koala colony. Other island attractions include a Dairy Centre, chicory kilns, Wool Centre, and a motor and antique museum.

Both day and overnight-coach trips are available from Melbourne to Phillip Island to view the penguins. The island is a 1½-hour drive from the city and is connected to the mainland by a bridge. There's also ferry service from Stony Point. People with limited time might want to take the Penguin Express tour, flying to the island from Melbourne in a light aircraft.

Phillip Island, a popular recreation area for Melbournians, has hotel and motel accommodations and camping and caravan facilities.

TASMANIA

The emerald isle where Australians escape to play

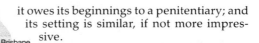

Dangling like a pendant south of Australia's mainland, tiny Tasmania often gets overlooked on world maps. Yet it is one of the country's most fascinating tourist destinations for overseas visitors—and a favorite holiday retreat for Australians.

The island's 427,000 residents prefer to be called Tasmanians rather than Australians. A sixth of the island's inhabitants are direct descendants of convicts. The island was settled in 1803 as a British penal colony, then called Van Diemen's Land. Most of its development was done by convict labor under military supervision; approximately 70,000 prisoners were sent here between 1803 and 1850. Convict traffic stopped in 1853, and in 1856 the island's name was changed to Tasmania in honor of its discoverer, Dutch explorer Abel Tasman.

For many visitors, though, the lure of Tassie (as it is affectionately called) lies not in historical mementos but in the island's scenic variety: from blustery western coastline, over rugged mountain ranges, through tranquil valleys, to east coast fishing ports and beach resorts.

Thanks to the second highest rainfall of any Australian state, much of Tasmania is covered by dense vegetation. Winter dusts mountaintops with snow; clouds of apple blossoms blanket lush, green hills and valleys in spring; and the autumn countryside glows with reds and golds of imported oaks, willows, poplars, and elms. Clear streams cascade through gorges and merge into rivers spawning enough trout to attract anglers from around the world.

Tasmania is graspable, a compact isle only 314 km/195 miles wide and 296 km/184 miles long (a bit smaller than Ireland). Most of its diverse attractions are easy to reach. Two good bases for exploring the countryside are Tasmania's capital, Hobart, in the south, and Launceston in the north.

Hobart—A capital city

Historic Hobart, capital of Tasmania, has a lot in common with Sydney: it was founded only a few years later (1804);

Children frolic among ruins of Port Arthur, infamous penal colony on tip of Tasman Peninsula. Guided tours of the buildings include nearby Isle of the Dead cemetery.

it owes its beginnings to a penitentiary; and its setting is similar, if not more impressive.

Surrounding one of the world's finest deep-water harbors, the city covers the broad lower valley of the Derwent River. Providing a spectacular backdrop is Mount Wellington—snow-clad in winter, forested and green the rest of the year. On a clear day, the 22-km/14-mile ride up to the Pinnacle (the 1,270-meter/4,166-foot summit) provides an unobstructed view of the harbor, the city's eclectic mixture of colonial architecture and modern high-rises, and a good portion of south and central Tasmania, as well.

Getting your bearings

Hobart proper lies on the west bank of the Derwent, linked to suburbs on the eastern shore by the soaring Tasman Bridge. Much of the town's historical heritage centers on the waterfront. Along the harbor, ships' bows loom over the side streets, and fishing vessels, draped with nets and green glass buoys, prove irresistible to photographers.

Sandstone warehouses and stores date back to the whaling days of the 1830s. Close by are the winding streets, Georgian cottages, and tiny gardens of the city's first settled area—Battery Point.

North of the city stretches the vast parkland called the Queen's Domain and the adjoining Royal Botanical Gardens. To the south lies Sandy Bay, about 3 km/2 miles from the city center, where the 21-story Wrest Point Hotel-Casino and adjacent Hobart Convention and Entertainment Centre dominate the scene.

First stop for visitors to this bustling city of over 180,000 should be the Tasbureau (downtown at 80 Elizabeth Street). Open weekdays from 8:45 A.M. to 5:30 P.M. and weekends and holidays from 9 to 11:30 A.M., the Tasbureau offers maps and brochures of major tourist attractions and accommodation information, operates city sightseeing tours, and arranges a variety of tours to other Tasmanian destinations.

Mementos of the past

Hobart's Georgian and Victorian eras have been preserved in many fine old buildings. Several museums also provide a peek into the past.

Battery Point. A number of early buildings remain at Battery Point, an apt name for a promontory once dominated by a gun battery overlooking the harbor. Hobart's original settlement is a fascinating district of narrow streets, winding lanes, and grassy squares. Its homes, public houses, and stores date back to the 1850s and days of sea captains, sailors, and shipwrights. On Saturday mornings there are Battery Point walking tours that leave from Franklin Square.

Constitution Dock and Salamanca Place. Sleek pleasure boats have taken the place of old whaling ships at Hobart's seaside doorstep. Constitution Dock marks the end of the famous Sydney/Hobart Yacht Race in December, and is the site of the annual Royal Hobart Regatta, largest aquatic event in the Southern Hemisphere, in February. Nearby Salamanca Place warehouses are now homes for restaurants and shops. On Saturday mornings the place becomes the open-air Salamanca Market, a colorful collection of stalls, singers, and bands, where locals and tourists browse for trash and treasure.

Collections of history. Van Diemen's Land Folk Museum, 103 Hampden Road, is housed in one of Hobart's earliest colonial homes. Built in 1836, the carefully preserved furnished residence shows how the gentry lived in those times. The museum is open weekdays from 10 A.M. to 5 P.M., weekends from 2 to 5 P.M.

Other museums downtown include the Tasmanian Maritime Museum, exhibiting historic material on seafaring in Tasmania, located at the rear of St. George's Church on Cromwell Street (open daily from 2 to 4:30 P.M.); the Tasmanian Museum and Art Gallery, containing tragic but fascinating relics of the state's extinct Aborigines as well as early colonial paintings and sketches, at 5 Argyle Street (open daily from 10 A.M. to 5 P.M.); and the Post Office Museum, housing historic information on the post and telegraph in Tasmania, at 21 Castray Esplanade (open weekdays from 9 A.M. to 5 P.M., and Saturday from 9 to 11 A.M.).

The Model Tudor Village, 827 Sandy Bay Road, will delight both adults and children. A faithful reproduction of an English 16th century hamlet, this scale model is historically authentic down to the clothing of the 2-inch-high residents. The village is open daily from 9 A.M. to 5 P.M.

You can have Devonshire tea at Shot Tower, located at Taroona 11 km/7 miles from Hobart. The landmark tower was erected in 1870; the adjacent factory (now containing a museum and gallery) was built in 1855.

Shopping around town

Articles made from the island's natural resources make interesting mementos. The usual gimmicky souvenir finds its way onto store shelves, but you can find good substitutes by visiting art and craft shops, galleries, antique stores, and craft workshops. Look for local gemstones, wooden products made from Huon pine, pottery, metalwork, framed art, shellcraft, and antiques. Leatherwork is increasingly popular; best buys are handbags, wallets, and key cases.

You'll find several modern shopping centers downtown, including the Cat and Fiddle Arcade (Elizabeth to Murray streets) where an animated mural enacts the old nursery rhyme every hour on the hour. Look for antique shops around Battery Point.

Most shops are open Monday through Thursday from 9 A.M. to 6 P.M., and 9 A.M. to 9 P.M. on Friday. Some stores are open on Saturday from 9 A.M. to noon.

After dark

Hobart has a variety of good places to dine, ranging from the revolving restaurant atop the Wrest Point Hotel-Casino to more romantic little spots at Battery Point. However, in some cases restaurants may have early closing hours, and be closed on Sundays.

There are theaters, cabaret shows, and ubiquitous discos around town, but most of the nightlife centers around the casino. Here, you can watch a Las Vegas-type revue or join the throng at the tables. Most of the games people play are known world-wide, but there is one unique Australian game, Two-Up. Though it is played throughout the continent, it is played legally only in the casino. Two-Up is fast and fascinating. You bet on whether two coins will fall heads or tails after they have been thrown up in the air simultaneously by a "spinner" in a pit below the gambling circle. If the coins do not land on the same side, it's a "do-over"; after five "do-overs" in a row, everybody loses except the house.

Things to do outdoors

Tasmania is an outdoor playground for sports enthusiasts and spectators. Around Hobart visitors can enjoy golf, tennis, squash, swimming, and boating. Horse racing is held at Elwick Racecourse throughout the year; the Hobart Cup takes place in February. Major trotting events include the Tasmanian Pacing Championships held in December.

Courses, courts, and links. For a list of public tennis courts for hire in Hobart and around the island, contact the Tennis Centre, 2 Davies Avenue. Squash courts are listed in the telephone directory. Rosny Park, in Bellerive suburb, is a public golf course offering prebooked starting times and equipment rental. Here, you can pick up a list of island golf courses open to the public.

Aquatic sports. Bayside beaches close to Hobart include Nutgrove, Long Beach, Bellerive, Sandy Bay, and Kingston. The Derwent Sailing Squadron and the Royal Yacht Club invite members of an affiliated club to get on the water. Guests of the Wrest Point Hotel-Casino can rent boats; other boat rental agencies are found in Sandy Bay and Hobart.

During the summer months, various half-day and day sightseeing cruises operate to Bruny Island and New Norfolk and along the D'Entrecasteaux Channel. Check with the tourist bureau for more information.

Get into the bush. Mt. Wellington, crisscrossed by walking tracks, is a good introduction to bushwalking. Among the most popular is a 3 km/2 mile walk from the Springs to the Pinnacle, past the Organ Pipes. For walking tour maps and guides, stop by the National Parks and Wildlife Service, 16 Magnet Court, Sandy Bay. For more information on bushwalking throughout Tasmania, check with the Tasmanian Wilderness Society, Liverpool Street, Hobart 7018.

Fishing. Game fishing is big sport off the coast of Tasmania. Bluefin tuna run the year around at Eaglehawk

Neck (on the Tasman Peninsula south of Hobart); check with the Tasbureau on boat charters. Several surf-fishing beaches around Hobart, good for catching flathead, mullet, and perch, include jetties at Sandy Bay, Lindisfarne, and Bellerive. The fishing season opens in early January, but each area sets its own season closing date. For a copy of the brochure, "Fishing Code for Anglers in Tasmania," check with the Tasbureau office in Hobart.

One excursion from Hobart includes the Plenty Salmon Ponds. In spite of its name, this is where the first brown and rainbow trout were introduced into the southern hemisphere—in 1864. You can look at the fish here, but you can't go fishing. In addition to a piscatorial museum, the salmon ponds have a tea room and spacious lawns for strolling.

Excursions from Hobart

Radiating from Hobart are regions displaying Tasmania's diversity. To the southwest lies the Huon Valley, source of most of the state's apples. Westward is a wilderness area so rugged that it remains unpopulated and virtually unexplored. Northwest of Hobart are the mountains and national parks. The sheep-raising Midlands stretch due north from Hobart toward Launceston. Farther afield, there's good skiing in the inland mountains of the lightly inhabited northeastern corner, and resort towns and white sand beaches are scattered along the east coast. The Tasman Peninsula off the southeastern coast was the site of the Port Arthur penal colony.

You can explore many of these areas on day trips from Hobart, and most trips can be booked through the Tasbureau office.

Port Arthur's old penal colony

The last of the penal settlements, Port Arthur on the tip of the Tasman Peninsula 100 km/62 miles southeast of Hobart, is Tasmania's number one tourist attraction. Guides show visitors through the ruins of this monument to misery, abandoned in 1877.

Most of the 12,500 prisoners who spent time in this penal settlement were second offenders, under conviction for crimes committed after their deportation to the colony. Many spent their time at Port Arthur learning some trade and were later released to become useful citizens of the infant colony. For the incorrigible prisoners, however, there was harsh discipline.

Prisoners literally built their own prison. Ruins of the since-burned settlement include the prison church, an exile cottage, commandant's residence, and model prison where the "silent system" of punishment replaced the lash. The former lunatic asylum now houses an audio-visual theater and musuem.

Escape from this prison was not easy. On Eaglehawk Neck, the peninsula's narrow land bridge, vicious dogs were chained; only a few inches separated hound from hound. Guards patrolled the line continuously.

Within a few miles of Eaglehawk Neck, the sea has carved several interesting sights. Stretching from the rugged cliffs into the sea is the Tesselated Pavement, a vast plaza of rectangular paving blocks laid out by nature in one of her more orderly moods.

Nearby is an impressive blowhole, as well as Tasman's Arch, a bridge of land whittled away over the centuries by the crashing waves, now far, far below. At Devil's Kitchen you look straight down into a cauldron of churning, roaring surf, hemmed in on three sides by sheer cliffs.

The essentials

Getting there. Tasmania is served by air and sea from the mainland.

Air. Australian Airlines, Ansett Airlines, and East-West Airlines provide air service to Tasmania from Melbourne and Sydney. Air New South Wales also flies to Tasmania from Sydney.

In addition to Hobart International Airport, there are domestic airports at Launceston, Devonport, and Wynyard. Hobart's airport, 22 km/14 miles outside town, is served by bus and taxi.

Sea. The M.V. *Abel Tasman* passenger/vehicle ferry crosses Bass Strait three times weekly from Melbourne to Devonport. The crossing takes about 14½ hours.

Accommodations. Most major hotels are in Hobart and Launceston Major hotels in Hobart include Four Seasons Downtowner, Four Seasons Westside, Innkeepers Lenna of Hobart, Sheraton-Hobart, and Wrest Point Federal Hotel-Casino. Hotels in Launceston include Four Seasons Great Northern Motor Inn, Innkeepers Colonial Motor Inn, Innkeepers Penny Royal Watermill, and Launceston Federal Country Club Hotel-Casino.

Other types of accommodations include colonial cottages, host farms, guest houses, and self-contained villas and flats.

Food and drink. Tasmania has the country's freshest, tastiest fish, home-grown fruit, and some restored colonial buildings where memorable meals and fine Devonshire tea are served. The usual range of ethnic cuisine is available only in Hobart. Watering holes around the state include everything from licensed historic pubs to the posh Federal-Hotel casinos at Launceston and Hobart. Try the local cider, beer, and wine.

Getting around. Transportation on the island is good, with most main towns connected by daily coach service from Hobart. There is daily air service from Hobart to Launceston, and other cities around the island. Because the island is so compact, rental cars are a good bargain if you wish to explore out-of-the-way spots. Local drive-yourself firms usually offer one-way rentals. Tasmania is also good for camper-vans; a number of caravan parks are located throughout the island.

Tours. Half-day city tours of Hobart, Burnie, Devonport, and Launceston are available from the Tasbureau. Scenic air tours are a great way to see the island.

For more information. Tasbureau, 80 Elizabeth Street, Hobart 7000.

Orchards & seascapes

On a 145-km/90-mile loop trip southwest from Hobart—heading for the Huon Valley on Route B64 (the Huon Highway) and returning on Route A6 along the D'Entrecasteaux Channel—orchard views combine with seascapes. A winding side road branches off the Huon Highway, leading you up to the top of Mount Wellington.

The island's first apple tree was planted in 1788 by the botanist accompanying Captain Bligh on the *H.M.S. Bounty*, when the ship anchored at Adventure Bay off Bruny Island south of Hobart. Much of the island's history is recorded in the Bligh Museum at Adventure Bay. Car ferries operate between Kettering and Barnes Bay, North Bruny.

Route A6 continues south beyond the Huon district, past dairy farms, sawmill towns, and tiny seaside hamlets. A popular stop along the way is the vineyard and winery in Cygnet. From the end of the road at Southport, you can drive west about 16 km/10 miles into the hills to Hastings Caves. A number of guided tours daily lead spelunkers into the lighted caverns. Just a few kilometers away is a thermal pool with an average year-round temperature of 27°C/81°F. Also nearby are the Lune River, a haven for gem collectors, and the Ida Bay Railway, a narrow-gauge, open-sided excursion train that operates daily during the summer tourist season.

Also southwest of Hobart lies Hartz Mountains National Park, a superb hiking area of forests and lakes, with peaks rising above 1,255 meters/4,117 feet and providing sweeping views over southern Tasmania. Sir Edmund Hilary noted this park contained "some of the wildest and most spectacular scenery I have ever seen." Perhaps it will be here that you encounter your first Tasmanian devil, a ponderous marsupial who earns his name by his half-scream, half-snarl cry. More elusive would be the Tasmanian tiger (really a wolf); no authenticated sighting has taken place in years. Watch out for the Tasmanian snakes when you do any back-country bushwalking. There are only three, all poisonous: the copperhead, the whip, and the tiger.

Mount Field National Park

Another easy 1-day trip from Hobart by coach or car is through the Derwent Valley to Mount Field National Park, with its 16,260 hectares/40,180 acres of mountains, rain forests, lakes, and streams.

Passing through hop fields you reach New Norfolk, a town that has received "historic" classification by the National Trust. At the Oast House you can take tea after visiting a hop museum and art gallery. Other historical buildings include St. Matthew's Church, oldest in Tasmania; the Bush Inn, built in 1815; and the Old Colony Inn, chock-full of history and antiques.

About 40 km/25 miles beyond is Russell Falls; here you'll enjoy watching a beautiful series of cascades dropping 36 meters/118 feet into a lush gorge, green with rain forest plants and tree ferns. Between July and October, the slopes of nearby Mount Mawson become a popular ski resort; in summer the mountains are alive with hikers.

Beyond the park, the Gordon River Road continues westward about 80 km/50 miles into the wilderness, along a route that many people consider Australia's most spectacular mountain highway. Every turn of the road reveals another range of mountains.

At the end is Lake Pedder, a natural lake now filled beyond its shoreline as part of Tasmania's hydroelectric system. The lake and its companion, Lake Gordon, comprise the largest inland fresh-water storage in Australia. Popular among anglers for its giant trout, Lake Pedder has a number of boat ramps. A launch offers scenic lake cruises. Camping is available, as are motels and guest houses.

The Midlands

Ross and Oatlands—in the Midlands—and the town of Richmond, across the Derwent 27 km/17 miles northeast of Hobart, are probably the best preserved of Tasmania's villages.

Founded in 1814, Ross is noted for its three-arched bridge built by convict labor; a village store operated by the same family for more than a century; and the Scotch Thistle Inn, restored as a restaurant. Each year on the first Saturday in November, the town holds a 1-day rodeo that attracts riders from all over Australia.

Oatlands, 84 km/52 miles north of Hobart, was established in 1826 as a military camp and stopping place for coaches traveling between Hobart and Launceston, to protect travelers against the notorious bushrangers (highway robbers).

Richmond's special features include the six-arched stone bridge, Australia's oldest span, built across the Coal River in 1823; the oldest Roman Catholic Church in Australia, completed in 1837; and the Richmond Gaol (jail), built in 1825. You can wine and dine in one old home and buy antiques in another.

Elsewhere on the island

Beyond the Hobart area, scenic highway routes lead to Tasmania's other towns and attractions.

Launceston, the state's second largest city, is the hub of northern Tasmania. From here you can make a number of excursions to coastal resorts and the lake district in the center of the island. Fine beaches and rich farmlands line the northwestern coast, while the wild region of the west holds some of Tasmania's most spectacular scenery.

The Launceston district

Set in pleasant, hilly countryside 64 km/40 miles inland at the head of the Tamar River estuary, Launceston is a provincial city of 88,000. Three scenic highways and good bus connections link it with Hobart in the south. The city has a number of hotels and motels, including the Colonial Motor Inn, housed in a structure built in 1847.

The town's parks and private gardens are among the best in Australia. European trees, particularly oaks and elms introduced by early settlers, and flowering shrubs flourish in Launceston's mild, moist climate, reminding many travelers of rural England.

(Continued on page 80)

Early colonial architecture is found in Launceston. Tasmania's second largest city is also known for its fine gardens and parks.

Boats tie up at Constitution Dock in Hobart. Bush-covered Mount Wellington provides backdrop for Tasmania's largest city.

...*Continued from page 78*

The Tasbureau, at the corner of Paterson and St. John streets, is your best source of information about Launceston. The Explorer Bus is a good way to see the town. You can also book tours ranging from a half-day jaunt around town to day trips to a seaside resort.

Cataract Gorge. In 10 minutes you can walk from the city center to famed Cataract Gorge, an awesome rocky corridor chewed out by the South Esk River on its way to join the Tamar. The rapids are especially exciting after a heavy rain in the highlands. On the north face of the gorge, a path, illuminated at night, leads along the cliff to First Basin. Here, in a picturesque setting, are a restaurant and swimming pool. You can cross the river on a breathtaking chairlift ride or by a wriggling suspension bridge.

Parks and gardens. Stretching north of Tamar Street is City Park, the most centrally located of the town's parklands. This oasis harbors a miniature zoo and a conservatory displaying begonias, cyclamen, and other hothouse blooms.

At the Punchbowl Reserve and Rhododendron Gardens, south of the city along Punch Bowl Road, a large variety of native birds, beasts, and reptiles live among natural surroundings.

Historic beginnings. Penny Royal World, on Paterson Street, is a fascinating collection of restored buildings that include a working cornmill (vintage 1825), miller's quarters, wheelwright's shop, threshing room, windmill, blacksmith's shop, gunpowder mill, arsenal, cannon foundry, museum, tavern, and restaurant. A paddle steamer takes visitors for a cruise on the Tamar River. Penny Royal World is open daily 9 A.M. to 5 P.M.

Franklin House, 6 km/4 miles from Launceston, was built by convict labor in 1838. It later became a school house and is now restored with furniture and fittings of the era. The home is open daily from 9 A.M. to 5 P.M.

Entally House, 13 km/8 miles south of Launceston at Hadspen, is an excellent example of early colonial architecture. Built in 1820, the restored mansion was once the home of a Tasmanian premier. Exceptional antiques inside and other interesting estate buildings make this dwelling a Tasmanian showplace.

Ben Lomond. One of Tasmania's two major ski areas, Ben Lomond lies in a rocky mountain plateau in the northeastern part of the state, about an hour's drive from Launceston. During ski season (July, August, September) a daily bus runs between Launceston and Ben Lomond; there are no overnight accommodations.

The Great Lake. Southwest from Launceston 120 km/75 miles is one of Australia's leading trout fishing resorts. Lying 1,034 meters/3,392 feet above sea level, the lake is also part of Tasmania's hydroelectric system. Visitors' galleries are located at power stations around the lake.

East coast resorts

Tasmania's east coast, paralleled by the Tasman Highway, is famed for its mild climate, beautiful beaches, fishing, and swimming facilities.

Of numerous popular coastal holiday resorts, the principal ones are St. Helens, Scamander, Bicheno, Coles Bay, Swansea, and Orford. A variety of accommodations are available throughout this area and range from motels and older guest houses with cabins, to self-contained villa units. There are also caravan campgrounds.

St. Helens, 265 km/165 miles northeast of Hobart and 165 km/103 miles east of Launceston, has a large sheltered bay popular for fishing and boating. Good surf beaches line the open coast, and forest streams winding from the north and west offer excellent trout fishing.

Bicheno and Triabunna on the coast are old whaling towns where people still make their living from the sea. You can arrange for fishing trips with local fishers.

At Coles Bay you can explore secluded coves, swim from snow-white beaches, scale rocky cliffs, or stroll leisurely along quiet, bush-edged trails. The small guest house stands at the base of The Hazards, 305-meter/1,000-foot-high hills of red granite. Adjoining the town is Freycinet National Park—a combination seaside resort and bushwalking and mountain climbing haven.

Tasmania's best-known park

The best-known wildlife sanctuary and scenic reserve in Tasmania is Cradle Mountain-Lake St. Clair National Park in the western half of the state, covering an area of 126,148 hectares/311,725 acres. From Devonport on the north coast, the park is a 1½-hour drive. Lake St. Clair, at the southern end of the park, is 175 km/109 miles north of Hobart on the Lyell Highway.

A favorite among hikers is the 83-km/52-mile, 5-day trek through the park from Waldheim Chalet at Cradle Mountain to Cynthia Bay at the south end of Lake St. Clair, with overnight stops at huts along the way. Cradle Mountain Lodge near Waldheim provides accommodations in the lodge or in self-contained cabins.

The wild west

The most unusual and fascinating part of Tasmania is the island's wild western region. This part of the state ranges from tracts of unexplored wilderness, to bare, stark hills in the Queenstown area, and Aboriginal rock carvings at Marrawah in the far north.

Tasmania's western region has been put under the protection of the World Heritage Council. The Western Tasmania Wilderness National Parks World Heritage Area consists of three national parks—Cradle Mountain-Lake St. Clair National Park, the Franklin-Lower Gordon Wild Rivers National Park, and the South West National Park.

The area can be explored on guided hikes, 4-wheel drive expeditions, cruise boat and rafting trips, and scenic air tour excursions. In the mountains, beware of a phenomenon called the "horizontals." Saplings grow to a certain height, then blow over to lie parallel to, but above the ground. This creates an area that looks like solid ground, but isn't.

A good way to get a glimpse of the area is to take the Lyell Highway into Queenstown, 256 km/159 miles northwest of Hobart. En route, you'll pass through Cradle Mountain-Lake St. Clair and Franklin-Lower Gordon Wild Rivers national parks. From the nearby coastal town of Strahan, take a boat trip up the Gordon River.

Queenstown. This is the largest township on the west coast (about 4,500 people), prospering from nearby copper mining. Before the turn of the century, the surrounding hills were green with trees and dense undergrowth. But then the smelters started to process copper ore, the timber was cut for fuel, and resulting sulphur fumes denuded the slopes. Heavy rains washed away topsoil, and the rocks became stained in shades of chrome yellow, purple, gray, and pink. Ore processing changed in 1922, and plant life is slowly returning.

A wilderness boat trip. The only developed port on the west coast is Strahan, west of Queenstown on the northern shore of Macquarie Harbour. Fishing boats and ships handling lumber sail in and out of the port.

Strahan is the starting point for boat trips across the harbor toward Settlement Island, Tasmania's first infamous penal colony, and into the wilderness surrounding the Gordon River.

The northwest corner. From Queenstown, the Murchison Highway crosses rugged mountains to reach Burnie, a timber and agricultural center on the northern coast. From Burnie, Route A2 heads west across the Cape Country and ends at Marrawah, where ancient Aboriginal rock carvings can be seen inside caves overhanging the shoreline.

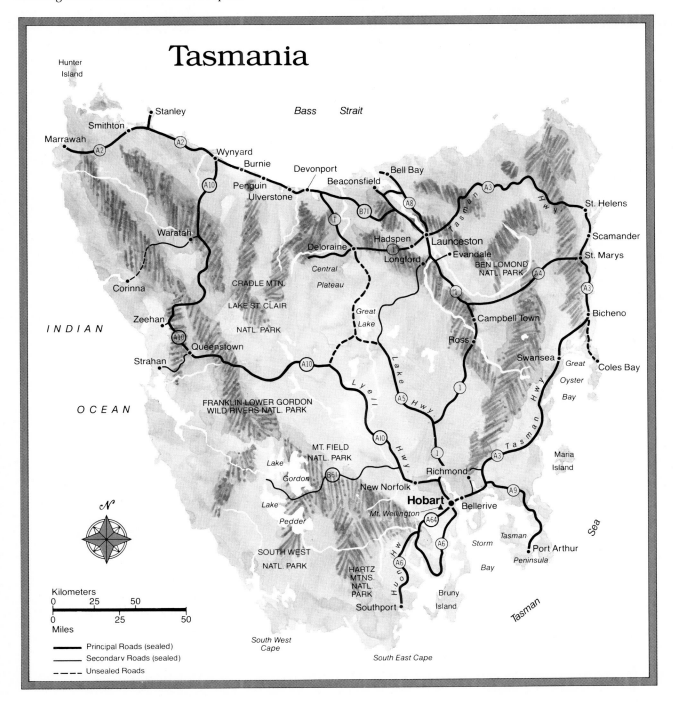

ADELAIDE

South Australia's beach resorts & wine valleys begin at town's edge

South Australia is at once a source of greater contrasts and smaller ones than its two great neighbors, New South Wales and Victoria. And, as a result, it is a much different place to visit.

Most Australian states have fertile coastal edges posed against bleak interior deserts, but in South Australia the line seems closer and sharper. It does not take long to get from the lush gardens of Adelaide to the bony, sun-bleached ribs of the Flinders Ranges, but the more dramatic point is that most of the journey is across rich, green agricultural land.

That greater contrast is also the key to the smaller contrast, which is that Adelaide does not dominate the rest of South Australia in the ways that Sydney and Melbourne dominate their states. Rather, farm districts ease through the suburbs and right into the edge of the city. Or, maybe, the city eases out into the farms. Either way, Adelaide is closely linked to the countryside around it. Visitors find themselves as much tempted to poke around in the countryside as downtown.

South Australians also manage to blur the boundary between land and sea. Sailors, swimmers, and surfers in and around Adelaide make the beaches of St. Vincent Gulf and other resort shores look as if fully a quarter of the population is amphibious. There remains plenty of room in the water for visitors.

The local populace is pleased that its state was not developed by convict labor. Philosopher Edward Gibbon Wakefield developed a plan to generate capital by paying laborers enough to encourage them to buy land. The successful idea must have come from the heart. Wakefield devised it while serving time in Newgate Prison in London, England.

Adelaide—A city of parks

Despite its sizable population (over 1 million), Adelaide manages to retain many of the charms of a much smaller city—partly because some of its streets are lined with colorful buildings that would not look out of place in Western movies, and partly because it has a superior park system even by Australia's high standards.

With implausibly fair weather, with a ring parks around town, open spaces in the Mount Lofty Ranges on one side and the spacious St. Vincent Gulf on the other, Adelaide is attuned to the outdoors. Adelaide revels in outdoor sports, including motor racing—the city is host to the annual Australian Formula One Grand Prix. However, both outdoor and indoor venues are used for the biennial Adelaide Festival, a 3-week art, music, and dance event.

Getting your bearings

Adelaide is an easy city to get to know. The key is compactness, the result of the well-designed 1836 plans of Colonel William Light, South Australia's first surveyor-general.

The business heart of Adelaide throbs within a square mile centering on Victoria Square. Many of Adelaide's corporate offices, banks, stores, hotels, and public buildings flank the wide, tree-lined streets and broad squares that seem to be the hallmark of every Australian city.

Circling this inner city are the great parklands that dominate the shape of Adelaide. Through the northern section of these parks flows the Torrens River, dammed in front of the Festival Theatre to form a lake.

Beyond the river is North Adelaide—a suburb of large, old homes and bluestone cottages. In this pleasant suburban area you will find Light's Vision. The statue of Colonel Light stands on top of Montefiore Hill. From the hill you can get a commanding view of the city.

Central Adelaide walking tour brochures are available from the South Australian Government Travel Centre at 18 King William Street. You can also pick up general information and maps on Adelaide and South Australia here.

Strolling through the park

Because Adelaide is so definitively shaped by its 688 hectares/1,700 acres of parks, they are the best places to begin an acquaintanceship with the city.

Showplace of Adelaide's parklands is the Botanic Gardens and Park in the northeast parklands. Here, you'll find 16 hectares/40 acres of native Australian vegetation.

Part of the vast greenbelt encircling Adelaide, the Torrens River adds to the city's recreational possibilities. Pedal boats can be rented near the Festival Centre.

(Continued on page 84)

. . . Continued from page 83

A world-renowned collection of water lilies grows in the park's lakes.

Next to the Botanic Park is Adelaide's compact zoo. It's open daily from 9:30 A.M. to 5 P.M. During summer months, a launch sails along the Torrens River between the zoo and the Festival Theatre.

The parklands not only provide a pleasant place to stroll, but also feature facilities for a number of recreational pursuits—golf courses, tennis courts, cycling paths, and jogging tracks.

Touring the central city

Within the square created by Adelaide's parklands, is the city's central shopping and business district—a conglomeration of 19th century architecture and modern high rises.

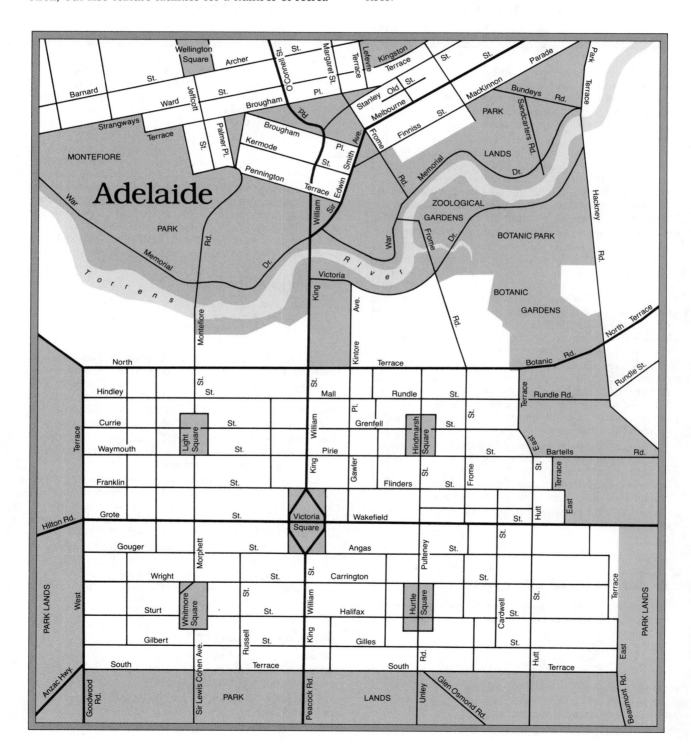

The city's parkland atmosphere extends into this commercial hub with numerous tree-shaded squares. Victoria Square—marking the exact center of the city—is filled with trees and features a statue of Queen Victoria.

One of the city's main thoroughfares—King William Street—heads north and south from Victoria Square. With its median strip of lawns and flowers, it is considered the widest capital city street in Australia. Lining King William Street are most of the city's banks, insurance offices, town hall, and post office. These latter two buildings—opposite each other—have imposing clock towers.

Another main tree-lined boulevard—North Terrace—runs in an east/westerly direction at the north end of city center. Important buildings along this thoroughfare include Parliament House, Holy Trinity Church (Adelaide's oldest), Government House, South Australian Museum, Art Gallery, State Library, and University of Adelaide.

Following are some of the major attractions for visitors.

Art Gallery. Located on North Terrace near its intersection with Pulteney Street, this gallery houses a fine collection of Australian paintings, ceramics, and sculptures as well as works of British, European, and American artists. The gallery is open daily from 10 A.M. to 5 P.M.

South Australian Museum. Near the Art Gallery, this museum houses large collections of regional natural history and Aboriginal and Melanesian artifacts. Take note of the giant Diprotodon skeleton on the ground floor of the museum. It's believed to be an ancestor of today's wombat. The museum is open daily.

Historic home. On North Terrace opposite the Royal Adelaide Hospital stands Ayers House. This beautiful 19th century bluestone residence was once the home of Sir Henry Ayers, one of South Australia's earliest premiers. Today it houses the headquarter offices of the South Australian National Trust, a historical museum, a posh restaurant, and a bistro. The house is open weekdays (except Monday) from 10 A.M. to 5 P.M. and on weekends from 2 to 4 P.M.

North Adelaide. On the north side of the Torrens River (a long walk from town center) is this interesting suburb with its bluestone cottages, old hotels, and new restaurants. North Adelaide was the city's first fashionable residential area. You can still see fine 19th century colonial mansions as well as simple cottages. Good streets to explore include Stanley, Melbourne, and Archer streets, and Le Fevre Terrace.

Shopping around

Adelaide's main shopping area is concentrated in the pedestrian-only Rundle Street Mall between King William Street and Pulteney Street. On it are many of the city's large retail department stores (Myer's, David Jones, John Martins of South Australia) as well as cafes, boutiques, and movie houses. Several small shopping arcades branch off tree-shaded Rundle Street with its flower boxes, sculptures, and fruit carts.

Shops in Adelaide are open weekdays from 9 A.M. to 5:30 P.M. and Saturdays from 9 A.M. to 11:30 A.M. On Fridays many of the downtown stores are open until 9 P.M.

The essentials

Here are a few basics to help you in planning and taking a trip to Adelaide.

Getting there. Adelaide is served by air, rail, and bus.

Air. Interstate domestic flights by Ansett and Australian airlines with intrastate service by Kendell Airlines. Adelaide International Airport is 6 km/4 miles from downtown by bus or taxi.

Rail. Interstate trains provide regular service to and from other state capitals. The terminal is 2 km/1 mile from downtown.

Bus. Ansett Pioneer, Greyhound, and Deluxe have regular service between Adelaide and other capitals.

Accommodations. Most major hotels are in the downtown area; try the Adelaide Parkroyal, Gateway Inn, Hilton International Adelaide, Hotel Adelaide, Adelaide Travelodge, Meridien Lodge, South Park Motor Inn, Old Adelaide Inn, and Town House.

Food and drink. Seafood from nearby waters heads the list of local specialties—crayfish, prawns, whiting, yabbies, and rock lobsters. One local dish, a "floater," is also a favorite. It consists of a meat pie floating upside down in pea soup with a dab of tomato sauce on top. Pie carts, operating nights and Sundays, are adjacent to the General Post Office.

South Australia has five good wine districts—the Barossa, Southern Vales, Clare, Murray River, and Coonawarra—whose wines are featured on Adelaide restaurant menus. Major local beers include West End, Southwark, and Coopers.

Getting around. Extensive city-operated bus system in city as well as out to suburbs. Free "Bee-line" bus follows downtown shopping circuit—Victoria Square to Railway Station along King William Street. City's only tram travels between Victoria Square and beach suburb of Glenelg. Extensive surburban train system operates from Adelaide. City circle bus links tram, rail, and bus services. Also several rental car agencies in town rent both cars and motor scooters.

Public transport maps available at South Australian Government Travel Centre.

Tours. Half-day tours include city sights. Regional tours (some half-day, some full-day) include Mount Lofty Ranges (see page 86), Victor Harbor (page 89), Kangaroo Island (page 91), the Murray River (page 93), Barossa Valley (page 92), and Southern Vales (page 92). Also available are longer tours to Flinders Ranges (see page 93) and cruises on Murray River (page 93).

For more information. South Australian Government Travel Centre, 18 King William Street, Adelaide 5000. Can also arrange tours and accommodations. Open Monday through Friday from 8:45 A.M. to 5 P.M., Saturday from 8:45 to 11:30 A.M., and Sunday from 10 A.M. to 2:15 P.M.

Buying an opal. South Australia's opal mines (see page 88) make Adelaide one of Australia's best cities for opal shopping. Small workshops in the city cut and polish opals on the premises to make custom jewelry you can purchase. Most of the major jewelry stores and department stores also stock a good range of opal jewelry.

Antique hunting. On North Adelaide's Melbourne Street, several old buildings have been restored to house antique shops. (There are also a number of exclusive boutiques in the area.) Other antique dealers can be found along Unley Road and King William Road near Hyde Park.

Arts and entertainment

The focus of Adelaide's entertainment scene is the Festival Centre. Many of Adelaide's cultural events are held in this modern complex on the banks of the Torrens just north of North Terrace off King William Road.

The Festival Centre, built for the Adelaide Festival, includes a 2,000-seat auditorium (Festival Theatre), a 612-seat drama theater (The Playhouse), a 360-seat experimental theater (The Space), a 2,000-seat open-air amphitheater, and a broad plaza with concrete sculptures. Hourly guided tours are held weekdays from 10 A.M. to 3 P.M. and Saturdays from 10:30 A.M. to 3 P.M.

Both the Adelaide Symphony Orchestra and State Theatre Company perform at the Festival Centre. The center also hosts international performers on tour. (The Stuttgart Ballet and Vienna Boys' Choir are among recent visitors.) During the summer months the open-air amphitheater is the venue for free concerts.

The State Opera of South Australia performs at the Opera Theatre on Grote Street.

Adelaide Festival. Biennially—during the first 3 weeks of March in even-numbered years—the Adelaide Festival brings together fine performers of every kind from Australia and abroad. Rudolph Nureyev, Dave Brubeck, the Royal Shakespeare Company, London Philharmonic, and the Kabuki Theatre of Japan are among the roster of past performers.

The list of activities during the festival includes opera and ballet performances, jazz and symphony concerts, folk dancing, comedy, and drama. Art and sculpture fill the galleries and spill over into outdoor exhibits. Floral displays provide color in the gardens. Processions and pageantry complete the festival's calendar.

The core of all the events is the Festival Centre but activities occur everywhere—streets, parks, smaller theaters, sports arenas, and playgrounds.

Adelaide Casino. This city's only casino is housed in the beautifully refurbished former railway station on North Terrace. In addition to gaming tables, the casino has a restaurant and five bars.

Sports to watch

The city's main sports ground is the Adelaide Oval, in parklands on the north side of the Torrens River. During the summer months cricket is played here and during the winter months fans enthusiastically gather to support Australian Rules football.

Horse races are run weekly at Victoria Park Racecourse, in parklands southeast of the city or at Morphetville near Glenelg. Other tracks include Cheltenham, 8 km/5 miles to the northwest. There's harness racing from October through July at Globe Derby Park in Bolivar.

Recreational possibilities

The city's parklands offer a rich range of activities.

Boating. The Torrens River—flowing gracefully through the city's northern parklands—is ideal for quiet boating. You can hire rowboats and pedal boats on the river bank near the Festival Centre.

Golf. It's just a short walk from city center to the Municipal Golf Links in the northern parklands; there are two 18-hole courses.

For more information on Adelaide's golf courses check with the South Australian Golf Association on War Memorial Drive in North Adelaide.

Tennis. Adelaide is one of the last great bastions of lawn tennis in the world. The city also has a number of hard courts. (The most notable public complex is Memorial Drive Tennis Courts next to the Adelaide Oval in the northern parklands.) For-hire courts are listed in telephone book Yellow Pages. For information on club play contact either the South Australian Lawn Tennis Association, P.O. Box 220, Goodwood 5034, or the South Australian Hard Court Tennis League, Inc., P.O. Box 202, Goodwood 5034.

Beautiful beaches

Adelaide's beaches stretch along the coast from Outer Harbor in the north to Seacliff in the south. Along their 32-km/20-mile expanse, you'll find good swimming in the calm waters of St. Vincent Gulf. Most of these beaches are less than a 30-minute drive from the city. A special streetcar even takes beachgoers from Victoria Square in downtown Adelaide to St. Vincent Gulf. Buses and trains also serve the area.

Principal resorts along this coast include Largs Bay, Semaphore, Grange, Henley Beach, Glenelg, Brighton, West Beach, and Seacliff.

Peaceful, quiet hill country

The sometimes steep, sometimes rolling hills that hem Adelaide tightly against the sea are serene pleasures within themselves. Along winding roads, green meadows with grazing sheep give way to orchards, which in turn give way to tiny villages tucked into forested folds.

Called the Mount Lofty Ranges, these hills hold some predictable charms in the form of parks and wilderness reserves, and some unpredictable ones in the forms of art colonies, a German village that holds one of the largest beer fests outside of Bavaria, and a museum of motorcars and other machines.

Spring and fall are the finest seasons for visiting the district. In spring the orchards come alive with fragrant blossoms; in fall, poplars, birches, and maples light the hillsides with fiery reds and golds.

Driving distances are easy. There also are full and half-day tours into the region from Adelaide.

With regal waves and smiles, queen and court parade through city streets at the Barossa Valley Vintage Festival. This great Australia winemaking region lies north of Adelaide.

Froufrous and furbelows adorn century-old Botanic Hotel on North Terrace in Adelaide.

Cleland Conservation Park. This inviting concept in wildlife sanctuaries allows people to walk among animals that roam free in natural habitats. The park is divided into five areas, each featuring animals that live together in the wild. Visitors can meet more or less eye to eye with red and gray kangaroos, tammar wallabies, swamp wallabies, red-necked wallabies, and such waterfowl as pelicans, cormorants, and black swans. A walk-through aviary gives close-up looks at rosellas, parrots, and lorikeets in flight. (Wombats, koalas, and dingoes must live in enclosures for the protection of one or both parties.) The park, 13 km/8 miles southeast of Adelaide, is open daily from 9:30 A.M. to 5 P.M.

Hahndorf is home to the great beer festival, held each January on Australia Day. All year around it is home to the descendants of settlers who fled to South Australia in 1839 to escape religious persecution in their homeland.

The half-timbered German cottages and houses lining the main street have been converted to an array of shops, crafts galleries, and restaurants. Of particular note are the Hahndorf Academy, which houses a German folk museum and the adjoining Heysen Art Gallery, which holds paintings by Sir Hans Heysen.

Hahndorf is 40 km/18 miles southeast of Adelaide.

Birdwood Mill. Northeast of the city, an old flour mill built in 1851 now houses Australia's Museum of Technology's collection of Australiana.

Inside the mill, you'll find old diving equipment, washing machines, stoves, gramophones, and drinking glasses. An adjacent new building houses the National Motor Museum's 135 old jeeps, racing cars, fire engines, and automobiles.

Birdwood is about a 50-minute drive from Adelaide.

A diverse shore

The coast of South Australia around Adelaide looks as if it had been cut with a scroll saw. Deep bays and peninsulas alternate in bewildering numbers—all to the benefit of sailors, surfers, fishers, and scenery watchers.

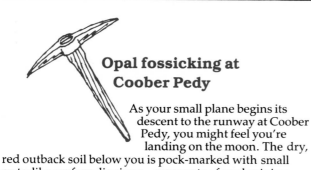

Opal fossicking at Coober Pedy

As your small plane begins its descent to the runway at Coober Pedy, you might feel you're landing on the moon. The dry, red outback soil below you is pock-marked with small craterlike surface diggings—remnants of opal mining.

More than 100 million years ago, the sea covered this area of Australia, laying down sediment and entrapping the silica solutions that developed into opals. The gems are found in sandstone, below layers of rock and jasper.

Miners at Coober Pedy, and Andamooka to the southeast, dig out more than $4 million worth of opals annually. About 75 percent of the world's opals come from these areas. Some miners use modern equipment such as blowers to bring up earth from the mines. Others scar the ground with giant earth-moving equipment, making deep cuts in search of opals. Still others rely on the old mining techniques, using just picks, shovels, windlasses, and buckets.

Above the ground, it's impossible to distinguish on sight persons who have struck it rich and those living off credit. Everyone avoids displaying wealth, for fear of claim jumping.

In Aborigine, Coober Pedy means "man in hole." It's an appropriate name, for nearly half of the 3,000 residents of Coober Pedy live underground—even the church is underground. The reason for this molelike existence is the area's soaring summer temperatures, which can reach 49°C/120°F. Average underground house temperatures stay around 19°C/65°F the year around.

These underground homes are usually quite spacious and comfortable. The prosperous miner might even have wall-to-wall carpets, a stereo, and a cocktail bar. The largest such dugout, Aladdin's Cave, has 11 rooms and a huge workshop-store.

If you're feeling lucky, you may want to dig for opals too. In addition to a Precious Stones Prospecting Permit from the Mines Department in Adelaide, you'll need a pick and shovel and a strong back. If you try this during the heat of summer, take heed from local miners who work their claims while temperatures are cooler— between 3 and 10 A.M.

Tours of Coober Pedy usually include an underground home, the church, nearby mining fields, and the Umoona Mine. You can tour this old mine and purchase opals from the underground shop. Opals, mounted or unmounted, are available in Coober Pedy at prices considerably lower than in larger cities.

Coober Pedy is 966 km/600 miles north of Adelaide. You can get there from Adelaide by bus or Opal Air, which operates eight-seater Cessnas on a regular schedule. Packaged tours on Opal Air can include Coober Pedy, Ayers Rock, and on to Alice Springs on Connair. Coach tours and 1-day air tours are also available from Adelaide. There are bus and air tours to Andamooka too. Accommodations in Coober Pedy and Andamooka are limited to a few motels and a guest house.

In addition to Coober Pedy and Andamooka, you can visit gem mining areas at Lightning Ridge in far northern New South Wales (home of the famous black opals) and in the Anakie District of Queensland, an important sapphire-producing area where good stones can still be found near old diggings.

For visitors from afar, there are two main choices south of Adelaide, and two more northwest. The southerly choices are the Fleurieu Peninsula and Kangaroo Island. The northerly options are Yorke and Eyre peninsulas. All four offer resorts and wilderness with equal ease.

Fleurieu Peninsula

The Fleurieu Peninsula coast touches the waters of both St. Vincent Gulf and the Southern Ocean. A varying sea- scape includes secluded bays with calm waters, broad beaches with rolling surf, and rocky headlands where waves crash endlessly. Inland are wine vineyards, al- mond orchards, forests, and undulating pasturelands.

You can visit the Fleurieu Peninsula on a 1-day tour from Adelaide. If you wish to stay longer, you'll find ac- commodations at Victor Harbor, Port Elliot, and Goolwa.

Victor Harbor. The largest and most popular seaside re- sort on the peninsula is Victor Harbor, 84 km/52 miles south of Adelaide. On Encounter Bay, the town's harbor

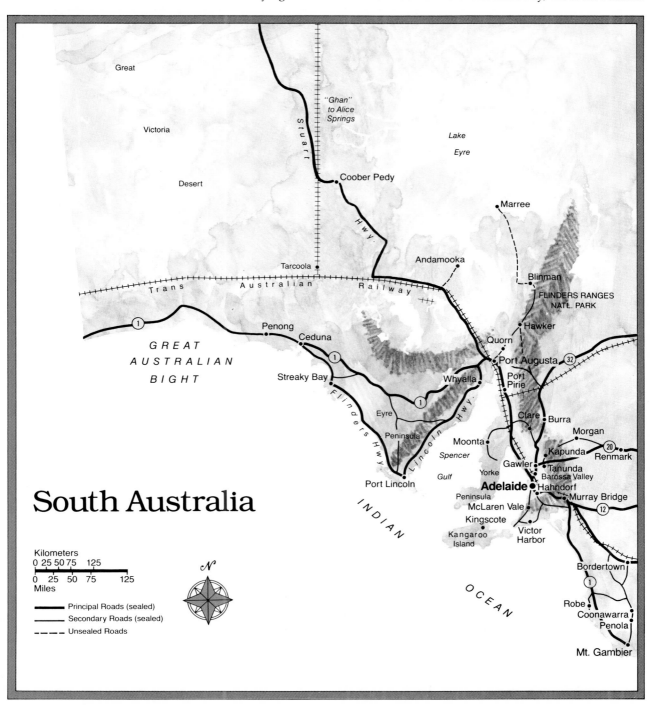

South Australia

Kilometers
0 25 50 75   125

0   25   50   75   125
Miles

—— Principal Roads (sealed)
— Secondary Roads (sealed)
--- Unsealed Roads

Slowing to cross a waterhole, four-wheel-drive vehicle ventures deep into the Flinders Ranges, a land of peaks and ravines tapering into desert.

Amusing to tourists, sign is no laughing matter to people who know the danger of hitting a kangaroo. Outback drivers protect cars with "kangaroo guards."

is protected from the ocean by Granite Island. This rocky knob, joined to the mainland by a causeway, is buffeted by giant rollers crashing against its windward side, throwing spray high into the air. On the island's harbor side—facing the town—you can swim and study marine life in sheltered pools along the causeway.

Urimbirra Fauna Park. In the natural setting of this park—5 km/3 miles from Victor Harbor—you can see many of Australia's animals, some enclosed and some not. Wandering among giant gum trees, you'll see kangaroos, wallabies, emus, koalas, dingoes, wombats, and Tasmanian devils. The park also has an excellent Nocturnal House where you'll see Australia's night creatures.

Coorong National Park. Winding around Encounter Bay and heading south, you'll come to Coorong National Park. It consists of a narrow sandspit of sand dunes plus a shallow salt-water lagoon behind the beach area. This lagoon is the breeding rookery for pelicans, crested terns, and silver gulls.

You can best view the lagoon breeding area from Princes Highway (1).

Unspoiled Kangaroo Island

Australia's third largest island lies 113 km/70 miles southwest of Adelaide at the entrance to St. Vincent Gulf. Much of the island's original character remains—abundant wildlife, splendid beaches, secluded coves, rugged headlands, and wind-sculptured boulders. Here you can also enjoy Australia's animal kingdom. Walk among the seals at Seal Bay or explore Flinders Chase National Park and see the koalas and platypuses.

It's a 40-minute trip by air to Kangaroo Island from Adelaide. A car ferry from Port Adelaide makes the journey in 6 hours. And there's a one-day aerial tour from Adelaide.

Main centers. Largest of the island resorts is Kingscote on the north coast. It offers many safe beaches, a sea front swimming pool, jetty, and the main shopping area.

American River, southeast of Kingscote, is a holiday resort in a woodland setting. The waterway is not really a river, but an arm of the sea separating Dudley Peninsula from the rest of the island.

Penneshaw, on the Dudley Peninsula, looks 13 km/8 miles across the strait (called Backstairs Passage) to the mainland. An attractive town with a white sandy beach, jetty, and sheltered anchorage, it has a rocky promontory populated with fairy penguins.

A ferry service operates between Cape Jervis and Penneshaw; coach service links Cape Jervis and Adelaide.

Flinders Chase National Park. At the western edge of the island—about a 1½-hour drive from Kingscote—you can explore this refuge for Australian fauna and flora. Roads wind through the 54,950-hectare/135,787-acre park, and there are trails for bushwalking. Here you'll find kangaroos, wallabies, emus, Cape Barren geese, and goanna lizards. The animals are so tame that visitors have to guard their picnic hampers against hungry marauding kangaroos. Emus will even peck on your car window begging for handouts. Visitors can dine in an enclosure while the kangaroos and emus look on beseechingly from the other side of the fence.

Beautiful Yorke Peninsula

Like a long leg, the Yorke Peninsula stretches into the sea between St. Vincent Gulf and Spencer Gulf. With beautiful beaches along both these waterways, the peninsula is an ideal spot for a coastal holiday with activities like surfing, fishing, swimming, and boating. Inland, good roads wind through golden wheat and barley fields and lush pasturelands.

The peninsula's towns, including Wallaroo, Kadina, Moonta, Maitland, Ardrossan, and Port Vincent, are just a few hours' drive from Adelaide. Accommodations in the area include hotels, motels, and caravan parks.

One of the best times to visit Yorke Peninsula is in springtime when the wildflowers decorate the landscape. The peninsula is ablaze with yellow daisies, brilliant red flame bushes, and golden wattles.

Copper mining towns. In the late 1800s, copper was discovered on the Yorke Peninsula, and the resulting boom lasted for about 63 years. Boom towns included Kadina, Moonta, and Wallaroo.

Men from Cornwall, England, immigrated to work the mines, and you can still see their Cornish miners' cottages as well as abandoned mines and slag heaps. In Moonta, you can visit the Mining Museum located in the former Mining School.

The area's Cornish heritage is evident during the celebration of Kernewek Lowender. This Cornish festival—held on the long weekend in May in odd-numbered years—features wheelbarrow races, street dances, a Cornish feast, a village green fair, crowning of a festival king and queen, and the eating of Cornish pasties. Activities are centered in Wallaroo, Kadina, and Moonta.

Innes National Park. At the "toe" of the Yorke Peninsula, you can explore this 6,000-hectare/14,827-acre wilderness of mallee scrub and spectacular coastal scenery. There are wonderful beaches, coves, and bays.

Eyre Peninsula, a water playground

Lying between Spencer Gulf and the Great Australian Bight, Eyre Peninsula forms a giant triangle, with the towns of Port Augusta in the northeast, Ceduna in the northwest, and Port Lincoln at the southern tip.

The Eyre Peninsula's landscape includes grainfields, bushlands, and sheep pastures. In the northeastern part of the peninsula are iron ore mines at Iron Knob and Iron Monarch, and steel factories along the eastern coast.

Coastal offerings. As with the Yorke Peninsula, the area's greatest attractions are its shores. The coast surrounding Port Lincoln—the peninsula's major resort town—is long and deeply indented, with great seas for yachting, quiet inlets for swimming, and endless beaches with rolling waves for surfing. People who fish usually find the sea generous whether tackled from beach, jetty, rock, or boat.

A festival. The calm waters of Boston Bay where Port Lincoln is situated provide safe anchorage for Australia's biggest tuna fleet. Each year on the last weekend in January, this fleet is heralded with the Tunarama Festival. Honoring the opening of the tuna fishing season, the 4-day festival includes the blessing of the fleet, a sailpast of boats, parades, and feasting.

Getting there and accommodations. The hub of the peninsula's resort activities is Port Lincoln. Daily air service links this town with Adelaide. There's also bus service via Port Augusta. Motels, hotels, and guest houses are located in Port Lincoln, and there's a nearby caravan park.

Mount Gambier's crater lakes

Mount Gambier, a large commercial center near the Victoria border 483 km/300 miles southeast of Adelaide, takes its name from an extinct volcano rising above the town. Inside the mountain's shattered top are three beautiful crater lakes.

Perhaps the best known of the lakes is Blue Lake. Annually at the end of November, Blue Lake mysteriously changes color from slate gray to bright blue. Between January and March, the lake slowly reverts to its former gray.

You can get to Mount Gambier by daily air or coach service. There is also rail service from Adelaide. There are hotels, motels, and campgrounds.

Wine country

In this, Australia's largest winegrowing state, vineyards begin at the edges of Adelaide and sprawl everywhere sea breezes reach, and a few places where they don't.

The most famous single district in the country, the Barossa, is a broad, shallow upland valley little more than an hour's drive north of the city. Its near neighbor and one of its closest competitors is the Clare Valley. Flanking Adelaide on the south is the district called Southern Vales, where vines and suburban houses compete for space on a narrow shelf above the sea.

South Australia's other two wine districts demand longer travels. Far to the south is Coonawarra, a tiny but treasured source of red wines. It is most easily visited as part of a trek to Mount Gambier. Inland, south and east of Adelaide, the largest district of them all flanks the Murray River. It is as much visitable for rides on paddle wheel passenger boats and for fishing as for winery touring.

Barossa Valley

Heading the list of well-known wine-producing regions not only in South Australia but in the entire country is the Barossa Valley. This premier winemaking region is located only 64 km/40 miles northeast of Adelaide. The valley with its gentle rolling hills, vineyards, orchards, and market gardens stretches 29 km/18 miles from Lyndoch in the south past Nuriootpa in the north.

A bit of history. The valley was originally settled in the 1840s mainly by Prussians and Silesians. Lutherans, they came to Australia to escape religious persecution in their homeland. These settlers planted the first vines in 1847 near Tanunda and Rowland flats.

The valley's towns have retained an old-world look, with solid stone houses, old German cottages, and carefully cultivated gardens set along neat tree-lined streets. The Lutheran religion still predominates, and at the center of each town is a Lutheran church with its belfry.

Area wineries. The valley has about 40 wineries. Included in this lengthy list are Orlando, Chateau Yaldara, Penfolds/Kaiser Stuhl, Seppelt, and Yalumba.

Many of the Barossa Valley wineries are still family owned. Some boast castlelike buildings and clock towers reminiscent of the winegrowing districts of the fatherland. You'll find impressive stone buildings at Yaldara, Tanunda, Seppelt's, Yalumba, and Penfolds.

Behind the handsome facades, the wineries of the Barossa Valley offer hospitality. Many have guided tours showing the various steps of wine production from grape crushing (in season) through fermenting to bottling. You can also taste and purchase the wines they produce. The Barossa is noted for its fine table wines, but also produces sherry and brandy. Check locally for the hours the wineries are open.

During odd-numbered years, the Barossa Valley celebrates the vintage with a large-scale, 7-day festival in late March or early April. Activities include processions, feasting, wine sampling, grape stomping contests, folk dancing in German costumes, and crowning of a Vintage Queen. Headquarters for all these activities is Tanunda.

You can drive to the Barossa on your own or take a full-day coach tour from Adelaide. You'll find accommodations (hotels, motels, and caravan parks) at Lyndoch, Tanunda, Nuriootpa, and Angaston.

Clare Valley

About 136 km/83 miles north of Adelaide is a smaller district with considerable charm. Within Clare Valley are the towns of Clare and Watervale.

Clare—named after County Clare, Ireland—is a peaceful agricultural center with unusual bluestone cottages and other buildings dating back to the area's settlement in the early 1800s. The surrounding countryside offers vineyards divided by woodlands and scenic gorges. One unique way to explore the area is in a Cobb & Co. horse-drawn coach. A special weekend tour, starting at Waterloo, includes gourmet dinners, picnic lunches, and a 4-hour coach journey to historic Martindale Hall near Mintaro. This Georgian-style mansion was featured in the Australian film *Picnic at Hanging Rock*.

There are in the district about 12 wineries, including Chateau Clare, Mitchell Cellars, Sevenhill Cellars, Robertson's Clare Vineyards, and Wendouree Cellars. Wines produced in the area include whites, reds, and sherries.

You'll find accommodations (hotels, motels, and caravan parks) in Auburn, Watervale, Penwortham, Sevenhill, and Clare.

Southern Vales district

Still another wine district—the Southern Vales—is to be found about 32 km/20 miles due south of Adelaide on the Fleurieu Peninsula (see page 89). The charm of this area is the large number of small, family-owned wineries you can explore. Nearby are the southern coast's beaches.

Winery touring. About 40 wineries have regular visiting hours Monday through Sunday. Area wineries include Reynella, Old Clarendon, Maxwells, Hardy's, Kay Bros., and Sea View. The Southern Vales district is known for its red wines in particular.

Bushing Festival. McLaren Vale is the scene of this 7-day festival in October. Activities include wine tasting, winery tours, dancing, and an Elizabethan feast in costume.

Ol' Man Murray

Rising in the Australian Alps between Melbourne and Canberra, Australia's longest river—the Murray—flows for much of its 2,589-km/1,609-mile route between Victoria and New South Wales, forming those states' boundaries. However, near the end of its run, it meanders through 644 km/400 miles of South Australia. Just before it terminates its course at Encounter Bay, it widens into Lake Alexandrina.

Constantly changing its course over the centuries, the river has left a wide swath of rich bottom land now used for vineyards, orchards, and dairy farms. The riverfront towns serve not only as farming centers for these agricultural regions, but also as river resorts. The river provides excellent opportunities for fishing (no license required in South Australia), water-skiing, and boating.

From Adelaide, there's a coach tour to Goolwa at the mouth of the Murray River. There's also regular coach service from Adelaide to Goolwa, Murray Bridge, Loxton, Renmark, Barmera, Berri, and Mannum.

You'll find accommodations (hotels, motels, caravan parks, and campgrounds) all along the river. Fully self-contained houseboats are also available for rent.

Wineries. The development of irrigation along the Murray River opened this great river valley to productive vineyards between 1915 and 1930. Extensive vineyards around the towns of Barmera, Berri, Loxton, and Renmark provide the grapes for a number of winery cooperatives, as well as for small, independent wineries. All are open for inspection; check locally for visiting hours.

Dessert and appetizer wines were the early specialties of this area, but table wines of sound quality and reasonable price are rapidly increasing in volume.

River cruises. At one time the Murray River was an important trade route for Australia's inland cities. Wool, grain, and timber were transported down the river and supplies shipped up the river. With the advent of rail transport, this river traffic died. Today's river traffic consists mainly of pleasure craft and small passenger boats.

A variety of passenger vessels cruise the Murray. Among the favorite trips: The *Murray River Queen*, an 86-passenger, diesel-powered paddle wheeler, takes 5½ days on a trip from Goolwa to Swan Reach. The 120-passenger, paddle wheeler *Murray Princess* cruises from Renmark to Loxton and back. The paddle wheeler *Proud Mary* offers both 5-day and weekend cruises on the river.

Coonawarra

The most southerly of South Australia's wine districts, Coonawarra, lies 435 km/270 miles southeast of Adelaide close to the Victoria border. The rich volcanic soil of this region produces some of Australia's most sought-after red wines.

The area remains unspoiled farm country. Among area wineries are Mildara, Wynn's, Lindeman's Rouge Homme, Penfold's, Hungerford Hill, Redbank, and Brand's. Most have weekday visiting hours.

The rugged outback

Few places on the face of the earth are less hospitable to man than the Australian outback, that vast area occupying all but the coastal rim of the continent.

Nearly two-thirds of South Australia is outback, yet only 1 percent of the state's populace lives in it. A handful of station owners and opal miners endure a place where temperatures can touch 49°C/120°F and where rains come so seldom that the huge watershed called Lake Eyre goes for years at a time without so much as a puddle to justify its name. But when the rains come, they come. The lake gets deep enough for swimming every so often, and once it even had enough water to allow a shipwreck.

Dry or wet, the outback is no place to go alone as a stranger. Distances are cruelly long, roads few, and water questionable. But if the outback appeals to you at all, go, for this is dramatic country. Settlements in the Flinders Range and at the old silver mines of Broken Hill provide quick samplers. There are also tours from the Flinders area that get you deep into the outback.

The colorful Flinders Ranges

The Flinders Ranges provide a majestic slice of the outback. Rising abruptly from the plains near Crystal Brook (193 km/120 miles north of Adelaide), these spectacular mountain ranges offer 800 km/500 miles of multicolored cliffs, granite peaks, and razor-backed ridges. Steep gorges, many cut by creeks and cooled by deep water holes, have majestic gum trees.

The beauty of the Flinders lies not only in their ruggedness, but also in colors that change with the light of day. At sunrise, they are flaming rust and red; as the day progresses they mellow to blues, purples, and rich browns. Still more color comes to these mountains in September and October when wild hops, daisies, and Sturt peas all brighten the terrain after a spring rain.

You'll find that the Flinders Ranges' coolest months are April through October. Six-day coach tours from Adelaide provide the easiest way to visit the Flinders Ranges. Secondary roads can be primitive and treacherous after heavy rains; floods are not uncommon. Hotels, motels, caravan parks, and campgrounds are available in the main resorts of Wilpena Pound and Arkaroola, and in other smaller towns throughout the ranges.

Broken Hill—City of silver

To the world's mining community, Broken Hill represents one of the greatest mineral discoveries of the past 100 years. Chanced upon in 1883 by a range-rider, it has since become known as the world's largest silver-zinc-lead lode—152 meters/500 feet wide and as much as 610 meters/2,000 feet deep.

Though Broken Hill is located in New South Wales (1,190 km/739 miles west of Sydney), it is only 48 km/30 miles over the border from South Australia and most easily reached from Adelaide (402 km/250 miles southwest). Kendell Airlines operates between Adelaide and Broken Hill. There's also rail and bus service.

PERTH

In Western Australia, a pleasant city & rich hinterlands

Perth is the principal urban area on Australia's west coast, and it's one of the country's prettiest and most livable cities. In and near Perth, miles of uncrowded beaches bask beneath a reliable sun. Not far inland, good wine is made, and the remains of a great gold rush still cough up an occasional nugget.

The vast state of Western Australia is three times the size of Texas. With more than a million square miles of land and a population not much over one million, it makes the American West look crowded. Eight out of 10 people live in or near Perth, making for a startling difference between cosmopolitan city and hinterland.

For many years Western Australia found itself left off the itineraries of many foreign visitors to Australia because it is so remote from the major east coast cities. However, now that Perth is Australia's gateway to Asia and a growing headquarters for mining, visitors have become numerous. Perth received still more recognition as a travel destination when it hosted sailing enthusiasts from around the world during the America's Cup races in 1986–87.

Perth—A booming capital

In 1829, Perth's founders chose their city's location for its beauty. They plotted their first few streets in low, rolling hills on the right bank of the Swan River where it broadens almost into a bay just before running into the Indian Ocean. Little did they realize their small start would grow to a thriving metropolitan area with 1 million people.

The first wave of growth and prosperity didn't come until the turn of the century, when gold was discovered east of Perth, in Coolgardie and Kalgoorlie. The second wave has yet to crest; with the recent discovery of iron and other minerals in the north, the city booms anew.

In spite of its growth, Perth retains the beauty that first attracted its founders. Residents still enjoy the Swan River for its swimmable waters, and its banks as public parklands. Throughout Perth, in fact, parks with flower gardens and ornamental lakes soften the harshness of urban concrete and glass.

In town or out, it is easy to be outdoors. The city enjoys a year-round average of 8 hours of sunshine a day, yet temperatures remain mild. Even in the hottest month, February, the thermometer averages a comfortable 24°C/75°F. When temperatures start to soar, a cooling, after-

noon sea breeze—affectionately called the "Fremantle Doctor"—regularly blows in from Fremantle on the Indian Ocean. It's no wonder, then, that even the city's musicians and actors move outdoors for part of their seasons, and that the whole populace swims, surfs, sails, or otherwise plays in the sun.

With the city's downtown charms amplified by mile after mile of sweeping sandy beaches along the Indian Ocean, and the Darling Range offering limitless bushwalking possibilities a short distance to the east, it's no wonder Perth is so oriented to the outdoors.

The urban core

Perched on the far edge of Australia, Perth looks toward Asia as well as back to Australia's European or English heritage. The result is a diverse cosmopolitanism reflected in every aspect of life from music to food to sport.

Landmarks. Downtown Perth is a city of old and new. Because of today's prosperity in Western Australia, countless high-rises have sprung up in the downtown area. Preserved in the shadows of these glass and steel towers are some of Perth's first major buildings, richly textured classics painstakingly built by convict labor imported a few years after the city was founded. Many of these reminders of Western Australia's pioneers can be found downtown in the Barrack Street area.

At the corner of Hay and Barrack streets, Perth's Town Hall resembles an English Jacobean market hall complete with clock tower. It was built by convicts between 1867 and 1870. Around the corner on St. George's Terrace is the colonial-style Treasury Building dating from 1874.

Perth's oldest public building, the Old Court House, sits sheltered among trees in the Supreme Court Gardens. Built in 1836, the Georgian-style building today houses the Law Society of Western Australia behind its stately columns.

At the head of tree-lined St. George's Terrace, Barracks Archway stands in front of the modern brick home of the state parliament. Built in Tudor style, the brick arch is all

Christmas decorations add color to Perth's Hay Street Mall. Pedestrian promenade between William and Barrack streets allows car-free shopping and provides umbrella-shaded spots for resting.

that remains of barracks that housed soldier settlers in the 1860s. When Parliament is not in session, visitors can tour Parliament House at 11:15 A.M. and 3:15 P.M. Monday through Friday.

Across the Narrows Bridge in South Perth, the Old Mill, where Perth's first flour was ground, today houses a folk museum of early colonial artifacts. Visitors are welcome on Saturdays from 1 to 4 P.M., and on Sundays, Mondays, Wednesdays, and Thursdays from 1 to 5 P.M.

Museum and art gallery. The Western Australia Museum (entrance on Francis Street) features exhibits from the state's gold rush days, the skeleton of a blue whale, the Mundrabilla meteorite, and an Aboriginal gallery. Perth's first jail, built in 1856, has been extensively restored and is now part of the museum complex. The Old Perth Gaol, one of the city's best examples of colonial architecture, houses historical displays on western Australia's early days.

Hours are 10:30 A.M. to 5 P.M. Monday through Saturday, and 1 to 5 P.M. Sunday.

Near the museum, you can browse through the Western Australia Art Gallery (47 James Street). The collections include both traditional and contemporary paintings, prints, drawings, and sculptures. The gallery is open daily from 10 A.M. to 5 P.M.

Shoppers' paradise. Opals and other gemstones, Aboriginal arts and crafts, and Western Australian iron ore jewelry are the most distinctively local products. Shops and stores are equally distinctive.

Three blocks of Hay Street, between William and Barrack streets, have been set aside as a pedestrian promenade where shoppers can stroll or stop to relax on seats beneath giant parasols. Where cars once parked, trees in movable pots add a softening touch of greenery.

Branching away from this central mall are traffic-free shopping arcades called Piccadilly, National Mutual, City, Trinity, Plaza, and Wanamba. London Court is of special note. This narrow walkway may make you feel you have stepped back in time to 16th century London. In it, some 50 small shops are housed in Tudor-style buildings. Noteworthy clocks mark the court's entrances.

Normal shopping hours are from 8:30 A.M. to 5:30 P.M. Monday through Friday, 8:30 A.M. to noon on Saturday. Most stores stay open until 9 P.M. on Thursday.

After the sun goes down. During the Festival of Perth—February and March—the city is alive with plays, films, and music in both indoor and outdoor settings. But festival time isn't the only busy time for the performing arts.

The Perth Concert Hall on St. George's Terrace and the Perth Music Shell in Supreme Court Gardens hold concerts by the Western Australia Symphony and other well-known orchestras.

Both the Hole in the Wall and the Playhouse Theatre offer dinner with a show. And in nearby Crawley, the University of Western Australia's Dolphin Theatre stages drama, dance, and string ensemble music.

On Wellington Street, the 8,000-seat Perth Entertainment Centre hosts performances by pop performers (and is also the site of tennis tournaments and boxing matches). Some of the city's larger hotel cocktail lounges book live entertainment. The Burswood Island Resort casino is one of the world's largest.

A useful source of entertainment possibilities is *This Week in Perth,* available in hotels or from the Western Australian Government Travel Centre.

Things to do outdoors

The people of Perth spend as much time outdoors as they can. The mild climate lends itself to a multitude of recreational endeavors, many of them water-related. Australian Rules football, horse races, yacht races, and lawn bowls are favored spectator sports.

All aboard the Indian-Pacific

In today's fast-paced world where speedy transportation is the key, it's nice to know that Australia offers visitors a more leisurely form of travel on a great train—the *Indian-Pacific.*

As it makes its runs between Perth and Sydney, this train allows its passengers to really see some of the Australian countryside. During its 3,959-km/2,460-mile journey, the *Indian-Pacific* stops at places like Kalgoorlie, a town with an interesting gold rush past, and streaks across the Nullarbor Plain, a treeless expanse with the longest straight stretch of railroad track in the world.

There are times when you think that Australia's entire landscape is nothing but clumps of blue green bushes, a scattering of gum trees, and endless red earth. Then the scene from the train window changes and becomes a more pastoral green, with rolling hills and grazing sheep. Throughout the journey, there is always the possibility of spotting Australian wildlife—perhaps even an emu or kangaroo.

Passengers making this 65-hour journey from coast to coast ride in air-conditioned comfort. Both first-class and economy fares include all meals as well as sleepers. Among other luxuries are an observation lounge, bar, and music room complete with a piano.

If you want to climb aboard for a ride on the *Indian-Pacific,* be sure and make your reservations well in advance for this popular trip. The *Indian-Pacific* runs three round trips a week between Perth and Sydney.

The *Trans-Australia Express* makes the run between Perth and Port Pirie two times a week with connections to Adelaide.

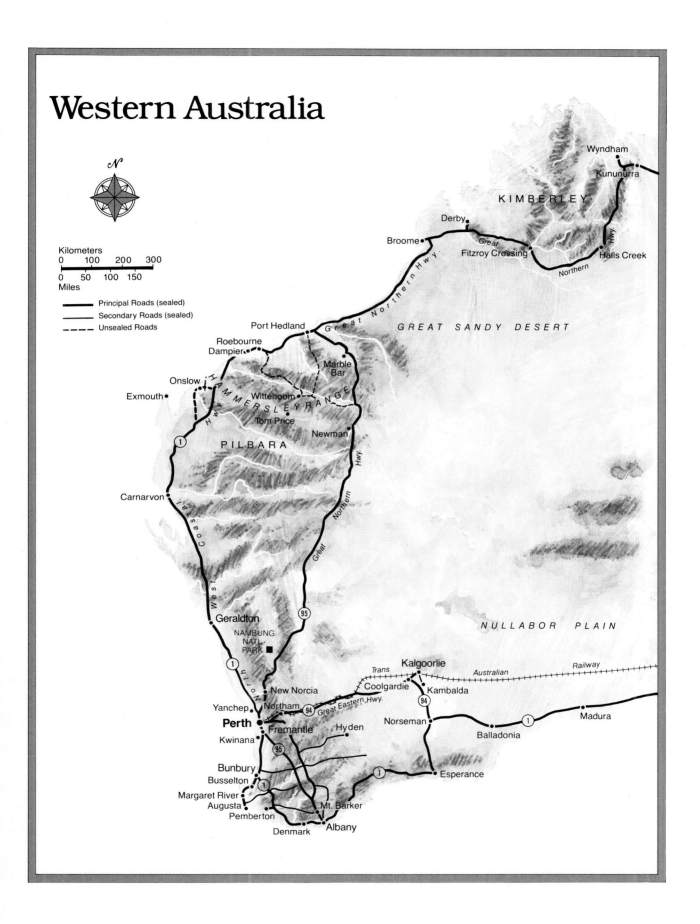

Western Australia

Kilometers
0   100   200   300
0   50   100   150
Miles

—— Principal Roads (sealed)
—— Secondary Roads (sealed)
- - - - Unsealed Roads

KIMBERLEY

Wyndham
Kununurra
Derby
Broome
Great Fitzroy Crossing
Halls Creek
Northern

Great Northern Hwy.

GREAT SANDY DESERT

Port Hedland
Roebourne
Dampier
Marble Bar
Onslow
HAMMERSLEY RANGE
Wittenoom
Exmouth
Tom Price
Newman
PILBARA

Carnarvon

West Coast Hwy.

Great Northern Hwy.

NULLABOR PLAIN

Geraldton
NAMBUNG NATL. PARK

Kalgoorlie
Trans   Australian   Railway
Coolgardie
New Norcia
Kambalda
Yanchep
Northam
Great Eastern Hwy.
Perth
Norseman
Madura
Fremantle
Hyden
Kwinana
Balladonia
Bunbury
Busselton
Esperance
Margaret River
Augusta
Mt. Barker
Pemberton
Albany
Denmark

High-necked black swans, native to Australia, eagerly accept food from cautious visitors at Lake Monger outside Perth.

Zooming in for a closer look, vacationers watch boat heading into Lake Argyle. Australia's largest man-made lake is a recreation area for bush walking, fishing, and water sports.

Strolling through the park. Perth offers a variety of verdant parklands. The pride of the city is King's Park—a short bus trip or drive southwest of downtown. The 405-hectare/1,000-acre reserve features both natural and cultivated bushland.

Footpaths and roads wind through the park. You can purchase guidebooks and a map at the entrance kiosk. Mount Eliza, at the northeast end of the park, provides views of Perth and the distant Darling Range.

From August through October, you can delight in a myriad of wildflowers—labeled with wonderfully descriptive names such as bacon and eggs, kangaroo paw, one-sided bottle-bush, and white spider orchid.

At the eastern end of Hay Street, you can retreat into Queen's Gardens with its lakes, footbridges, lily ponds, sloping lawns, and weeping willow trees. Children will adore the Peter Pan statue—a replica of the one in London's Kensington Gardens.

The Zoological Gardens in South Perth house rare native animals in a garden setting. Don't miss the walk-through aviary, the wallaby enclosure in a bushland setting, and the nocturnal animal house. The zoo is open daily from 10 A.M. to 5 P.M. You can reach the zoo via the Barrack Street ferry or a bus crossing the Narrows Bridge.

Sports to watch. In Perth, as in Melbourne, Adelaide, and Tasmania, Australian Rules football has an avid following: nearly a million spectators a year pack club ovals.

Cricket matches (including International Test Matches) are held at the Western Australia Cricket Association Oval at the end of Hay Street in East Perth.

Saturday horse race meetings—another popular Perth pastime—are held winters at Belmont Park and summers at Ascot. Gloucester Park Raceway in East Perth features Friday evening harness racing October through July. Richmond Raceway in Fremantle also hosts monthly harness races. To see greyhounds racing, go to the Cannington Dog Track on Albany Highway on a Saturday night.

Fun in the sun. Perth is an ideal city in which to enjoy outdoor sports. Water activities head the list.

West of the city stretch miles of Indian Ocean beaches. Skilled surfers will want to check out Cottesloe, City, and Scarborough beaches. For gentler waters try Leighton or North Beach.

The Swan River supports all forms of aquatic sports—yachting, speedboat racing, swimming, canoeing, rowing, and water-skiing. Crawley Beach near the University of Western Australia and Como Beach south of Perth are both ideal for sun-bathing.

Those who fish can work fresh or salt water. Deep-sea catches include blue marlin, mackerel, and tuna. Charter boats berth at Barrack Street Jetty and Fremantle. Fresh-water fishers will find good summer trout fishing in rivers and dams south of Perth.

You'll need a license for fresh-water fishing or for catching crayfish and prawns. For more information about licenses and fishing in Western Australia stop by the head office of the Fisheries and Fauna Department at 108 Adelaide Terrace in Perth.

For golf, Wembley—one of a dozen public courses in Perth—is a challenging 18-hole test. For a quick workout, the 9-hole Embleton course serves well.

Public tennis courts are scattered throughout the city. Contact the Perth City Council Parks & Gardens section for information on booking a court.

Downriver to Fremantle

Fremantle, just 19 km/12 miles downriver from Perth, is the city's port and Australia's main western gateway to the Indian Ocean. Yachts competing in the America's Cup challenge races in 1986–87 docked at Fremantle's expanded marina facilities.

Established as a colony in 1829 by Captain Charles H. Fremantle, the town retains the feeling of those early colonial days—narrow streets, a city square with a fountain, and architecture emphasizing Dutch gables and Gothic cloisters. Many of the early stone buildings were built by convict labor.

Museums. The colony's first insane asylum, built in the 1860s, now houses the Fremantle Museum. The old building, located on Finnerty Street, is considered one of the finest examples of convict colonial architecture in Western Australia.

One wing of the building features a living arts center where local artists can work and exhibit their creations. During the summer months, the building's courtyard serves as an open-air stage for performances. Museum hours are 10:30 A.M. to 5 P.M. Monday through Thursday, and 1 to 5 P.M. Friday through Sunday.

Still another example of Fremantle's early architecture is the Round House Gaol at the end of High Street. Built in the 1830s, this 12-sided building with eight cells served as the colony's first jail. Today, it is a historical museum, open weekend afternoons.

The Maritime Museum, in a restored building on Cliff Street, houses memorabilia from wrecked ships, antique weapons and armor, and old photographs. It is open afternoons, Friday through Sunday.

Fremantle Markets. More than 100 stalls filled with an exotic array of seafood, fruits and vegetables, herbs and spices, jewelry, and handicrafts lure passers-by into Fremantle Markets at Henderson Street and South Terrace. Operating since 1898, they resemble old European markets. You can browse through the market on Fridays from 9 A.M. to 9 P.M. and on Saturdays from 9 A.M. to 1 P.M.

How to get there. Suburban trains and buses connect Perth and Fremantle. Half-day tours feature a river cruise to Fremantle from Perth.

Escape to Rottnest Island

This popular summer resort lies just offshore from Fremantle opposite the mouth of the Swan River. The tiny, low-lying island offers beautiful beaches and clear waters teeming with colorful marine life.

In 1917 Rottnest was declared a permanent public reserve and wildlife sanctuary. The island is home for the rare marsupial known as a *quokka*. The first Dutch seamen to see this midget-size kangaroo mistook it for a rat, thus the island's name—"Rats' Nest."

From 1850 to 1903, the island served as a penal settlement. Convicts built many of the limestone buildings you'll see in your island exploration.

The essentials

Perth serves as Australia's gateway to the Orient, and so is a busier transportation hub than its isolation might suggest.

Getting there. Perth is served by air, sea, rail, and bus.

Air. International service by Qantas and foreign flag carriers. Domestic flights to and from other states by Ansett, Australian, and East-West airlines. Flights within the state by Skywest and Ansett W.A. airlines. Perth's airport is 11 km/7 miles from downtown; bus and taxi services are available.

Sea. International cruise and passenger/cargo ships call at Fremantle, 19 km/12 miles west of Perth. Taxis, trains, and buses link piers with city center.

Rail. The famous *Indian-Pacific* train connects Sydney with Perth. The *Trans-Australia Express* connects Perth with Port Pirie. (See page 96.)

Bus. Ansett Pioneer, Greyhound, and Deluxe travel between Perth and Adelaide on the Eyre Highway. Hardy visitors may consider driving this same highway, but the desolate Nullarbor Plain makes the trip a grueling one.

Tours. Eastern-based tour operators offer package trips to Perth and rest of Western Australia as supplements to regularly scheduled trips.

Accommodations. Major Perth hotels include the Ansett International, Burswood Island Resort, Merlin, Parmelia Hilton International, Perth Ambassador, Perth Parkroyal, Orchard, Sheraton Perth, and Transit Inn.

Food and drink. Local seafood is abundant and savory. Try Westralian Dhufish (succulent white meat), rock lobster (locally named crayfish), crab, and tiger prawns. The usual range of ethnic and national cuisines plus some unusual Asian cookery are to be had; restaurants of all types cluster in downtown area.

Local wines from Swan River Valley vineyards include Houghtons and Sandalford. Major local beer is Swan Lager. (Unlicensed restaurants allow customers to bring own bottles for modest corkage fee.)

Getting around. Metropolitan Transport Trust operates bus, train, and ferry services within city and to suburbs as distant as Fremantle. For map and information, visit that office's information bureau, 125 St. George's Terrace. The free clipper-bus service circles the city Monday through Saturday; trips to Perth's scenic spots are made Sunday mornings and afternoons. Ferries to South Perth use Barrack Street Jetty. Taxis are plentiful.

Tours. Full and half-day city tours are available. Also available are tours to Fremantle (see page 99), Rottnest Island (page 99), Swan Valley vineyards (this page), Yanchep Park (this page), Darling Range (this page), and to a number of beach towns south of Perth (page 101).

For more information. Holiday W.A. Travel Centre, 772 Hay Street, Perth 6000.

Accommodations and activities. Even the island's accommodations reflect the history of Rottnest. The Lodge was the original prison complex and the Quokka Arms Hotel was once a summer residence for Western Australia's governors. Other island accommodations include cottages and a camping area where you can rent tents or bring your own camping gear. It's advisable to reserve accommodations well in advance.

Since the island has no private cars, bicycles are the most popular form of transportation. The less energetic can take a half-day bus tour.

How to get there. Ferries and hydrofoils travel daily to Rottnest, many by way of Fremantle. The ferry takes about 2 hours; by hydrofoil it's only 65 minutes. There is also air service to the island from Perth.

Other nearby jaunts

By bus tour or car, it's easy to visit a number of other interesting destinations during your stay in Perth. Here are a few trips you might want to consider.

The Darling Range. A trip to the Darling Range, 26 km/16 miles east of Perth, takes you into the 1,619-hectare/4,000-acre John Forrest National Park. Its scenic drives wind through the park, and hilltop view points provide sweeping vistas out across the plains to the sea. Facilities include a swimming pool, picnic areas, walking tracks, and sport grounds.

This wooded country, laced with streams and waterfalls, and ablaze with wildflowers in spring, was once an Aboriginal camping ground. Nearby is the Mundaring Weir (dam), starting point for a 563-km/350-mile pipeline to the eastern gold fields. The old No. 1 pumping station for the weir has been turned into a museum.

Yanchep Park. This 2,428-hectare/6,000-acre bushland reserve preserves not only wildlife and flora but also beautiful limestone caves. Located only 51 km/32 miles north of Perth, the coastal park has several small hotels, a golf course, tennis courts, a man-made lake, an aquatic entertainment center, and a swimming pool.

Daily tours explore the caves. In Crystal Cave—the main grotto—a quiet underground stream reflects images of stalactites and stalagmites. Other park attractions include a large koala colony and spring wildflower walks.

Swan Valley vineyards. A half-hour trip up the Swan River from central Perth brings you to the heart of Western Australia's wine country. There you can visit over 20 wineries including Houghtons, Sandalford, and Valencia. Bus and boat tours are available from Perth.

Beyond Perth

Perth and its environs, however attractive, are only a small part of Western Australia. The rest includes a southwest coast rich in beach resorts, explorable caves, forests, and wildflowers. To the northwest, colorful fishing villages dot the coast. Inland, rich mineral deposits have resulted in other attractions, and Lake Argyle provides recreational facilities. Due east are gold fields and ghost towns.

Into the southwest

Perth's residents flock to the southwest on vacation. Though they can sun-bathe, swim, surf, fish, sail, and play golf and tennis at home, in the southwest they can enjoy the same pleasures far from city pressures.

The major coastal resort towns all have hotels, motels, caravan parks and campgrounds near their beaches. Bunbury and Busselton are just down the coast from Perth; Augusta sits at the tip of the continent where the Indian Ocean gives way to the Great Australian Bight. Albany is on the bight. All of these towns are served by buses and trains; tour operators even make loop trips of the area.

Spelunkers' paradise. At the southwestern tip of the state stands a limestone cliff riddled with caves for almost 97 km/60 miles.

Along with stalactites and stalagmites, viewers can see rarer shawls—thin sheets of limestone projecting at right angles from the cave walls. Beautiful underground rivers flow through some of these caves, while quiet lakes mirror the fragile beauty of others. Four of these caves—Yallingup, Mammoth, Lake, and Augusta Jewel—have been developed with walkways and lights for tourists.

Hardwood giants. In a rain-soaked region near Pemberton, magnificent forests of karris loom out of the landscape. The karri is a huge species of eucalyptus. One giant, the Gloucester Tree, cradles one of the world's highest natural fire lookouts—61 meters/200 feet above the forest floor.

Wildflower country. Few places can boast such a profusion of wildflowers. Indeed, many of the species are unique to Western Australia.

From August to October, large areas of the southwest are carpeted with brightly colored spring wildflowers. While blue is the predominant color, you'll also see brilliant yellows, pale pinks, and glowing reds. One of the most notable places to find flowers is around Albany.

East to the gold fields

In the 1890s the shout of "Gold" rang out from the tiny communities of Coolgardie and Kalgoorlie, and the rush was on. Eager for riches, prospectors came in droves from the eastern Australian colonies and other parts of the world. From Fremantle, they rode on horseback or in camel-drawn coaches. Many even walked the entire 550 km/342 miles behind their wheelbarrows.

Towns appeared overnight at the peak, when as many as 200,000 prospectors roamed the rolling plains. Once the easy pickings on the surface were gone, these communities died as quickly as they were born. Coolgardie has become a ghost town, leaving Kalgoorlie the only active community.

At the turn of the century, Kalgoorlie's "Golden Mile" was known as one of the world's richest square miles of rock, yielding more than 34 million ounces of gold. Today the take is greatly reduced. But even if the easy pickings are gone, it's still worth looking around. In 1979, a local father and son prospecting team found a nugget weighing about 120 ounces worth $50,000 the day they dug it up. Visitors are allowed to poke about for the price of a miner's right.

For the quieter gold speculators, the former British Arms Hotel, which once housed the miners, now serves the public as the Golden Mile Museum, housing mining memorabilia. A short distance south of town, the Hainault Tourist Mine lets visitors descend 62 meters/203 feet into the earth by elevator on several daily tours.

Coolgardie, located west of Kalgoorlie, is probably Australia's most famous ghost town. Today, all that remains of the roaring boom town of 15,000—once known as the queen of the gold fields—are a few hotels, the Railway Station Museum, the Goldfields Museum, and a few crumbling stone buildings. Coolgardie is currently being restored as a gold rush memorial.

If possible, visit the gold fields during the winter months of June, July, and August. Summers—December through March—can be unbearably hot. Accommodations include campgrounds, small motels, and hotels.

A train rightly called *The Prospector* makes the 8-hour journey from Perth to Kalgoorlie. Passengers on the *Indian-Pacific* or *Trans-Australia Express* trains may stop off at Kalgoorlie. There's also air service from Perth. Local tour operators offer a variety of tours as well.

The remote north

The northern part of Western Australia is a frontier giant just beginning to feel its strength. Machines are beginning to tap rich deposits of iron ore and other minerals that could determine the financial future not only of the state, but also that of all of Australia.

For visitors, the principal charms range along the coast in a series of sweeping beaches and fishing villages. Inland, on the Kimberley Plateau, a manmade lake with nine times more water than Sydney Harbour is the main attraction. The mining district around Pilbara is at once surprisingly civilized and astonishingly beautiful with gorges and other natural scenery.

Nambung National Park. Located 257 km/160 miles north of Perth, Nambung is famous for its Pinnacles Desert. The "pinnacles" studding this coastal desert were once forest trees—but the forest is petrified now, the trees turned into odd-looking limestone pillars by the forces of time, wind, and weather. The pillars range from 1 to 5m/3½ to 17 feet in height; bright white sand surrounds them. Tours from Perth explore this area.

The Kimberley Plateau. The broad, high plains of the plateau have been carved by an unexpected wealth of water into pyramids and other dramatic shapes. But the most unexpected feature of the whole region is Lake Argyle. The harnessing of the Ord River and other northern streams formed the lake, which dwarfs Sydney Harbour. Lake Argyle Tourist Village has ample accommodations.

The Pilbara. The reason behind the quickening development of Western Australia is the mineral wealth buried in the Hamersley Range.

The Hamersley Iron Company's model town called Tom Price has such comforts as public swimming pools and tennis courts to cheer visitors, but the red-rock gorges of the Fortesque River System are the major attraction in this region. A rough but passable mine road between Tom Price and Wittenoom touches the finest gorges: Dales, Wittenoom, Yampire, and Hamersley.

NORTHERN TERRITORY

From the tropics of Darwin to the outback of Alice Springs

Australia's Northern Territory is one of the world's last frontiers. Massive and empty, it stretches roughly 1,600 km/1,000 miles from north to south and 933 km/580 miles east to west. Covering nearly a sixth of Australia's land area, the Northern Territory provides a multitude of scenic contrasts. In the north, commonly referred to as the Top End, there are tropical bushlands and swamps. Farther south is the Centre, in the heart of Australia. Here you'll find the rugged beauty of the MacDonnell Ranges, the massive bulk of Ayers Rock, and a landscape of scrub and gum trees.

Only two towns of any size will be found in the territory—Darwin, the capital on the northern coast, and Alice Springs, in the geographic center of the continent.

Darwin, a tropical capital

Darwin is not only the governmental center for the Northern Territory, it is also the gateway to a land rich in tropical vegetation and wildlife. Within easy reach of the capital, you can visit areas where wild water buffaloes roam and crocodiles bask in the sun.

Nearly half the Top End's residents (64,000) call Darwin home. Darwin is an international gateway to Southeast Asia. It is also a strategic commercial center.

Built on a peninsula on the eastern shore of Port Darwin, the city has not always had a happy history. The town, located in the middle of the Indian Ocean cyclone belt, has been hit directly by devastating cyclones (hurricanes) three times—in 1897, 1937, and most recently in 1974. During World War II, Darwin was the target of numerous Japanese air raids. But like the phoenix, each time the city meets destruction it rises anew.

Today, Darwin is a modern city of well-planned commercial and residential areas, attractive public gardens, recreation parks, and tree-lined streets.

When planning a trip to Darwin, take into account that the Top End has just two seasons—"the Wet" and "the Dry." The season known simply as "the Dry" (April to October) has warm, cloudless days and balmy nights. It's a pleasant time to visit Darwin and its environs. Heavy rains and high humidity, however, prevail during "the Wet" or monsoon season from November through April. Roads become flooded and impassable and excursions impossible.

Sightseeing in Darwin

Darwin offers sightseers modern city buildings; a few historical buildings including the Government House; the N.T. Museum of Arts and Natural Sciences with its historical displays; the Artillery Museum at East Point, complete with World War II blockhouses, command posts, and observation towers; and the Indo Pacific Marine, a collection of tanks filled with sea life.

Parks and gardens. Darwin's 14-hectare/34-acre Botanical Garden features tropical flora—frangipani, hibiscus, coconut palms, poinciana, and bougainvillea. In contrast, Yarrawonga Park, 21 km/13 miles southeast of town, is a small, private zoological garden that allows you a close look at wild water buffaloes, brolgas, emus, dingoes, and snakes.

A little shopping. Darwin's stores offer a wide range of Aboriginal products. The Arnhem Land Aboriginal Art Gallery, corner of Knuckey and Cavenagh streets, carries fabric designs, woodcarvings, and paintings.

Fun in the sun

Warm tropical weather makes Darwin ideal for swimming, skin-diving, water-skiing, sun-bathing, sailing, fishing, and beachcombing. Among the best of the silver-sand beaches are Mindil, Casuarina, and Dripstone. Swimming is impossible, however, between October and May because of the sea wasps (jellyfish) floating near the surface; their poisonous tentacles can produce fatal stings.

Ascending Ayers Rock is only for the physically fit, though chain rail gives climbers a boost. The less active can await companions' return on thoughtfully placed benches at base.

THE CLIMBING OF THE ROCK
IS DIFFICULT AND DANGEROUS.
THE PARK AUTHORITY ACCEPTS
NO RESPONSIBILITY FOR INJURY
OR LOSS OF LIFE TO ANY PERSON.
RESCUE GEAR IS AVAILABLE AT
THE RANGERS OFFICE.

· BY ORDER OF THE BOARD · AL ROSE CHAIRMAN ·

Fishing. Deep-sea fishing is ideal off the coast of Darwin. Catches include queenfish, Spanish mackerel, and coral trout. Fresh-water offerings include barramundi.

Tennis and golf. For information on tennis, contact the Northern Territory Tennis Association on Gilruth Avenue. The Darwin Golf Club on McMillans Road allows public play.

Sports around the clock

The hot climate fails to dampen the Australians' zest for recreation, with some 40 active and spectator sports available. Three codes of football are played. Both men and women compete in hockey. Basketball is played at night; during the day, baseball, cricket, and softball keep people busy.

One event unique to the area is the Beer Can Raft Regatta. The regatta is held in early June each year at Mindil Beach. Some 60 to 80 boats, built only of beer cans or soft drink cans, hold a 1-day regatta. Some are sailing craft, some paddle boats, some speed boats with 100-horse-power motors—all competing in different classes. Some of the boats use six to eight thousand empty cans in their construction, but with Darwin such a hot and thirsty land, there's no real shortage of building material.

Excursions from Darwin

Darwin serves as an excellent base from which to explore the surrounding countryside. Your excursions can include geological and wildlife phenomena and Aboriginal rock paintings.

The outback region of the Northern Territory is a living museum, populated by animals and birds that are—in many cases—the last remaining specimens of some of the world's most unusual wildlife. You can watch emus running through the mulga and saltbush, kangaroos standing up to survey the land, and dingoes circling safari camps like trained dogs. Along the swamp coastline and near water holes, you'll find the air thick with birds. Pelicans catch fish in the shallows of the swamps and long-legged spoonbills dabble in the marshes. Lagoons and northern rivers abound with giant barramundi (a superb table fish), saratago, catfish, mullet, and saw fish.

Darwin tour operators arrange excursions including the best of these attractions, with travel by coach, launch, car, jeep, or light aircraft. For a full listing of trip possibilities, contact the Northern Territory Government Tourist Bureau in Los Angeles (see page 16 for address).

Close-in excursions

Several close-in attractions may be reached on your own, or on a local tour.

Magnetic anthills. These wedge-shaped architectural wonders can be found at Howard and Berry springs, 24 km/15 miles and 64 km/40 miles south of the city. You'll see thousands of these hard mud mounds, some reaching 6 meters/20 feet in height and 2 meters/6 feet in width. White termites (not ants) construct these hill nests on a north/south axis—thus the name "magnetic anthills."

Fogg Dam Bird Sanctuary. Thousands of birds gather in and around the water lily-covered reservoir of this sanctuary, 58 km/36 miles southeast of Darwin. Nearby, wild buffalo tread the open plains. Sunrise is a good time to visit the sanctuary—just before the light of day, an eerie quiet pervades the area. As the sun brightens the landscape, this quiet gives way to a deafening sound of animals awakening to a new day.

Nearby are the remains of an experimental rice farm at Humpty Doo.

Aboriginal rock paintings

Among the wild red rocks and forests of the Northern Territory, Aborigines dream of times now past. Their cultural roots in Australia go back more than 30,000 years—that's how long ago scientists think the first Aborigines began to arrive from the north.

The Aborigines recorded their dreamtime (beginnings of time) with paintings on cave walls and on the sides of smooth cliffs beneath outcroppings. These were the same places where elders instructed young men in tribal ways, and where a *corroboree* (dance festival) enacted their story in music and dance.

The rock paintings were made with colors created by mixing pulverized rock with water—yielding white, red, brown, pink, and yellow ocher. There seems to be two styles of art: X-raylike paintings depicting both internal and external organs, and realistic paintings. The paintings chronicled great hunts and included intricate designs involving kangaroos and other marsupials. Some portrayed misfortunes, which the artists blamed on a colorful array of evil spirits or on the half-human, half-animal ancestral beings they believed were the inhabitants at the beginning of time.

Tribesmen claim that many of the older, single-line drawings were not done by men at all but by a spirit people called Mimi. They were credited with the ability to melt into cliffs by blowing on the rocks and to leave their shadows on the wall.

For centuries, retouching and new rock painting kept alive the myths of the secret places. With the shifting of tribes and passing of elders, though, many of the secrets of the Aborigines remain locked within the paintings.

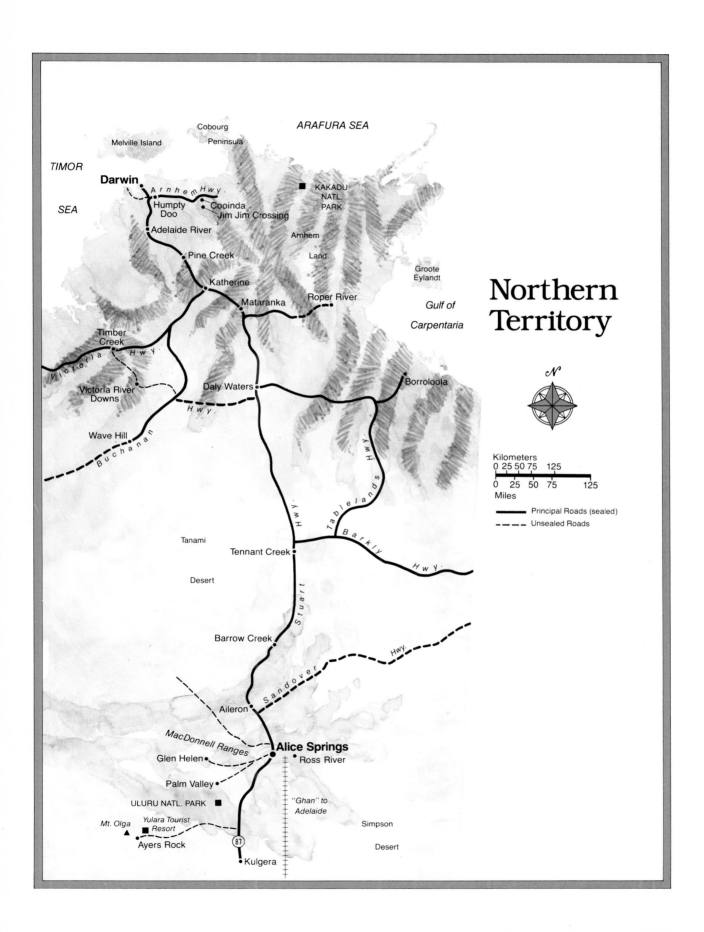

Melville Island

Cobourg
Peninsula

ARAFURA SEA

TIMOR

Darwin

SEA

Arnhem Hwy.

Humpty
Doo

Cooinda
Jim Jim Crossing

KAKADU
NATL
PARK

Arnhem

Adelaide River

Land

Pine Creek

Groote
Eylandt

Katherine

Mataranka

Roper River

Gulf of
Carpentaria

Northern
Territory

Timber
Creek

Victoria

Hwy.

Victoria River
Downs

Daly Waters

Borroloola

Hwy.

Buchanan

Wave Hill

Kilometers
0 25 50 75   125

0   25   50   75   125
Miles

——— Principal Roads (sealed)
- - - - Unsealed Roads

Tanami

Tennant Creek

Stuart Hwy.

Tablelands Hwy.

Barkly Hwy.

Desert

Hwy.

Barrow Creek

Sandover

Hwy.

Aileron

MacDonnell Ranges

Alice Springs

Glen Helen

Ross River

Palm Valley

"Ghan" to
Adelaide

ULURU NATL. PARK

Mt. Olga

Yulara Tourist
Resort

Simpson

Ayers Rock

(87)

Desert

Kulgera

Bottomless boat races are a feature along dry bed of the Todd River (below) at Alice Springs. This annual Henley-on-Todd Regatta was once cancelled because of water.

At Katherine Gorge, flatbottom excursion boats take passengers gliding through waterways edged by high cliffs. Aboriginal paintings cover canyon walls.

Ancient Aboriginal rock paintings awe visitors in Kakadu National Park. Fascinating art is believed to be more than 30,000 years old.

Kakadu National Park. The dry season (May through October) is the best time to visit this national park. The area is noted for its abundance of wildlife including birds, kangaroos, wallabies, and wild water buffaloes. The park's varied landscape includes swampy marshlands, a eucalyptus forest, dramatic sandstone escarpments, and several waterfalls.

The Aboriginal paintings found at Nourlangie Rock Artsite and Obiri Rock Artsite are prime attractions. There's also a boat cruise on the Yellow Waters Lagoon, home of saltwater crocodiles.

You can reach Kakadu National Park via the Arnhem Highway. Accommodations include campgrounds and two motels. In addition to local coach and flightseeing tours from Darwin, many Northern Territory tours, featuring Ayers Rock, Alice Springs, Katherine, and Darwin, also include Kakadu National Park in their itineraries.

Katherine & Katherine Gorge

The town of Katherine, 354 km/220 miles south of Darwin, is the gateway to Katherine Gorge National Park. Here you'll find hotel, motel, and caravan park accommodations. There's also tourist park accommodations 13 km/8 miles from the gorge at the Springvale Homestead. Built in 1878, this homestead on the Katherine River is thought to be the area's oldest building.

You can reach Katherine by air or express bus from Alice or Darwin.

Katherine Gorge is located 35 km/22 miles northeast of Katherine. It features waterways edged by 61-meter/200-foot cliffs. During the dry season, 2-hour flatbottom boat tours take you along the Katherine River through the gorge. Canyon walls have Aboriginal paintings; trees grow at strange angles; and bird nests are tucked away small caves. Other canyon wildlife includes kangaroos, wallabies, crocodiles, dingoes, and echidna. The park also has a number of marked walking trails.

A town called Alice

"Down the track" from Darwin lies Alice Springs, the Northern Territory's other major town. Located in the center of the continent, isolated Alice Springs is surrounded by Australia's outback—a vast wilderness of spinifex grass, mulga trees, and rambling cattle stations. Alice's nearest neighbor of any size to the south is Adelaide, 1,320 km/820 air miles away. Darwin is 1,532 km/952 road miles to the north.

An oasis in Australia's "Red Heart," Alice is an attractive town of 22,000 nestled in a bowl of ancient, weather-carved red rock mountains. Its main streets are lined with modern buildings of concrete and glass.

For the visitor, Alice Springs is a "two-stage" town. The first stage concerns points of interest in the town itself, and the second, attractions in the surrounding area.

The tourist season for Alice Springs extends from April to October, a period of warm days (about 27°C/80°F), little humidity, and cool evenings—much like the winter season in Arizona. Days are clear and bright with about 9 hours of sunlight. During the rest of the year, temperatures soar to 38°C/100°F and above.

Exploring the town

Alice is a compact town, easily explored on your own or on a half-day tour. You might want to begin your exploration on Anzac Hill where you'll get a panoramic view of the city. The following are some other sights you'll want to explore.

The Old Telegraph Station. Alice Springs really began 3 km/2 miles from its current location. An overland telegraph repeater station was established here in 1872. The nearby water hole was named Alice Springs after the wife of the superintendent of telegraphs, Charles Todd. The tiny town which sprang up near this telegraph station was called Stuart. When the post office moved to Stuart, the town's name was changed to Alice Springs.

Today, the buildings of the old telegraph station—in operation from 1872 to 1932—have been restored and are part of a national park. The park—a favorite with picnickers—is open from 9 A.M. to 7 P.M. daily.

Royal Flying Doctor Service. The Flying Doctor base is located on Stuart Terrace between Todd and Simpson streets. From here, doctors give medical advice by radio to ranchers a long distance away. When needed, these doctors can fly in light aircraft to the scene of an emergency. The base is open for tours weekdays and Saturday mornings.

School of the Air. Two-way radios at the outback cattle stations are used for education as well as for emergency medical information. From the School of the Air headquarters on Head Street, school lessons are broadcasted to station children in remote areas. On weekday afternoons between 1:30 and 3:30, you can hear tapes of children at outback homesteads as they take part in lessons conducted by two-way radio.

Panorama Guth. The beauty of Central Australia is captured in an extraordinary circular (360°), 61-meter/200-foot painting exhibited in this gallery. Dutch artist Henk Guth created it to be viewed from a specially constructed platform. The floor in front of the painting is covered with rolling sand hills and shrubbery, adding dimension to the artwork.

Pitchi Richi. This unusual name belongs to a most unusual bird sanctuary 3 km/2 miles south of town. Here you'll find some of the dreamlike sculptures of William Ricketts. Placed in an outdoor setting of trees and rocks, his sculptures of Aborigines possess a haunting beauty. (The William Ricketts Sanctuary near Mt. Dandenong in Victoria also features sculptures by this famous Australian artist.)

Open 9 A.M. to 5 P.M. daily, Pitchi Richi also serves as an open-air museum for pioneer equipment.

Emily Gap Camel Farm. It hasn't been that long since Alice was supplied by camel caravans. These "ships of the desert" were the prime means of transportation for explorers, prospectors, and other pioneers in the area during the 19th century. When motorized vehicles finally came to the Centre, the camels were released to run wild. It's estimated that more than 20,000 camels roam wild today in the outback.

The Emily Gap Camel Farm just outside Alice has recaptured and domesticated some of these camels. You can ride a camel here. It's open daily from 9 A.M. to 5 P.M.

Araluen Arts Centre. Just minutes from downtown Alice is the town's art center; its definitely "outback" architecture blends well with the surrounding landscape. In addition to an art gallery, the center contains a 500-seat theater, a convention center, and a bistro.

Close to the arts center, you'll find the Central Australian Aviation Museum.

Shops in Alice are normally open from 9 A.M. to 5:30 P.M. Monday through Friday, and Saturday morning from 9 A.M. to noon. Some shops extend hours to 9 P.M. on Friday nights.

The essentials

The information below will help you plan your trip.

Getting there. The Northern Territory is served by air, rail, and bus.

Air. Regularly scheduled flights by Ansett and Australian airlines travel to and from most state capitals into Darwin and Alice Springs. Air New South Wales and East-West Airlines fly to Ayers Rock from Sydney. Ansett N.T. files within the Northern Territory and to Ayers Rock from Alice Springs. International service into Darwin by Qantas and foreign-flag carriers. Each town's airport is about a 20-minute trip from downtown.

Rail. Interstate trains providing regular service to Alice Springs from other state capitals are *The Ghan* from Adelaide and *The Alice* from Sydney.

Bus. Ansett Pioneer, Greyhound, and Deluxe have service between Alice Springs and Adelaide with connecting service to more distant capitals. All three companies travel between Alice and Darwin, and Alice and Ayers Rock.

Accommodations. Major hotels in Darwin: Sheraton Darwin, Beaufort Darwin, Diamond Beach Hotel-Casino, Four Seasons Darwin, Darwin Travelodge, and Crestwood Phoenix. In Alice Springs: Diamond Springs Casino & Country Club, Sheraton Alice Springs, and Alice Springs Gap Motor Inn. In the Yulara Tourist Resort at Ayers Rock: Sheraton Ayers Rock, and Four Seasons Ayers Rock.

Food and drink. Darwin's local specialty is barramundi, a fresh-water fish with a delicate flavor. Other local specialties in the Northern Territory include buffalo steaks and dates grown near Alice. Chateau Hornsby, located 15 km/9 miles southeast of Alice Springs, is Central Australia's only winery.

Getting around. Alice Springs has no public transport, but there are plenty of taxis. Darwin has bus service as well as taxis. Both towns are easily explored on foot.

Tours. Tours of Alice Springs include city sights, MacDonnell Ranges' attractions, and Ayers Rock. Special camel treks are also available, including a trip to Chateau Hornsby for dinner. Tours of Darwin can include Kakadu Park and Katherine Gorge.

For more information. The Northern Territory Government Tourist Bureau offices are located at 31 Smith Street, Darwin 5790 and 51 Todd Street, Alice Springs 5750.

Sports to enjoy

You can enjoy a game of golf at the 18-hole Alice Springs Golf Club, or hire a public tennis court at Traeger Park (courts can be reserved at the Council offices on Hartley Street). If you enjoy spectator sports, you'll be glad to know that Alice Springs residents are avid followers of Australian Rules football and competitions are held on Sundays, April through September, at the Traeger Park sporting complex.

Horse racing is another favorite. Every Saturday the horses race at the Central Australian Racing Club south of town. Picnic race meetings, held annually, are a real social occasion for those who live in the sparsely populated outback. Picnic race meetings are held in May at Aileron and Renner Springs, in June at Barrow Creek and Brunette Downs, and in early August at Harts Range. Often the picnic is as important as the horse race.

Other Alice Springs spectator sports include baseball, cricket, and rugby.

Festival time

Rousing, rollicking annual events in Alice Springs include the Bangtail Muster and Camel Cup in May, and the Henley-on-Todd Regatta in late August.

Bangtail Muster. The name Bangtail Muster dates back to the early cattle station practice of cutting the tips off the tails of cattle. After mustering, these tips were collected and counted to determine the number of cattle being shipped. Events at a Bangtail Muster include a light-hearted procession and a series of sporting events.

Camel Cup. This event features a full day of camel races. The results of some of the races can be hilarious since camels can be quite unpredictable. Parties and fireworks follow the races.

Henley-on-Todd Regatta. This "regatta" is held in the dry river bed of the Todd River which "flows" through Alice Springs. It consists of a full program of "aquatic" events—races of skiffs, yachts, and bottomless canoes—but minus the water. Instead of wind or oar power, these makeshift craft are propelled over the course by the legs of their occupants. A highlight of the regatta is the Australia Cup—a battle between yachts representing Australia, the United States, and other international competitors.

Excursions from Alice

The MacDonnell Ranges—running in dramatic parallel ridges east and west of Alice—harbor tree-shaded canyons, steep-walled chasms, deep reflecting pools, and stands of stark, white-barked ghost gums. Beyond the drama of these mountains, visitors can travel further south to awesome Ayers Rock and the Olgas.

Roads to all of the closer MacDonnell Ranges' attractions are paved. Other attractions are reached by dirt road and, in some cases, four-wheel-drive track. The best way to see many of the attractions is on a tour. Alice Springs tour operators offer both short and long tours to points of interest in the MacDonnells. You can tour Ayers Rock by air, air and coach, or coach.

East of Alice

Although much of the MacDonnell Ranges are west of Alice Springs, the East MacDonnells have both scenic and historic value.

Emily and Jessie gaps. Just 8 km/5 miles east of Alice is the natural break of Emily Gap. Steep, jagged cliffs rise from a narrow sandy plain flooded by Emily Creek during heavy rains.

Another 11 km/7 miles east is Jessie Gap—another dramatic cut in the Heavitree Ranges of the MacDonnells. In your exploration of the MacDonnell Ranges, you'll discover that gaps like Emily and Jessie are common. Each cleft in these rocky mountains has its own character and beauty.

Trephina Gorge. Beautiful red cliff walls soar above the broad, sandy expanse of Trephina Creek in this reserve 80 km/50 miles east of Alice. Huge red gum trees line the usually dry creek bed. Nearby are the John Hayes Rockholes where steep rock walls shelter a series of inviting pools.

Ross River Homestead. If the prospect of a visit to a central Australian "dude" ranch appeals to you, try a stay at the Ross River Homestead located about 80 km/50 miles east of Alice Springs. A stay at the homestead offers time to explore points of interest in the East MacDonnells. Other possible activities at the homestead are horseback riding, swimming, lessons in boomerang throwing, a bush barbecue, and a chance to sample damper bread and billy tea.

You stay in rustic, comfortable cabins and dine in the old homestead—a whitewashed mud and stone-wall home built in 1898. Ross River Homestead, formerly the Love's Creek Homestead, is located on working cattle property.

To the west of Alice

A series of dramatic gorges lie west of Alice. As with sights in the East MacDonnells, access to points of interest is not always by paved road. Many of the sights might be better seen on a tour.

Simpsons Gap National Park. Just 19 km/12 miles west of Alice is this gap with walls that soar to 150 meters/492 feet in height. This area of dramatic scenery is home to rock wallabies.

Standley Chasm. The walls of this spectacular chasm are no more than 5 meters/18 feet apart at their widest point. Midday, when the sun reaches into this narrow chasm—normally cloaked in shade—these walls glow a brilliant red and gold. Standley Chasm is 53 km/33 miles west of Alice Springs.

Ormiston Gorge. Some say this feat of nature, 132 km/82 miles west of Alice, is more impressive than the Grand Canyon. Towering red and purple rock walls are reflected in permanent pools. In places the floor of this gorge is a chaotic jumble of huge boulders, worn into rounded shapes by Ormiston Creek—a raging torrent when it floods.

Palm Valley. About 145 km/90 miles west of Alice, the Finke River has carved out a huge rock canyon of rich red walls. Groves of lush prehistoric palm trees—some be-

lieved to be 5,000 years old—thrive in this canyon. A natural rock amphitheater in the valley is the site of many ancient Aboriginal rituals.

Ayers Rock, a massive monolith

The huge bulk of Ayers Rock rises abruptly from a flat plain 451 km/280 miles southwest of Alice Springs. It looms above the plain like a sleeping monster, some 348 meters/1,143 feet high with a perimeter of 8½ km/5½ miles. It is one of the world's largest monoliths—a spectacular natural wonder.

Touring the Rock. You can experience the majesty of the Rock on a walking, coach, or car tour.

Aborigines called it "Uluru" and considered it a holy place surrounded by legends. You can see Aboriginal rock paintings in some of the caves at its base. Actually, this monolithic wonder is pitted with caves, depressions, crevices, and holes carved by wind and weather. When it rains, water quickly fills the depressions near the top and then cascades down the Rock's sides in glistening waterfalls. To appreciate its spectacular colors, view the Rock at either sunrise or sunset. At these times, if the sun isn't covered by clouds, the Rock will glow a brilliant red.

Climbing the Rock. For the fit, climbing Ayers Rock is an important part of the "visit to the Rock" ritual. On the Rock's western face, a path has been marked to the top. There's also a sign at the start of the climb warning people that it can be dangerous; this is especially true when the Rock is wet or there are strong winds. Rubber-soled shoes are a must.

The first section of the climb is made easier by a post-and-chain safety rail along the steepest section of the Rock. A faded white line then marks the way along the last two-thirds of the trek which includes the negotiation of some steep holes and valleys. Only some of these depressions have helpful post-and-chain safety rails. At the summit, you can sign a guest book, rest, and enjoy the views below—endless flat plains and red sand dunes covered with spinifex, mulga, eucalyptus, and desert oak, relieved by the domes of the Olgas in the middle distance. The way down isn't much easier than the climb up, and it's not uncommon to see people clinging to the chain rail while they slowly make the last section of the steep descent on the seat of their pants.

The Olgas

About 32 km/20 miles west of Ayers Rock rise the spectacular domes of the Olgas. This group of more than 30 smooth-faced, dome-shaped monoliths of varying sizes separated by deep ravines covers a 36-square-km/14-square-mile area. Mount Olga, the largest, rises 549 meters/1,800 feet above the plains.

There are coach tours from Ayers Rock to the Olgas.

Both Ayers Rock and the Olgas are part of Uluru National Park. In years past, many park visitors traveled round-trip from Alice Springs, an arduous journey. Accommodations at Ayers Rock were few and rustic. Today, the Yulara Tourist Resort complex, 20 km/12 miles northwest of Ayers Rock, has modern accommodations, restaurants, and shops. The resort was built outside the park's boundary to protect the environment.

GREAT BARRIER REEF

A watery wonderland of coral reefs & tropical islands

Most maps of the world show a dotted line off the northeast coast of Australia, running from the continent's waistline all the way north to Papua New Guinea. Labeled the "Great Barrier Reef," it encompasses a series of coral reefs, shoals, cays, and islands—the biggest collection of coral in the world, 2,012 km/1,250 miles long and ranging in width from 16 km/10 miles to 241 km/150 miles.

Most of the vast area enclosed by the Great Barrier Reef is water. A long series of detached reefs—true coral islands (some submerged, many awash with booming surf, a very few topped with sand and perhaps some shrubbery and trees)—define the eastern edge or Outer Reef.

Between the mainland and the Outer Reef is a north-south passage dotted with rock-and-soil islands, once part of the mainland's coast ranges. Most of these larger, high-rise islands (tops of partly submerged mountains) also have coral reefs in the water around them. Of the island tourist destinations listed in this chapter, only Green and Heron islands and the Low Isles are true coral cays; Lizard Island, though situated on the Outer Reef, is a continental island.

At its northern end (along the Cape York Peninsula) the Outer Reef is barely 10 km/6 miles offshore; to the south, opposite Gladstone, the reef lies 100 km/62 miles or more from the coast.

Barrier Reef ecology. The unassuming architects of this "eighth wonder of the world" are coral polyps, colonies of tiny anemonelike creatures thriving in the tropical waters off the Queensland coast. Succeeding generations secrete protective limestone shells upon the skeletons of their forebearers, but at such a slow rate that the creation of the Great Barrier Reef took millions of years.

As in other habitats, a fierce, competitive, yet finely balanced food chain exists among the many creatures of the reef. Sharks and turtles feed on lesser marine life; the survivors feed on still smaller creatures, and so on.

Unfortunately, something went very haywire in nature's balance of feeder and food on the reef. A sudden incursion of crown-of-thorns starfish, the coral's worst enemy, wiped out entire coral communities. Government skin divers fought and destroyed about 50,000 of the spiny invaders before too big a dent was made in the reef. According to some environmentalists, the imbalance was caused by the over-hunting of the giant triton clam (a natural enemy of the starfish and prized for its shell) and by pollutants carried to reef waters by Queensland rivers.

When to visit. Time and tide are important if you're going to make the most of any reef visit. Weatherwise, late August through November is best for cruising, "reefing" (wandering along the exposed coral barrier), and viewing; some say May is good. At all times, winds are unpredictable. Caution is advised from late November through March when coastal beaches can be plagued with venomous sea wasps (jelly fish); and January through March is monsoon season, with winds at their worst.

The reef puts on its best monthly show during the full or new moon, when the tide is at its lowest. Tide tables are published in advance for the year. For reef walking, check tide depths; low tide on the reef usually means a foot or so of water—more than 1½ feet makes difficult walking. Snorkelers and scuba divers can see even more of the underwater wonders of the reef; in some places, the reef is a vertical wall of living coral. Glass-bottom boats and semi-submersible viewing vessels make it easy to see coral while staying dry.

Reef offerings

Island resorts between the mainland and Outer Reef—as well as numerous scheduled cruises, sightseeing trips,

Setting sail from Shute Harbour on the northern Queensland coast, boat heads through Whitsunday Passage toward island resorts along the Great Barrier Reef.

and package tours—make it easy to enjoy the wondrous Great Barrier Reef.

Planning your stay is important. Visitors can decide on a cruise among the islands, a flight around the reef, or a resort stay at one or more islands.

Reef walking is a revelation to those who have never done it—a chance to actually see coral formations and marine life first hand. Giant sea clams spit water at you, plants shrink inward if touched, and sea anemones wave wickedly. Best color and formation are at the reef's outer edge—a solid coral runway interspersed with pools of stranded multi-colored fish.

When exploring, wear rubber-soled shoes—coral cuts are painful, infect easily, and heal slowly. Walk carefully

The essentials

Here is basic travel information to help you reach and explore the gateway cities to the Great Barrier Reef.

Getting there. The gateway cities are served by air, rail, and coach.

Air. Ansett, Australian, and East-West airlines provide daily flights from the south, primarily via Brisbane, to Cairns, Townsville, and other tropical centers. Air Queensland provides service within the state. Both Cairns and Townsville have international airports. Qantas flies to Cairns from the U.S. west coast (via Honolulu).

Rail. Australia's extensive rail system reaches as far north as Cairns. The Sunlander and Queenslander operate between Brisbane and Cairns on a regular basis; the Sunlander making the trip in 37 hours and the Queenslander in 34 hours. The Capricornian journeys between Brisbane and Rockhampton in 14 hours.

Bus. Ansett Pioneer, Greyhound, and Deluxe coachlines travel daily between Brisbane and Cairns, making intermediate stops along the Queensland coast.

Accommodations. Major Cairns hotels include the Pacific International, Tuna Towers, Ramada Reef, Kewarra Beach, and Harbourside Village; in Townsville try the Sheraton Breakwater Hotel-Casino, Townsville International, and Townsville Travelodge. (For island resorts, see pages 115–117.) Book all accommodations in advance.

Food and drink. The area's specialties are fresh seafood and fresh tropical fruit. The price of island accommodations generally includes full board.

Getting around. Island resorts are reached by plane, helicopter, or launch from nearby coastal cities. Boats and local airlines make regular trips to the Outer Reef from coastal cities and island resorts.

Tours. Coastal Queensland and Great Barrier Reef island tours depart from Brisbane and major cities.

For more information. Check with the Queensland Government Travel Centre, 12 Shields Street, Cairns, 4870, or the Far North Queensland Promotion Bureau Ltd., 44 McLeod Street, Cairns 4870.

and test the coral for solidity before putting your weight on it. Do not disturb formations, and replace anything turned over. If you plan to touch anything, it's a good idea to wear gloves. And don't break off a piece of coral—it's protected by law.

Cruising the reef

Great Barrier cruises—4 to 5 days in length—sail through the Whitsunday Passage calling at resort island beaches and exploring reef areas.

The M.V. *Elizabeth E* sails from Mackay Harbour Mondays and returns Thursdays, and the M.V. *Roylen Endeavor* sails Mondays and returns Fridays. Both visit Whitsunday islands and reef areas. The M.V. *Coral Princess* departs Townsville Mondays, returning on Fridays. This trip includes visits to Hinchinbrook and Dunk islands, a 2-night stay on Magnetic Island, and reef viewing in the *Yellow Submarine*. Special packages are available that include the standard cruise plus additional nights at a resort.

One-day cruises to the Outer Reef depart regularly from island resorts as well as Queensland coastal towns.

Reef flightseeing

Many visitors discover that the most dramatic way to experience the beauty of the reef—other than gliding through its waters as a skin diver—is to skim the surface in a low-flying plane or helicopter.

Between the Queensland coastal cities and the Outer Reef, passengers get a memorable view of transparent, iridescent waters revealing the mass of coral beneath. Thousands of islands, heaps of coral sand, and lagoon-crowned reefs sparkling like gems can be seen along the deep channel-threaded waterway.

Seaplanes fly out to the reef at low tide. Reef walkers are transferred to a boat and ferried to a point on the coral platform where they can step ashore.

Underwater observatories

Visitors who want to see the reef's underwater life without getting their feet wet will enjoy the Underwater Coral Observatory adjacent to Hook Island in Whitsunday Passage.

Sunk in the midst of inner coral reefs, the steel chamber of the all-weather, air-conditioned, carpeted observatory has a viewing floor 10 meters/32 feet below deck level. Through its huge glass windows, visitors enjoy an extraordinary underwater view of coral polyps, exotically colored tropical fish, and other sea life, all undisturbed in their natural habitat.

Another coral observatory is on Green Island, off Cairns (see page 115). It is not as large as the Underwater Coral Observatory, but it boasts views of even more spectacular formations and reef life.

Island life

On the resort islands, life revolves around the sea, the tides, the reef, and cruising. Varied activities mingle to create a fascinating vacation. You can go reefing (if the weather and tides are right) or sports fishing; sailing, windsurfing, or snorkeling; take a lazy swim or go skin diving; go for a long walk on the beach or climb hills lush with pine forests, rain forests, or bush; do a little bird watching; or just sit under a coconut palm and watch the surf.

Evening entertainment ranges from luaus to nightclub shows and dancing. Some islands feature guided reef-walking tours and bird watching. Some resorts offer tennis, golf, and even horseback riding.

Away from the hotel, you will find your island much the way nature left it. A National Parks Act protects flora and fauna; trails are well-kept and markers unobtrusive; native bush and birds are undisturbed.

Island dress is casual. The atmosphere is casual, easy, and relaxed. Visitors roam the islands in swimsuits, loose shirts or shifts, and thongs (or bare feet).

For reefing, wear rubber-soled sandals, tennis shoes, or even boots. As we've mentioned previously, coral cuts are painful, infect easily, and heal slowly. Slacks and long-sleeved shirts provide additional protection against scrapes and cuts should you slip and fall.

Island vacationers may also want a shade hat, sun glasses, large beach towel, a sweater for cool evenings or late launch outings, flashlight, camera, lightweight rain-coat, and suntan lotion. Many islands have a shop where you may pick up miscellaneous items, in addition to coral specimens, shells, and shell jewelry.

Resorts, plain and fancy. Accommodations run the gamut from rustic to modern, but there are no high rises. A few islands are limited to salt-water showers.

Relaxed comfort rather than luxury is the keynote, with a few notable exceptions. Daily rates per person vary; most but not all resorts include all meals in their rates. Usually each island has only one resort, reinforcing the atmosphere of restful isolation.

Island resorts serve a full range of food, with emphasis on fish of all kinds and tropical fruit. If you like, you can gather some of the huge local oysters yourself, eating them raw or tossing them into a fire to steam.

During winter (April through September), the reef islands and adjacent coast are prime vacation spots for Australians, so reservations should be made well in advance. Some resorts close down from January to March; others lower their rates during off-season.

Your travel agent can be helpful in arranging your accommodations and transportation. Full schedules and booking information can be obtained from the Queensland Tourist and Travel Corporation in Los Angeles (see page 16).

For the sports-minded

Island resorts and gateway cities offer a wide range of activities for the ocean lover. Game fishing is spectacular; diving gets you down into the life of the reef; and boating on your own lends mobility.

Game fishing. Whether you've been fishing for years or have yet to experience the thrill of your first strike, the Great Barrier Reef ranks among the world's best places to enjoy the sport. An ever-increasing number of game fishers, attracted by record catches of black marlin and sail-fish, are drawn to this area.

The major deep-sea fishing center for Great Barrier Reef

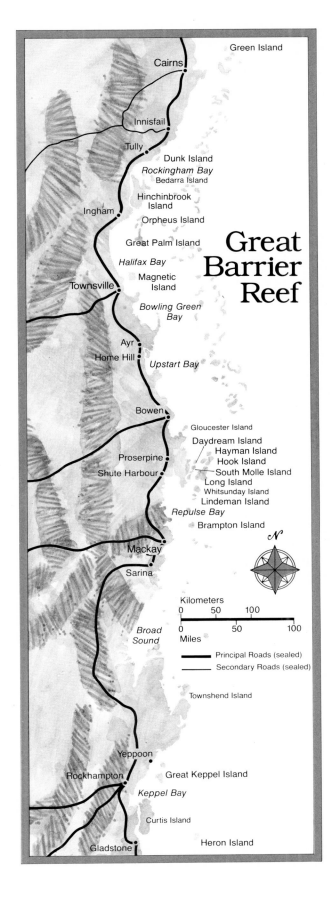

Low tide reveals wonders of Green Island's coral reef. Resort islands off the Queensland coast offer easy-going vacations that revolve around the sea.

Divers discover an underwater coral world miles from shore. Amphibians fly from coast for reef exploring.

waters is Cairns, with its big boating complex. Townsville and Innisfail are well equipped for the sport, and several Great Barrier Reef resorts operate game-fishing launches. For more information on boat charters, contact the Queensland Government Travel Centre, 196 Adelaide Street, Brisbane 4000.

More than a dozen species of game fish flourish in reef waters: barracuda, black marlin, sailfish, wahoo, giant trevally, yellowfin tuna, dogtooth tuna, cobia, rainbow runner, barramundi, threadfin, Australian salmon, small tuna, and Spanish mackerel (kingfish).

Spanish mackerel increase in coastal waters between Gladstone and Mackay from April to June, and farther north between Townsville and Cairns from July to September, when sailfish also seem to peak. Giant black marlin (1,000 to 2,000 lbs.) begin to appear at Cairns in late August and September, continuing until early December. Barracuda season usually starts in August and peaks in December.

Diving. Getting down along the reef appeals to many divers. The water temperature is pleasant, and the underwater world is alive with tempting coral displays and multitudinous marine life. Island resorts often supply equipment, including air for tanks. In addition to island diveboats and day diveboats departing from the mainland, there are live-on-board diveboats for longer trips.

Boating on your own. All major ports on the Queensland coast, and many island resorts, offer vessels for charter. The largest number of boat rentals in northern Queensland are found between Shute Harbour and Cairns.

After a checkout of your sailing expertise and experience you can self-skipper a boat with a "bareboat" charter or participate in a skippered program.

The gateway cities

From Lizard Island in the north to the Capricorn Islands opposite Gladstone, a number of tropical island resorts provide bases for reef exploring. Access to the islands is via a series of coastal cities—first Cairns (northernmost gateway), then Townsville, Proserpine (rhyming with *porcupine*), Mackay (usually pronounced to rhyme with *eye*), Rockhampton, and Gladstone. These cities are reached by plane, train, and express coach service from Brisbane.

The busy port of Cairns

Cairns—itself a popular winter tourist resort, busy port, and commercial center—is the departure point for trips to Lizard and Green islands; for some interesting jaunts into tropical jungle country; for day cruises; for diving excursions; and for expeditions in search of the fighting deep-sea fish.

Around town. Cairns is a true tropical town with broad palm-sprinkled streets, stage-set architecture, and a dramatic seaside setting. Despite its location on the bay, the city has no beaches, but some of the world's greatest stretches of sand lie just north and south of town. Behind the beaches a ring of sugar cane fields reaches to the steep mountain slopes. During crushing season (June to December) cane fires light up the night.

Lodging ranges from beach resorts just up the coast, to hotels and motels in town, and caravan parks. Dining spots are plentiful and, not surprisingly, much of the fare comes straight from the sea.

Most of the daytime action is outdoors. Down at the waterfront, the Hayles Cruises' catamaran departs mornings for a tour of Green Island and a trip to the Outer Reef.

During the 3 hours spent at the reef, passengers can go coral viewing in a semi-submersible vessel or go snorkeling from a special floating platform.

The Visitors' Information Centre (44 McLeod Street) offers a brochure describing historical sites in and around town. Especially interesting are the House of 10,000 Shells (a shell museum at 32 Abbott Street) and the Laroc coral jewelry factory (82 Aumuller Street).

A train ride to Kuranda. One of Australia's best, and most inexpensive, outings is the scenic rail excursion from Cairns to Kuranda. It took four years for hundreds of men wielding picks and shovels to hack a way through the lush jungle, build spans over deep gorges, and tunnel through rocky mountains to reach Kuranda in 1888. Each turn of the track unfolds a new view—the rugged splendor of Barron Gorge, Stoney Creek Falls, Barron Falls, and Victorian-style Kuranda railroad station with its profusion of tropical plants and flowers.

Trains depart Cairns at 8:30 A.M. and 9 A.M. daily, and return to Cairns at noon and 3 P.M.

The Atherton Tableland. Inland from Cairns lies the scenic Atherton Tableland, a rich volcanic area on the plateau of the Great Dividing Range. Many visitors consider it North Queensland's most spectacular area with tropical rain forests, volcanic lakes, and sparkling waterfalls.

Exploring the tableland is possible by rental car or coach, but perhaps the best way to get into the rain forest is by arranging a 1-day, four-wheel-drive safari. Safaris can be booked through Air Queensland or through the Queensland Government Travel Centre.

Up the coast. The Captain Cook Highway meanders north from Cairns to Port Douglas, less than an hour away. A good road by Queensland standards, the highway is given to unexpected loops and twists. A number of beautiful beaches with quiet resorts, caravan parks, and campgrounds line the coast.

From the quiet town of Port Douglas, the M.V. *Quicksilver* catamaran takes visitors to the reef for snorkeling, diving, and coral viewing in a semi-submersible vessel.

North of Port Douglas lies Cooktown—Australia's first British settlement, established by Captain Cook in 1770. Still farther north is the remote Cape York Peninsula. A road links Cooktown to Port Douglas, and four-wheel-drive safaris explore the area—but flying is still the best way to reach this historic town. Air Queensland in Cairns offers charters that include Cooktown; 5-day round-trip cruises from Cairns also stop here.

Green Island. Tropical plants flourish on this heavily wooded, 12-hectare/30-acre island that rises only 3 meters/10 feet above sea level. Low tide exposes miles of the reef for exploration. Glass-bottom boats and the portholes of Green Island's famous Underwater Coral Observatory also afford first-hand views of marine world wonders.

Anchored on the seabed in the midst of a living coral garden, the observatory is a steel-and-concrete chamber with 22 large portholes. If you're not a skin diver, this is a good way to enjoy the reef's underwater life. At Marineland Melanesia you'll find a crocodile pool, a 17-tank fish "arcade," a deep tank for large fish, and a coral grotto. There are also glass-bottom boat trips.

Green is one of the reef's true coral cays that has guest facilities. The year-round resort has 26 units, a restaurant, and a variety of water-sports options. You can reach Green Island from Cairns by high-speed catamaran (40 minutes) or launch (1½ hours).

Lizard Island. The most northerly resort in Queensland waters, Lizard lies northeast of Cooktown. Today a national park, Lizard was first explored by Captain Cook in 1770. Stranded inside the Outer Reef, Cook climbed Lizard's highest peak to find a break through which he could steer the *Endeavour* into deeper waters.

A coral reef surrounds the island; its waters teem with big game fish such as black marlin. Air Queensland provides service into Lizard daily from Cairns. The Lizard Island Lodge has 32 units. There's also a dining room and swimming pool. Activities include glass-bottom boat excursions, day cruises to the reef for snorkeling and diving, bush walks, fishing, water-skiing, tennis, sailing, windsurfing, and golf. The island has about two dozen isolated beaches.

Townsville, another gateway

Townsville is Queensland's third largest city and one of Australia's tropical centers. It is also the departure point for trips to Magnetic Island (reached by launch), Orpheus Island (reached by air and launch), Hinchinbrook Island (reached by launch via Cardwell and by air), and Dunk Island (reached by launch and air). Outer Reef cruises and fishing boat trips also depart from Townsville.

Magnetic Island. Almost a suburb, Magnetic is just off the coast near Townsville. Comfortable holiday accommodations are available at a number of resorts which nestle in secluded bays around the island.

Now a national park, the island is noted for its colorful tropical shrubs and groves of coconut palms, tamarinds, and mangoes. It is laced with hiking paths leading to the summit of Mount Cook with its far-reaching view.

Orpheus Island. A secluded, peaceful island, Orpheus belongs to the Palm Group near beautiful Hinchinbrook Channel, and lies south of huge Hinchinbrook Island near the Outer Reef. Accommodations are in 25 beachfront rooms including two separate cottages. The resort is designed for couples and small families. Access is by launch, seaplane, and helicopter.

Hinchinbrook Island. A mountainous island with beautiful palm-fringed bays and sandy beaches, Hinchinbrook is 26 km/16 miles from the mainland resort of Cardwell. It is a national park, one of the world's largest island parks. The resort, situated on its northernmost tip, offers bungalow accommodations. Launch service operates between Cardwell and the island and there's air service from Townsville. The island is a virtually unexplored wilderness with waterfalls and superb beaches. Elevated walkways lead through the mangroves at Missionary Bay.

Dunk Island. Like so many of the area's islands, Dunk was discovered and named by Captain Cook in 1770 during his famous voyage along Australia's east coast. Covering only 17 km/6½ square miles, Dunk still retains an unspoiled tropical beauty. Penetrating the heavy jungle foliage are miles of graded mountain tracks where you see numerous species of birds and giant butterflies. The island's shell-strewn beaches make it a beachcomber's dream.

Dunk Island's full-board resort has 138 rooms in bungalows and two-story complexes. Amenities include a restaurant, pools, tennis courts, golf course, and water-sports facilities. Guests can go horseback riding or take reef trips. You can reach Dunk by air from Townsville or Cairns, by launch from Clump Point (midway between the two towns), or by water taxi from South Mission Beach.

Proserpine and its island quartet

Proserpine is surrounded by acres of sugar cane fields. From here you catch a bus to Shute Harbour for the launches that transport you to Hayman, Daydream, South Molle, and Long islands. There's air service from Shute Harbour and Proserpine to Hayman and Daydream islands. To get to South Molle and Long islands, you can fly from Proserpine to Hamilton Island and take a launch.

Hayman Island. This well-known Great Barrier Reef resort has been recently remodeled and is now called the Ansett International Hotel, Hayman Island. It's open all year and provides cool, spacious accommodations in over 200 rooms including suites and penthouses, all situated around a beach lagoon. Island amenities include a filtered saltwater swimming lagoon, freshwater pools, marina, tennis courts, bowling green, health club, and dive shop.

When night comes, you can relax in quiet, attractive lounges or enjoy live entertainment including dance bands, cabaret performances, or special shows. The resort has several restaurants featuring a variety of cuisine.

Hayman Island is reached daily by the sleek boat, *Goddess*, from Shute Harbour or Hamilton Island. Ansett flies to Hamilton Island. There's also air service from Proserpine and Shute Harbour.

Daydream Island. This Whitsunday Group resort can be reached by daily launch from Shute Harbour or by air from Proserpine or Shute Harbour. There's also air service via Hamilton Island.

The buildings of the 100-room, two-story hotel curve around a huge, free-form swimming pool with its own island bar in the center. Each room has a panoramic view of the Whitsunday Passage. South Sea Island decor and entertainment highlight evening activities. The year-round resort features a badminton court, fishing, snorkeling, water-skiing, diving, tennis, sailing, windsurfing, and day cruises.

South Molle Island. Known for its carefree and relaxed atmosphere, South Molle nestles in a sheltered bay amid varied scenery—mountains, valleys, tropical gardens, and a sparkling series of beaches. This 405-hectare/1,000-acre island has 202 rooms.

Visitors have easy access to bush walks among lush forests with sparkling views of the Pacific. Free cruises and reef visits, aquaplaning, fishing, tennis, golf, and dancing are offered. Other island facilities include a dining room and four bars, a well-stocked store, a small arcade of shops, and even a store for divers which carries compressed air.

Long Island. This island's two small resorts, one at Happy Bay and the other at Palm Bay, offer activities to appeal to all ages—water-skiing, bush walking, tennis, fishing, and glass-bottom boat trips.

Long Island is reached by launch from Shute Harbour and by air from Proserpine to Hamilton Island with a connecting launch.

Mackay, base for cruises & islands

The attractive city of Mackay, with its wide, palm-shaded streets and tropical flower gardens, lies at the mouth of the Pioneer River. It is the airline embarkation point for trips to Brampton and Hamilton islands, and for two Whitsunday Passage cruises.

Brampton Island. One of the prettiest of the high-rise islands, this national park and wildlife sanctuary offers a view extending across the southern end of the Whitsunday Passage. Great stretches of palm-lined, white coral sands invite swimmers and sunbathers. Cruises can be arranged to other islands and the Outer Reef. In the evenings you can take in a movie, do a little dancing, or enjoy the entertainment.

Set in a coconut grove facing the beach, the modern all-year resort has 68 rooms. It is easy to reach by small plane or launch from Mackay.

Lindeman Island. Visitors to this mountainous national park can explore grassy hillsides, jungle gullies, and steep beach cliffs fringed with coral reefs. From Mount Oldfield, the view takes in more than 70 islands.

Guests keep busy with a selection of activities—bush-walking to deserted bays, watching flocks of multicolored parrots sweep over the groves, free cruises, shopping, golfing, picnicking, and coral viewing. Planes for flight-seeing and launches for special cruises or big-game fishing are available at extra charge.

The 90-room resort has a large dining room, two cocktail lounges, a games room, dance floor, golf course, and swimming pool—all in a tropical setting a few minutes walk from the beach.

The Lindeman Aerial Service, operating daily on demand, flies between Lindeman and Hamilton Island, Shute Harbour, and Proserpine. Lindeman Aerial Service also conducts scenic flights of the area.

Hamilton Island. This large resort complex has an airstrip with facilities capable of handling both commercial and private jets. The resort's 381 rooms include condos, Polynesian-style bures, and hotel accommodations. Other facilities include restaurants, tennis courts, spas, saunas, a native animal park, underwater reef exhibit, and marina with full water-sports facilities. Hamilton also serves as a base for trips to the Outer Reef on the *Coral Cat.*

Rockhampton, for Keppel and cruises

Rockhampton, on the Tropic of Capricorn, is the departure point for trips to Great Keppel Island. Scenic flights to the reef also depart from Rockhampton.

Great Keppel Island. Situated 13 km/8 miles off the Queensland coast and 56 km/35 miles northeast of Rockhampton, Great Keppel attracts many overseas visitors.

The resort, located on a protected bay with an inviting, white sandy beach, has begun to build a reputation for fine service and good food and wine. Accommodations include 160 modern motel-type units. Graded walks, leading to secluded bays and beaches, traverse the island. Coral-viewing is made easy in a glass-bottom boat or semi-submersible vessel. Guests on Great Keppel Island can also go cruising, fishing, water-skiing, diving, windsurfing, snorkeling, and golfing.

Launches to Great Keppel depart Rosslyn Bay mornings and afternoons. Local flights to the island are also available from Rockhampton Airport.

Gladstone, gateway to Heron

About 483 km/300 rail miles north of Brisbane, Gladstone lies on the shores of Port Curtis, a near-perfect natural harbor. This fast-growing town, ranking among Australia's busiest cargo ports, is also the departure point for trips to Heron Island.

Heron Island. Surrounded by many miles of perhaps the best, most easily accessible coral beds of the entire reef area, this well-known, thickly wooded, low coral cay measures only 2 km/1¼ miles in circumference. Many varieties of birds nest in the island's pandanus groves and *pisonia* forest. They include noddy terns, herons, silver gulls, fairy terns, and the migratory mutton birds, which regularly return to the island in late October and leave exactly five months later.

From late October until April, giant turtles visit the island and lay their eggs in the warm coral sand. Within 10 weeks after the eggs are laid, the hatchlings emerge and head to the sea. Heron's Marine Biological Station displays many live specimens of colorful tropical fish and other marine life. The station's biologists have classified more than 1,150 varieties of fish and 200 varieties of coral in the vicinity.

Skin divers regularly meet at Heron. Special events include an annual Divers' Rally in June and July, and the Skin Divers' Festival each November. Experienced divers provide free instruction and guide outings to Heron, Wistari, and other adjacent coral reefs. Heron Island is considered to be one of the best dive spots in Australia.

Nondivers can test their fishing skills or go snorkeling. Other resort activities include a combined cruise and barbecue on a nearby uninhabited island, escorted bird watching, and low-tide reef walks.

Heron has 90 holiday units in one and two-story buildings facing the water. The facilities also include a dining room, bar and lounge, swimming pool, and dive shop.

Arrangements must be made in advance for the 30-minute scenic helicopter flight to Heron Island from Gladstone. There's also launch service from Gladstone.

BRISBANE

In subtropical Queensland, playground beaches & quiet highlands

More than half of Queensland lies above the Tropic of Capricorn. With a climate ranging from subtropical to tropical, this is Australia's vacation country.

From the urban center of Brisbane, Australia's third largest city and the state capital, the seaside resort towns of the Gold Coast stretch south to Coolangatta on the border of New South Wales. North of Brisbane, surfing beaches and fishing resorts edge the less-developed Sunshine Coast. Farther up, at the northeast corner of the state, are the undersea wonders of the Great Barrier Reef.

Balmy sea breezes, sandy beaches, and a lively resort life are the star attractions of the "Sunshine State." But swimming, sunning, and surfing are not all Queensland offers. On the north coast and along the river valleys to the south, dense tropical rain forests flourish, cleared in many places to provide space for pineapple and sugar cane plantations. Mountain resorts and national parks lie within easy reach of Brisbane. Not far inland, the Great Dividing Range stands sentinel over the entire length of the state. About 129 km/80 miles west of Brisbane, the western foothills of the range soften into the Darling Downs, 1.4 million hectares/3.5 million acres of rolling wheat and grazing lands where some of Australia's finest cattle, sheep, and race horses are bred. The Downs gradually merge into the plains, and still farther west, the land eventually dries out to become part of the great Australian outback.

In this chapter we cover the attractions of Brisbane and southern Queensland. For information about northern Queensland, including the Great Barrier Reef, see pages 110–117.

Brisbane, a city on the river

The busy port city of Brisbane is an ideal base from which to explore southern Queensland. A city of almost a million people, Brisbane spreads over both banks of the Brisbane River, 32 km/20 miles upstream from the river's outlet into Moreton Bay. The foothills of the Taylor and D'Aguilar ranges rise behind and a little west of the city. In their foothills, some of Australia's most beautiful homes are designed to take advantage of their view settings and tropical surroundings.

Gardens, parklands, and flowering trees border Brisbane's avenues. The river—trafficked by ferries, tugboats, freighters, ocean liners, and pleasure craft—winds through the city in deep, graceful curves. Six large bridges and eight ferry crossings link the north and south banks.

The city, just a few degrees south of the Tropic of Capricorn, has a subtropical climate. The best months to visit are from April through November, when the daytime temperatures range between 20°C/68°F and 27°C/80°F. Most of the rainfall comes during the summer months of December, January, and February. Temperatures then are very warm to hot, and humidity is high.

Getting your bearings

The center of Brisbane, bisected by Queen Street, occupies a peninsula bounded by the sea on one side and Brisbane River on the other. The main commercial streets follow a grid pattern. Streets running south to north have feminine names; those running west to east, masculine. The Parliament buildings and the Botanic Gardens nestle in a bend of the river at the tip of the peninsula.

At the south end of Queen Street, Victoria Bridge crosses the river to South Brisbane. The south river bank will be the site of Expo 88. Construction has already begun on the international exposition complex. Expo 88, with a theme of "Leisure in the Age of Technology," will be open from April 30 to October 30, 1988.

A helpful city map is available from the Queensland Government Travel Centre, 196 Adelaide Street. The National Trust, at 157 Ann Street, has a brochure detailing points of historic interest.

City sights

Like most state capitals, Brisbane has its share of fine parks, museums, dignified government and civic buildings, and monuments. You will see many of them on your downtown walking tour. Others are just a short bus or ferry ride away.

Architectural landmarks. City Hall is at Adelaide and Albert streets. This mammoth building on King George

Reflecting pool in Brisbane's Botanic Gardens mirrors contrasting architectural styles of Parliament House complex. Serene setting belies bustle of Queensland's capital city.

Lifeguards in surf boat crash through waves.

CONTENTS

Australia

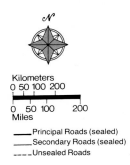

Kilometers
0 50 100 200

Miles
0 50 100 200

——— Principal Roads (sealed)
——— Secondary Roads (sealed)
- - - Unsealed Roads

How far is it?

Australia is a large country. Places that seem close to each other on a map might, in reality, be a good distance apart. The chart below indicates distances by road between certain towns.

Sydney/Melbourne	893 km/555 miles
Melbourne/Adelaide	755 km/469 miles
Sydney/Perth	4,135 km/2,569 miles
Perth/Albany	407 km/253 miles
Perth/Port Hedland	1,818 km/1,130 miles
Sydney/Brisbane	1,027 km/638 miles
Brisbane/Cairns	1,826 km/1,135 miles
Cairns/Mackay	786 km/488 miles
Mackay/Brisbane	1,044 km/649 miles
Alice Springs/Darwin	1,532 km/952 miles
Alice Springs/Ayers Rock	468 km/291 miles
Canberra/Sydney	309 km/192 miles
Canberra/Melbourne	661 km/413 miles